Politics and War in Meath 1913-23

*This book is dedicated to
my father and to my uncle Willie,
neither of whom lived to see it.*

Politics and War in Meath 1913-23

OLIVER COOGAN

with a foreword by Peter Connell

Comhairle Chontae na Mí
Meath County Council

First published by Oliver Coogan in 1983

Republished by Comhairle Chontae na Mí
Meath County Council in December 2013

ISBN 978 1 900923 26 2

Book Design and Typesetting by Anú Design, Tara
(www.anu-design.ie)

Cover images
Top, (l to r): Sean MacNaMidhe, Séamus Cogan, Seamus Finn, Willie Coogan
Bottom: British troops in Athboy, 1920

Contents

Foreword

The years 2012-2022 having been designated Ireland's 'decade of commemoration', we are drawn to reflect on the tumultuous events that occurred between 1912 and 1922 that shaped the destinies of the people of Ireland, both north and south. Of late there has been no shortage of publications dealing with the seminal events of these years, including the signing of the Ulster Covenant, the sacrifices and horror of the First World War, the 1916 Rising, the War of Independence, the Treaty and its aftermath, the Civil War.

It is a tremendous tribute to Oliver Coogan and his *Politics and War in Meath, 1913-23* that many of the themes explored in these books are pre-figured by research he completed over thirty years ago. In the early 1980s few professional historians ventured to write about this period in our history. For many the Easter Rising and the War of Independence were difficult subjects to tackle when violence and communal strife in Northern Ireland blighted so many lives.

Oliver's original intention, as he states in his prologue, was to 'record the history of the Old IRA in county Meath, particularly for the years 1919 to 1921'. But, like all good historians, he found that he needed to provide a context for what happened in those years and so he was drawn into a much wider story that includes the rise of the Irish Volunteers, the impact of the First World War, the Easter Rising and the social and industrial unrest that occurred from 1918 onwards.

Politics and War is the very best kind of history and reflects the character of the man who wrote it. It is down-to-earth, honest, judicious and original and infused with a passion for the people of Meath as they struggled through difficult times. Perhaps, above all, it tells a compelling story. Reading that story, one begins to understand how Oliver in his history classes in Dunshaughlin Community School could hold his students in the palm of his hand.

Oliver's passion for history, which defined his career as a teacher, was matched by his passion for Gaelic football, which ran as deep for the school teams he coached as for the Meath senior team. He was a loyal supporter of Meath teams that experienced many highs and some lows at Croke Park from the 1960s through to 2005 when Oliver attended his last game in May of that year, just a week before he passed away. An abiding memory is of a wet Sunday in July 1986 when Meath finally overcame Dublin to win their first Leinster title in sixteen years. Long years in the football wilderness were over and the future promised even greater victories. Joy was unconfined on the Hogan Stand at five to five that afternoon. At that moment if Oliver had been offered a choice between winning the lottery or handing the title back to Dublin there is no doubting what choice he would have made.

Being an avid supporter involves having definite opinions. Although usually quiet-spoken, and always self-effacing, when Oliver formed a judgement no amount of argument was likely to elicit a change of mind. Those judgements could be about a less than effective politician or a promising wingback on the Meath team. Definite opinions are not always the best starting point when approaching the business of researching history.

Politics and War is a master class in the considered use of historical sources and the recounting of a story that is fair to all sides. Many stories have been written about the exploits of the Old IRA which casts the men as unambiguous heroes. Oliver had the foresight to interview a number of the volunteers in their old age. And, as with all the best oral histories, the men are drawn into telling their stories in a natural way. Military witness statements from the time are now available on the internet but few of them capture the ordinariness and humour of the sometimes chaotic activities of men on the run recorded by Oliver. Jack Lynch from Carnaross, for example, recalled that while on the run 'some of the women of Cumann na mBan would bring us food. It is just as well they did because I remember that once a few of us killed and cooked a chicken but forgot to clean it out so it wasn't very nice to eat!'.

The book's portrayal of these young men reflected Oliver's own idealism. There is little doubt that he identified with men like Peter O'Connell and Charlie Conaty from Carnaross, Patsy and Johnny Bennett of Arbraccan and many more. His assessment of the activities of the Meath Volunteers in the years 1919-21 is shrewd and balanced and makes clear that the effectiveness of the campaign in Meath should not be judged by the scale of British army or RIC casualties (one soldier and two policemen). Oliver quotes approvingly from a discussion with Peter O'Connell – 'just because we were an army didn't mean we had to go round shooting people all the time. We could get our way by other means. We didn't want to kill anyone.'

Oliver had a reputation as an outstanding teacher. That reputation was built on a passion for his subject, a high regard for his students, skill as a communicator and a forensic attention to detail. That attention to detail is very evident in *Politics and War* as it carefully builds a picture of the gradual decline of the alliance around John Redmond and the Irish Parliamentary Party in Meath. Declining levels of activity on the part of organisations such as the United Irish League and the Ancient Order of Hibernians and increasing resistance to British army recruitment drives after 1916 are sketched in great detail from sources such as the *Meath Chronicle* and the *Drogheda Independent*.

Trawling through old newspapers to unearth these trends takes hundreds of hours of research but the evidence that is unearthed means that the story told is built on solid foundations. *Politics and War* presents the facts but here and there throughout the book Oliver produces a turn of phrase that suggests a true wordsmith at work and reveals something of the author – his distain for pretension of any sort. As someone who himself, despite his many talents, was self-effacing, he relished debunking those who unashamedly sought the limelight.

Patrick White was Home Rule MP for North Meath, first elected in 1900. The winds of change were sweeping through local politics as the 1918 general election approached and in an attempt to salvage his political career White attempted to jump ship and latch on to the growing popularity of Sinn Féin. In life and in conversation, Oliver was capable of a carefully honed phrase and he succeeds in demolishing White's pretensions by describing his fate as 'having bailed out of the sinking ship of Home Rule he found nothing waiting for him save the cruel sea of political anonymity'.

Others with grand strategies, no matter how well intentioned, are also brought down to earth. After the Russian revolution in 1917 he describes how some trade union and political leaders preached revolution to Meath's agricultural labourers whose single concern was a decent wage. Through the Irish Transport and General Workers Union some notable gains were made. But Oliver's sympathy obviously lay with workers in Dunboyne in 1920 when they 'served notice on local publicans that they would not pay more than 6d. for a pint of porter ... the publicans held out for only a week'. Their campaign, he notes, was "a far cry from Trotsky's fomenting of permanent communist revolution". As someone who enjoyed good conversation over a quiet pint we know this was a victory he was happy to salute.

Peter Connell, September 2013

Acknowledgements (2013)

Tá an-áthas ar Comhairle Chontae na Mí an leabhar fíor-tábhachtach seo a chur ar ais i gcló agus go mbeidh sé ar fail ar fud an chontae, ar fud na tire agus thar lear. Gach uile bhliain, cuirtear lenár dtuiscint ar fhás agus ar fhorbairt ár gcontae, trí réimse leathan foilseachán – stair áitiúil, irisí, bliainirisí agus dialanna.

In his foreword to the first (1983) edition of this book Oliver Coogan mentions that several of the men whose memories breathed life into his account of the period had since passed on. By recording those memories Oliver Coogan performed a significant service to the study of Meath's recent history, when he published *Politics and War in Meath 1913-23*. Our gratitude for the work of this patient chronicler cannot be overestimated.

Thanks are also due to Oliver Coogan's family for their support to this project, to Irene D'Arcy for her work on updating the maps, to Peter Connell for his warm and generous foreword, to the Local Studies department of Meath County Council Library Service for its work in preparing the text, to Julitta Clancy for her work on the index, and to Anú Design for their care and attention to detail in the preparation of this volume.

Meath County Council is delighted to restore *Politics and War in Meath 1913-23* to print, to be studied and enjoyed by a new generation of scholars of the revolutionary period in Meath's history.

Jackie Maguire, Bainisteoir an Chontae
Comhairle Chontae na Mí

John V Farrelly, Cathaoirleach,
Comhairle Chontae na Mí

Maps

Plates

Abbreviations

AOH	Ancient Order of Hibernians
Co.C.	County Council(lor)
For.	Foresters
FU	Farmers Union
GAA	Gaelic Athletic Association
Ind.	Independent
INF	Irish National Foresters
INV	Irish National Volunteers
IRA	Irish Republican Army
IRB	Irish Republican Brotherhood
ITGWU	Irish Transport and General Workers Union
ITU	abbreviated form of ITGWU
JP	Justice of the Peace
Lab.	Labour Party
LGB	Local Government Board
MFU	Meath Farmers Union
MLU	Meath Labour Union
MP	Member of Parliament
O/C	Officer Commanding
PLG	Poor Law Guardians (same as Board of Guardians)
PP	Parish Priest
RDC	Rural District Council(lor)
RIC	Royal Irish Constabulary
SF	Sinn Féin
TD	Teachta Dála
TT	Town Tenants (Association)
UIL	United Irish League
UDC	Urban District Council(lor)
UVF	Ulster Volunteer Force
VG	Vicar General

Sources & Acknowledgements (1983)

It would have been impossible to have compiled this account without help from a variety of sources. Of central importance amongst these were the *Meath Chronicle* and the *Drogheda Independent* for the years under review. Both provided information on a multitude of subjects and also gave an exact chronology for events remembered clearly but sometimes with only approximate dates by those who lived through them.

Much appreciation is due to Meath County Council Library Service in Navan, especially to William Smith, County Librarian, and to Andy Bennett who dredged up from the County Archive numerous bulky and dusty minute books of the various local government councils – County, Urban, Rural, and Boards of Guardians. These gave a clear insight into the membership, deliberations and business of these bodies during the years in question.

Thanks are also due to the staff of the National Library of Ireland in Kildare Street, Dublin, for their kind help.

Published works on topics of both local and national interest contributed much by way of filling in background or clarifying certain points. Invaluable in this respect was David Fitzpatrick's *Politics and Irish Life 1913–21* (Gill & Macmillan, 1977), an outstanding study of these years with particular reference to county Clare. Numerous quotes have been pillaged from this book and indeed many ideas as to the structure of the present account have been taken from it.

Regarding the Home Rule movement the following works were consulted: *Parliamentary Elections in Ireland 1801–1922* (Royal Irish Academy, 1978) by B.M. Walker (ed.), the North Meath and South Meath Election Petitions in 1892 as reprinted in the *Daily Irish Independent*; *The Irish Parliamentary Party 1890–1910* (Faber & Faber, 1951) by F.S.L. Lyons; Burke's *Irish Family Records*; *The Catholic Encyclopedia* (1965); and Manuscript 15553 in the National Library of Ireland which provided insight into the workings of the Kells corps of the Irish National Volunteers between July 1914 and December 1916.

For information on the republican movement the following published accounts were drawn on: *The Capuchin Annual* (1966) for the article 'The Fight at Ashbourne' by Colonel Joseph Lawless; *The*

Capuchin Annual 1968 for the article 'The First Sinn Féin Paper' by Niall Sheridan; *The Last Post, Republican Dead 1913–75*; *Ríocht na Midhe* 1978–79, for an account of the life of Brian O'Higgins by Josephine Murray; *Liam Mellows and the Irish Revolution* by C. Desmond Greaves (Lawrence and Wishart, 1971); *With the IRA in the Fight for Freedom* (The Kerryman, [? 1953]) for the chapter by Seamus Finn on the taking of Trim Barracks; Finn's own unpublished *History of the Meath Brigade of the IRA* as serialised in Garrett Fox's column in the *Meath Chronicle* between May 1971 and July 1972; and a copybook with the words *'An Uaimh Company IRA 1916–23'* on its cover, as well as handwritten lists of Old IRA and some letters of Seamus Finn and Mick Hilliard, all deposited in the County Archive, Navan.

Biographical details of some prominent figures were obtained from the *Magill Book of Irish Politics* edited by Vincent Browne and, from an earlier period, *The Oireachtas Companion and Saorstát Guide,* edited by William J. Flynn.

For the Labour movement, Manuscript 7282 in the National Library of Ireland lists branches of the Irish Transport and General Workers Union up to 1922, and gives founding dates of branches, names of secretaries and in some cases the numbers of members in each. Also useful were C. Desmond Greaves' *The Irish Transport and General Workers Union: the Formative Years 1909–1923* (Gill & Macmillan, 1982); and *Labour in Irish Politics 1890–1930: the Irish Labour Movement in the Age of Revolution* (Irish University Press, 1974) by Arthur Mitchell.

Consulted for miscellaneous topics were *The Green Flag: A History of Irish Nationalism* (Weidenfeld & Nicholson, 1972) by Robert Kee; *Francis Ledwidge: a Life of the Poet* (Martin Brian & O'Keeffe, 1972) by Alice Curtayne; *Local Government (Ireland) Act 1898* (Sealy, Bryers & Walker, 1899), by John J. Clancy; and two autobiographical accounts: *Ireland Forever* (Jonathan Cape, 1932) and *Impressions and Recollections* (T.W. Laurie, 1930) by Brigadier-General Frank Crozier. Jack Fitzsimons' *The Plains of Royal Meath* served a twofold purpose, as it was a guide to the correct spelling of place names as well as often indicating the whereabouts of obscure townlands.

Apart from written sources, many people were forthcoming with information. In this regard much gratitude is due to John Blake and Patsy Brady of the Navan branch of the Irish National Foresters, both of whom threw light on the history and workings of that organisation. My thanks also go to Peter Duffy of Dunshaughlin for providing biographical details on his father Michael Duffy.

Also of great assistance was Seán Boylan of Dunboyne who placed at my disposal some typed memoirs of his father of the same name. These were originally given to the Bureau of Military History in the late 1950s. The Bureau was set up by the then government to collect information regarding the Troubles from surviving Old IRA officers all over the country. It proved possible to obtain copies of the original statements from a few of those who gave them to the Bureau. Apart from Seán Boylan, these included Peter O'Connell and Charlie Conaty of Carnaross, and to both these men I am particularly thankful.

Others of the Old IRA who willingly gave of their time and reminiscences were Bobby Byrne, Mick Hilliard and Pat Fitzsimons of Navan; Peter Moran, Nick Moran and Christy Ennis of Dunboyne; Patsy and Johnny Bennett of Ardbraccan; Jimmy Sherry and Paddy Lalor of Trim; Matt Wallace of Batterstown; James O'Connell of Skryne; Owen Clarke of Oldcastle; Jack Lynch of Carnaross; Willie Coogan of Martry; Owen Heaney of Kilberry; Benny Carolan of Kells; Paddy Reilly of Moynalty and Tom Manning of Kilbride. In all cases, although frequently turning up unknown and unannounced, I was treated with great hospitality. The memories of these men served to breathe life into what were hitherto merely fleeting references to IRA activities in the local newspapers of more than sixty years earlier. It is unfortunate that several of these men have since passed away.

Thanks are due also to Sheila Dunne, Anne-Marie McEntagart, Geraldine Carey, Mary Moore and Claire Dolan for typing the manuscript; to Mary Hayes, Jeff Finlay and Alan O'hEadhra for helping with the proofreading; to Tom Keegan for drawing the maps of Navan, Trim and Ashbourne; to Fr. Gerry Rice and Peter Connell for reading the manuscript and suggesting certain changes; to Peter Walsh and Geraldine Reilly whose assistance at one stage ensured that a broken wrist did not unduly delay the work; to those who donated photographs; and finally to anyone who helped in any small way in the preparation of this book.

Oliver Coogan, August 1983

Prologue

The years 1913 to 1923 in Ireland were a time of such rapid change and great upheaval that historians are generally in agreement in terming them revolutionary. Amongst developments that this period witnessed were the rejection by the great majority of the Irish people of the moderate nationalism of the Home Rule movement in favour of the advanced republicanism of Sinn Féin; the resurgence of physical force republicanism – largely moribund for almost fifty years – in the form of the Irish Volunteers, also known as the Irish Republican Army; the appearance of an aggressive labour movement spearheaded by the ITGWU to supplant the hitherto more deferential and docile workers' associations; and much agrarian agitation on the part of farm labourers and smallholders as they sought the division of landed estates.

The original intention of the book was to record the history of the Old IRA in county Meath particularly for the years 1919 to 1921. However, as the work progressed it was found appropriate to extend the time limits backwards to 1913 and forward to 1923, and also to include discussion on other themes such as political happenings, labour developments and land troubles.

The book is divided into eight chapters. The first attempts to set the scene: it recounts the various political and quasi-political organisations in existence in the Meath of 1913 and it describes the unwieldy system of local government then in operation. Overall the aim is to show the Home Rule movement, initially, on the eve of its supreme triumph, and then in the paralysis of disillusionment which set in immediately afterwards.

Chapter Two deals with the Easter Rising as it affected Meath and also shows contemporary local reaction to this event. Chapter Three digresses briefly to describe the reverberations of the Great War in the county. Chapter Four returns to the political theme and charts the growth of Sinn Féin up until the general election of December 1918.

The fifth section represents the original intention of the book, as it recounts the struggle of the Meath Volunteers against British forces in the county until the Truce of 11 July 1921. The fact that this is far and away the longest chapter is due mainly to the reminiscences of almost two dozen survivors of that struggle; such oral testament was only fleetingly available in the cases of only some of the other chapters. The sixth chapter covers the same period of time as the fifth and has as its theme the concurrent campaign of passive resistance organised by Sinn Féin against British rule. Chapter Seven deals with the growth of the Labour movement – usually in accounts of these years either depicted as a mere adjunct of Sinn Féin or else totally ignored – and also examines briefly the long-forgotten work of the Back to the Land movement. Finally, the last chapter records attitudes to the Anglo-Irish Treaty of 6 December 1921 – which gave a substantial measure of freedom to most of the country – and also deals with the resulting split in the Meath IRA and the subsequent drift into civil war.

Well-known landmarks in Irish history for these years form, for the most part, the parameters of the chapters – the founding of the Volunteers, the Rising, the 1918 General Election, the Truce, the Treaty and the Civil War. But this book is meant as a purely local study and references to events at a national level are kept to a minimum and used only where it seems relevant to do so. These events have, moreover, been chronicled almost exhaustively, and the contributions of Redmond, de Valera, Connolly, Pearse, Collins, Griffith, Barry and Breen are well known.

It is often forgotten that the history of a nation is merely the sum total of the history of its constituent parts, and that a national profile cannot be built up without knowledge of local happenings. For many, history may seem very remote in time and in place as well as in the figures of those who people the history books. In the account which follows it is hoped that, occasionally at least, readers may find themselves reading about relations or neighbours or friends – almost all, albeit, now dead – and about places proximate to their homes or work.

This book then records the roles of Sir Nugent Everard, Seán Boylan, Francis Ledwidge, David Hall, Seán MacNaMidhe, Fr Robert Barry, Mick Hilliard, Séamus Finn, Seamus Cogan and many, many others in the Meath of their time. It should be a reminder that without the support of these small and anonymous men of the revolutionary years, the more illustrious figures listed earlier arguably may never have attained national prominence. As David Fitzpatrick puts it:

> The Irish Revolution was directed not by conspirators, thinkers and politicians but by great surges of opinion from below, expressed by countless forgotten spokesmen in countless bars and churchyards.
>
> (*Politics and Irish Life 1913-21*, ps 279-280).

County Meath -
Places mentioned in text

Administrative Boundaries -
Rural Councils and
Parliamentary Constituencies

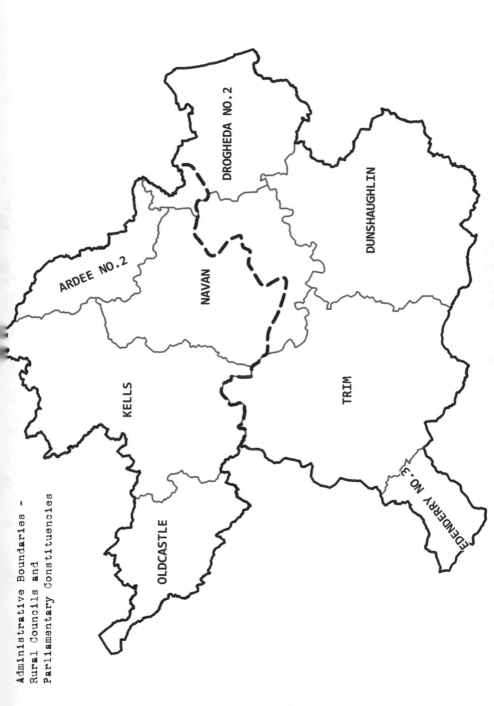

DROGHEDA NO.2

ARDEE NO.2

NAVAN

DUNSHAUGHLIN

KELLS

TRIM

OLDCASTLE

EDENDERRY NO.3

1

November 1913 - December 1915: Home Rule - Climax and Anti-Climax

In 1913 nationalist Ireland stood on the brink of a major triumph. The Home Rule Party, which had been striving since 1870 for the restoration of a parliament in Dublin, was now, under the leadership of John Redmond, finally about to realise that objective, since the Third Home Rule Bill was due to become law sometime in the middle of the following year. There was, however, one cloud on the horizon – the perennial opposition of the unionists. To reinforce their attacks on the Bill inside the House of Commons, unionists had since January 1913 begun to organise their own army, the Ulster Volunteer Force. It was from a fear that the Liberal government might back down in face of this pressure that the corresponding Irish Volunteers were founded in Dublin towards the end of the year.

On 8 November 1913 the *Meath Chronicle*, then varying in size from four to six pages, printed in Kells and costing one penny, carried on its second page a reprint of '*The North Began*' by Eoin MacNeill. This had first appeared a week earlier in the Gaelic League newspaper *An Claidheamh Soluis*, and it was this article which paved the way for the formal founding of the Irish Volunteers at the Rotunda in Dublin on the twenty-fifth of the month.

On 20 December the *Chronicle* published a letter from John Sweetman of Drumbaragh, enclosing the manifesto of the Volunteers which stated that its aim was "to secure and maintain the rights and liberties common to all the people of Ireland, without distinction of creed, class or politics." Sweetman had been a figure of political importance both inside and outside the county over the previous twenty years. In the general election of July 1892 he had stood as an anti-Parnellite Nationalist and won the seat in Wicklow County East. Early in 1895, however, having apparently undergone a change of heart, he resigned the seat and fought it as a Parnellite Nationalist but lost by sixty two votes. In the general election which followed a few months later, he contested Meath North but again lost, by the tantalising margin of thirty two votes, to James Gibney. This ended Sweetman's career at a national level but in 1899 he successfully contested the first election to Meath County Council and on Saturday, 22 April at the inaugural meeting of that body in Trim Courthouse, he became vice-chairman.

He remained a councillor until 1908 but thereafter his political career was on the wane and his letter to the *Chronicle* at the end of December evoked no immediate response to his call for the formation of the Volunteers in the county. Indeed over the next couple of months, about the nearest thing to extreme political action was the stoning of a Suffragette meeting in Navan by two men and a boy, all three of whom were later prosecuted at the local court.

Early in February 1914 it was reported by the *Chronicle* that a corps of the UVF had been formed on the Headfort Estate in Kells, that the Marquis had purchased rifles and that drilling and rifle practice were taking place every Friday. This was quickly denied by the Marquis and apparently the story was that just two of his employees were members.

It was in Kells that the first reported stirrings of Volunteer activity occurred when in mid-February about two hundred men were enrolled following a public meeting in the town. Navan soon followed. On

Sunday, 22 February a meeting was called in the Foresters Hall, a rented premises standing opposite the Church of Ireland. The meeting was chaired by Christopher Quinn, a member of Navan UDC, and was addressed by Eoin MacNeill who, it was reported in the *Meath Chronicle* on 28 February, emphasised that there was nothing secret about the movement, that they were not anti-English but aimed "at bridging over the gulf that had been created between Catholics and Protestants in Ireland." MacNeill "met with an enthusiastic ovation" and afterwards over one hundred and ten men enrolled.

Things moved quickly from then on. On Saint Patrick's Day in Athboy, two hundred men joined following a meeting presided over by Patrick O'Growney, a county councillor and brother of Fr Eugene O'Growney (1863–1899), one of the founders of the Gaelic League in 1893. By April the Volunteers had spread to rural areas such as Rathmolyon, Ballinacree, Castletown and Ardbraccan, and by May, there were companies in Stonefield, Bohermeen, Rathmore, Moynalty, Carnaross, Fordstown, Oldcastle and Martry, where the founding figures were James Coogan and Pat Lyons.

Local politicians and notables were strongly involved from the start. In Kells John Sweetman became president of the local Volunteer committee with Matthew Gartland, a county and urban councillor, as vice-president. In Navan, when a committee was formally appointed in April, its chairman was James Quigley, then County Surveyor; its secretary was John Gallen, also secretary to the County Committee of Agriculture, while the treasurer was a local businessman, P.J. McQuillan. Other members of the Navan committee included Michael Gaynor, James McNamee, Michael Smith, Thomas Walsh, Laurence Clarke (then secretary of the Meath County Board of the GAA) and Seán MacNaMidhe, a school teacher and prominent figure in Gaelic League circles as well as being chairman of the Meath GAA Board.

This involvement of existing political or quasi-political organisations was an early characteristic. For instance, when the Rathmolyon corps was formed in April, the meeting included representatives from local branches of the GAA, the United Irish League, the Ancient Order of Hibernians and the Irish National Foresters. And in Athboy it was proposed by O'Growney that the managing committee of the local corps should consist of three members from each of the Gaelic League, the Meath Labour Union and the AOH.

That the Volunteers embraced all social classes, as well as transcending political differences, is evident from the presence within its ranks of what might be termed as the gentry or titled upper class. Although by now in rapid decline, this class still commanded a certain amount of deference. Thus, on 21 March 1914 a notice in the *Chronicle* could report that "Sir William Rowse Boughton has returned to Blackcastle, Navan where he is fishing during the spring", and on 4 April 1914 that "the Marquis and Marchioness of Headfort have been at Cannes." In Meath in June Lord Dunsany and the Earl of Fingal wrote letters to the local press expressing their support for the movement, while in August Lord Gormanston, the Marquis of Conyngham and Lord Trimleston let it be known that they wished to be associated with support for the Volunteers. Another supporter was Sir John Dillon of Lismullin, a patron of the corps in Skryne. Indeed, the Earl of Fingal was soon appointed to the position of Inspector-General for county Meath.

During the summer of 1914 Volunteer corps spread like wildfire to every corner of the county. Enthusiasm knew no bounds. The first route march of the Navan corps took place early in May from the centre of the town out to Newgate and back again, involved four to five hundred men and was accompanied by a piper's band playing national airs. In Ballinacree they obviously meant business and were not content to be merely toy soldiers; when the corps was formed in April, a rifle club was formed at the same time "to prepare for any sudden emergency", according to the *Drogheda Independent*. By June, the *Meath Chronicle* was reporting that the Ballinacree men were:

> getting impatient for the arms ... a firm wrote offering to supply any amount of new German rifles, .22-bore, sighted with adjustable back, sight 200 yards, but they were not considered good enough.

Commercial interests were not slow to perceive the potential for business; Finucane's drapery in Ludlow Street, Navan, was soon advertising in the local papers that they were stocking "Volunteer equipment, uniforms, caps, bandoliers, haversacks, belts and special marching boots." And the rhymers were soon in evidence; in its first issue in June the *Chronicle* published some verses, among them 'Lines Addressed to the Irish National Volunteers' by Seumas O'Brien:

> I can hear your trampling feet,
> Marching down the village street,
> With a step so light and neat,
> > Volunteers.
>
> When the green flag waves on high
> In the clear blue sunny sky,
> 'Neath its folds will live or die,
> > Volunteers.
>
> Now that Home Rule's close at hand,
> Let us form an army grand.
> To defend our motherland,
> > Volunteers.

This was the first issue of the *Chronicle* to include a column devoted specifically to Volunteer meetings and activities. This column remained a feature for several months and, as much as anything else, it marks the arrival and acceptance of the Volunteers as a significant movement.

This significance was acknowledged by the first county convention of the Volunteers, organised to put some order on the rapid growth. It met in the CYMS Hall in Navan on Sunday, 12 July and was presided over by Patrick Sheridan, a county councillor from Oldcastle. About thirty corps from every part of Meath were represented at this. The convention did not last too long; the main business was, as reported in the *Meath Chronicle* on 18 July, an expression of "unqualified confidence" in John Redmond and a call "on the Irish Parliamentary Party to demand the immediate withdrawal of the proclamation prohibiting the importation of arms into Ireland." A small committee, including Sheridan and P.J. McQuillan, was appointed to lay the foundations for a permanent county structure for the organisation.

The work of this steering committee came to fruition the following month. On 9 August the Volunteers reconvened in Navan and a county board of twelve was selected. Sheridan continued as chairman, with McQuillan as treasurer while James Quigley became county secretary. In addition, one man was appointed to represent each of the nine areas into which the county was now divided. These areas and their representatives on the County Board were: Navan, James Kelly, a rural councillor; Kells, P. Fox; Trim, P.J. Coady, an urban councillor; Athboy, F.M. Reilly; Oldcastle, Patrick Sheridan (chairman); Dunshaughlin, P.J. McCarthy; Duleek, P.J. Corry, a Justice of the Peace; Nobber, James McGlew, a county councillor; and Slane, Patrick Boyle, also a county councillor.

Although the previous convention had been held just a month before, the number of corps represented had, even in such a short time, almost doubled. The full list of corps who sent delegates to the August convention was:

(1) Navan area: Navan, Kentstown, Johnstown, Martry, Bohermeen, Gibstown, Kilberry and Ardbraccan.

(2) Kells area: Kells, Oristown, Moynalty, Carnaross, Kilbeg and Carrickleck.

(3) Trim: Trim, Summerhill, Rathmolyon, Boardsmill, Kilmessan and Enfield-Rathcore.

(4) Athboy: Athboy, Rathmore, Ballivor, Fordstown, Dunderry and Higginstown.

(5) Oldcastle: Oldcastle, Virginia Road, Ballinacree and Killallon.

(6) Dunshaughlin: Dunshaughlin, Skryne, Kilmoon, Drumree, Dunboyne, Ratoath and Kilcloon.

(7) Duleek: Duleek, Hilltown, Donore, Gormanston, Clonalvy, Julianstown and Ardcath.

(8) Nobber: Nobber, Tierworker, Drumconrath, Castletown, Wilkinstown and Kilmainhamwood.

Irish Volunteer Corps,
August 1914.

7

(9) Slane: Slane, Lobinstown, Grangegeeth, Yellow Furze, Stackallen, Rathkenny and Monknewtown.

Then, within a week, the men of Robinstown affiliated to the Irish Volunteer Corps, August 1914. This brought the total number of corps to fifty-eight, a remarkable growth in the six months since the first reported activity in Kells.

The high point of the Volunteer movement in Meath came on the following Saturday, 15 August, when a military-style review and parade were held in Slane. On 22 August the *Chronicle* reported that twenty-five corps participated in this, involving about 2,500 men and a similar number of spectators. On the reviewing stand were county Inspector-General Fingal, Lord Dunsany, the Marquis of Conyngham and Patrick White, MP for the Meath North constituency. Also present was Sir Nugent T. Everard of Randlestown, one of the foremost public figures in Meath.

Born in 1849, Everard had been educated at Harrow and Trinity College, Cambridge. Returning to Ireland, he had been appointed High Sheriff of Meath in 1883, and by this time had been elevated to the position of Lord Lieutenant of the county. He had been a member of the county council continuously since its inauguration in 1899, always taking his place as one of the two members that this body was entitled to co-opt following the elections every three years. Apart from his political role, Everard carried out much pioneering work in agricultural matters in Meath, particularly in relation to tobacco growing. With the coming of the Volunteers he offered his services to the Kilberry Corps and his involvement was doubtless a great boost to the movement. The speeches after the parade struck a confident and triumphal note with constant allusions to the imminence of Home Rule. However, the Volunteer movement was never again to attain the same dominance in Meath as it did on that sunny August afternoon on the historic Hill of Slane.

The Home Rule Party in Meath in 1914 was represented by two MPs because the county had been divided into two constituencies since 1885. In the course of the nineteenth century Meath voters had at various times returned the three outstanding figures of contemporary Irish history, Daniel O'Connell (1841), Charles Stewart Parnell and Michael

Davitt. Parnell's political career, in fact, was launched with a by-election victory in Meath in April 1875, and he continued to represent the constituency until the next general election in 1880. Davitt was elected by Meath voters on two separate occasions (1882 and 1892–1893), but for both of these his tenure was brief and troubled. Other men who represented Meath's interests in Westminster in the nineteenth century included Frederick Lucas (1852–55), a leading figure in the short-lived Independent Irish Party of the 1850s, A.M. Sullivan (1880–82) a strongly nationalist journalist, and John Martin (1871–1875), a one time Young Irelander who had served five years in Van Diemen's Land.

Following the downfall and death of Parnell (1890–91), Meath had witnessed a major political furore arising out of the general election of July 1892 when, in both Meath North and Meath South, the anti-Parnellite candidates won narrow victories over those still loyal to the uncrowned king. In the North Michael Davitt defeated Pierce Mahony, the man, incidentally, after whom the O'Mahony's Football Club in Navan is called, by 2,549 to 2,146 votes. In the South Meath constituency, Patrick Fulham had just thirteen votes to spare over his opponent James Dalton, winning by 2,212 to 2,199. However, in both instances objections were made alleging bribery, intimidation and clerical interference; this last arose out of a notorious pastoral letter issued by Bishop Thomas Nulty (bishop from 1866 to 1898) on the eve of the election. In this letter Nulty stated, among other things, that "Parnellism is sprung from the foul root of sensualism and sin", that "Parnell had disgraced himself by the crime of vile, habitual and persistent adultery" and even that,

> no man can remain a Catholic as long as he elects to cling to Parnellism. The dying Parnellite himself will hardly dare to face the justice of his Maker till he has been prepared and anointed by us for the last awful struggle and the terrible judgement that will immediately follow it.

Strong stuff indeed and not surprisingly the objections of the Parnellites were upheld. An enquiry took place and both Davitt and Fulham were unseated and a new writ issued. The rearranged elections, however, held in February 1893, changed nothing. In both constituencies the anti-Parnellites once again emerged victorious; in the north, Jeremiah Jordan (2,707) defeated Dalton (2,638), while in the south James Gibney (2,635) had a comfortable enough margin to spare over Mahony (2,377).

Time helped to heal the wounds and Redmond emerged as the leader of a reunited party in 1900, a position he was to maintain until his death in 1918. In 1914 the Meath constituencies were represented by two men who come across as different from each other in background and outlook.

David Sheehy (Meath South) was very much one of the old guard of the party, having lived through and participated in the heady times of Parnell's leadership, the Land War, the First Home Rule Bill and the Plan of Campaign, all during the 1880s. Born in Limerick in 1843, Sheehy was educated in the local Jesuit seminary and then at the Irish College in Paris. Married in 1876 he made his living as a mill owner in Templemore, county Tipperary. However, political affairs soon began to take up most of his attention and from the late 1870s he was active in both the Land League and the extreme Irish Republican Brotherhood. His activities earned him eighteen months in prison in 1888–89 arising out of his leading role in the Plan of Campaign when he 'collected' rents on the Clanricarde Estate in county Galway. The following year he was among those who urged a temporary retirement on Parnell following the publication of Gladstone's letter which narrowed down the choice open to the Irish party to either Parnell as leader or Home Rule.

When the split came he became a member of the provisional committee set up to direct the business of the anti-Parnellite Home Rule Party. Sheehy had had a chequered parliamentary career. He was returned unopposed as MP for Galway County South in the elections of 1885 and 1886; lost Waterford City (to Redmond) in 1892; was again returned unopposed for Galway County South as an anti-Parnellite in 1895; took no part in the election in 1900; won back his seat in a by-election victory over Parnell's brother, John Howard Parnell, in Meath South in October 1903; and thereafter was returned unopposed for this constituency in 1906 and in both elections in 1910. A man of great political experience then, his image was enhanced no doubt by the fact that he had served time in prison for the nationalist cause.

It is more difficult to find information regarding the member for Meath North, Patrick White who, unlike Sheehy, is not mentioned in Burke's *Irish Family Records*. Certainly he did not have the same pedigree as Sheehy. Born in 1860, his career as an MP dated back to 1900 when he gained a narrow victory over the incumbent James Gibney, the former anti-Parnellite now standing as an Independent Nationalist. Like Sheehy, White was returned unopposed at each of the next three elections. Up to 1914 his political career had been relatively quiet, the only 'incident' of note being in March 1901 when he was one of twelve Irish members forcibly removed from the House of Commons for causing a disruption following the abrupt termination by the government side of a debate on education.

These then were the two men representing Meath in the Imperial Parliament in 1914. One more point may be made about them. They differed also in the fact that White was a native of the county, having been born, reared and now still resident in Clonalvy, when not in London on parliamentary business. Sheehy, as we have seen, was Limerick-born but had long been resident in the Dublin suburb of Rathmines. These facts fit the general pattern in the Irish party at this time since only about fifty per cent of the seventy to eighty members were resident in their constituencies.

Although very much the junior of the two MPs, White was much more active than his colleague as regards his constituency work. Perhaps this was because he was a resident MP or perhaps because he was a much younger man than Sheehy, now aged over seventy. Whatever the reason, the local newspapers show White to be very energetic in fulfilling his constituency duties – presiding at meetings of the North Meath executive of the United Irish League, attending branch meetings of this organisation, addressing Volunteer rallies (we have seen that he was present at the big review in Slane in August 1914), mediating between the Meath Labour Union in their disputes with the Farmers Union and a real driving force behind the county's Back to the Land movement. This is not to suggest that Sheehy was an 'absentee' MP but, while a frequent visitor to his constituency, his work rate, again judging from the local press reports, did not compare with that of White in the years from 1914 onwards.

The total domination of the Irish Nationalist or Home Rule Party over political life in the country in the early years of the century cannot be understated. A few facts and figures in relation to the last general election, that of December 1910, held before the years under consideration should illustrate this pre-eminence. Ireland then returned 103 MPs from 101 constituencies, all of which were single seaters except Cork City and Dublin University; 83 of these MPs were Nationalists, of which 73 were Redmondites, 8 were members of a splinter group led by William O'Brien and the other two classified themselves as Independent Nationalists; in only 29 constituencies were candidates put up in opposition to Redmond's party, and 18 of these were followers of O'Brien, whose grouping was sprung originally from the Home Rule party itself. Yet this party, whose stranglehold on the country was almost total, was a most peculiar creation since, according to David Fitzpatrick, it had "no provincial branches, no rank-and-file party members, and no formal hierarchy." (*Politics and Irish Life 1913–21*, p 85).

The nearest thing to a party structure or machine was provided by the United Irish League. This had been set up in 1898 by William O'Brien with the aim of pressurising the government into accelerating the process of land redistribution in the west of Ireland, but it expanded so rapidly that by 1900 it was accepted by the reunited party as the official Home Rule organisation. The League, however, was always subordinate to the party despite the fact that it had well over a thousand branches by 1914.

In January 1914 at the annual meeting of the National Directory of the United Irish League the official returns showed Meath as having a greater number of branches than any other county in Leinster. There were twenty eight in all, located in Trim, Rathkenny, Kilskyre, Summerhill, Monknewtown, Kilmessan, Dunderry, Slane, Kilbeg, Kilmoon, Navan, Castletown, Dunboyne, Rathmolyon, Dunshaughlin, Boardsmill, Killyon, Oldcastle, Kells, Ballivor, Yellow Furze, Warrenstown, Girley-Cortown, Jordanstown-Rathcore, Stamullen-Julianstown, Oristown-Kilberry, Donore-Rosnaree and Moynalty-Newcastle. These branches were grouped into two sections, depending on whether they were located in the Meath North or South constituencies; delegates from the branches formed an executive in each constituency and it was with

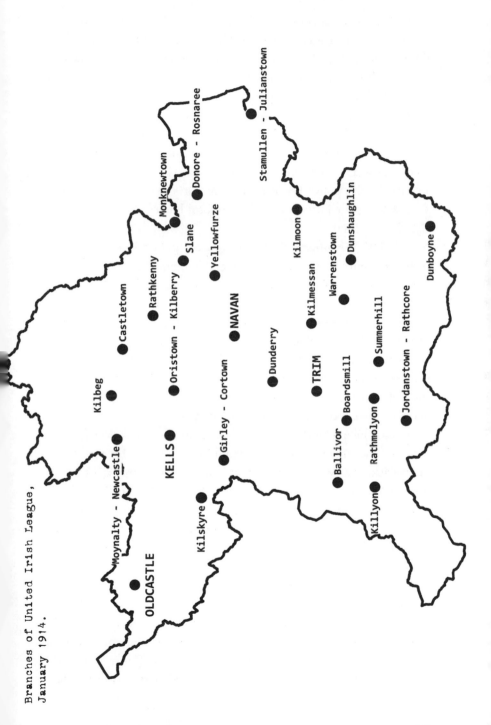

Branches of United Irish League, January 1914.

13

these executives that the two MPs liaised.

At the start of each year every UIL branch held a collection for funds in its locality; the amounts collected and those contributing were often published in the local newspapers. Almost without exception at the head of each list, as the biggest contributors, were the local Catholic clergy and in many instances Catholic priests were active members and frequent attendees of branch meetings in the parishes. Also high up in the subscription lists were county, rural and urban councillors for whom it was absolutely imperative to be seen to be involved in the UIL. Indeed, on this point, David Fitzpatrick states that support of Home Rule was "a prerequisite for election to local bodies" (*Politics and Irish Life 1913–21*, p 87).

The UIL was undoubtedly the foremost political organisation in early twentieth century Ireland but not far behind, and in some respects rivalling it in popularity, came the Ancient Order of Hibernians. The AOH can be traced back almost four hundred years when it was originally set up as a secret society designed to oppose England's rule. In penal times, according to *The Catholic Encyclopedia* (1965) "tradition had it that members stood as special protectors of the priest as he secretly celebrated Mass". This dual role of the AOH was summed up in its motto 'Faith and Fatherland'. The Order came to the USA in 1836 and took root in centres of Irish population.

In 1904 Joseph Devlin, a leading Home Rule MP, took over management of the organisation and remoulded it so that by 1913, states Fitzpatrick, the AOH "was a direct competitor of the UIL's as the principal launching pad for political office in Nationalist Ireland" (*Politics and Irish Life 1913–1921*, p 97). Its popularity was also enhanced by the fact that it was a designated organisation for administering sickness and unemployment benefits under the National Insurance Act passed in 1911.

In April 1914 the annual convention of the Meath AOH took place in Navan. The clubs represented were Kilmainhamwood, Navan, Breakey, Nobber, Kilbeg, Trim, Oldcastle, Kells, Moynalty, Newcastle, Rathkenny, Oristown, Ballivor, Wilkinstown, Drumconrath, Carnaross, Castletown, Kilskyre, Dunshaughlin, Boardsmill, Slane, Kilmessan, Enfield, Bellewstown and Meath Hill. This number, twenty five in all, is

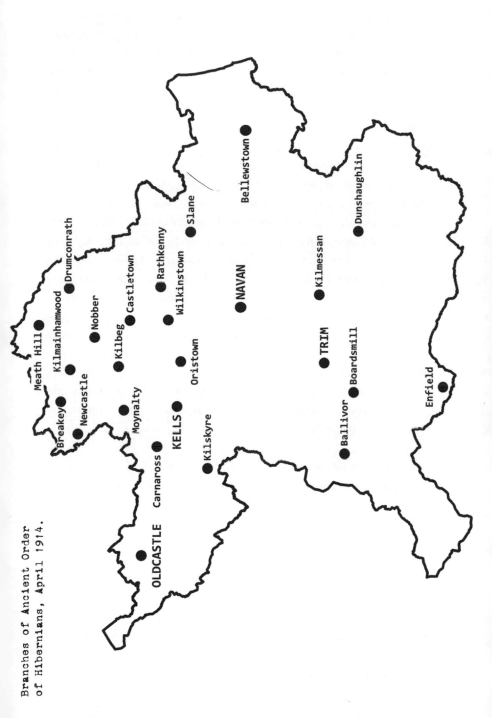

Branches of Ancient Order
of Hibernians, April 1914.

Bellewstown

Slane

Drumconrath

Rathkenny

Castletown

Kilmainhamwood

Dunshaughlin

Kilmessan

NAVAN

Nobber

Wilkinstown

Meath Hill

Kilbeg

TRIM

Boardsmill

Newcastle

Oristown

Breakey

Moynalty

Enfield

Ballivor

KELLS

Carnaross

Kilskyre

OLDCASTLE

just three short of the number of UIL branches recorded in the county for this year, and in the case of sixteen towns or villages there were units of both organisations in them. At this convention the following officers were elected: president, Joseph Madden, Oristown; vice-president, P.J. Newman, Trim; secretary, Michael McConnell, Navan; marshall, John Reilly, Castletown; trustees, Matthew Gartland and Thomas Lynch, both of Kells. Of these, we have seen that Gartland was a member of both the county council and Kells UDC; Lynch also was a dual councillor while Madden, a farmer, was a member of Kells RDC.

In the public mind the AOH are mostly regarded as the Catholic counterpart to the Orange Order. In Meath little attempt was made to play down the sectarian nature of the organisation. Speaking at the opening of a new AOH hall in Carnaross on Sunday, 1 February 1914, as reported in the *Meath Chronicle* on 7 February, Madden stated that "it was said that the Hibernians were intolerant". He made no apologies for this, going on to say that "he saw no reason why Irish Catholics should not unite and organise to look after their own interests", and that "he did not see why Catholics in this and every other parish should not come forward and join this great Catholic organisation". Another speaker on this occasion, T.P. O'Brien, Leinster organiser of the AOH, was more explicit, first stating the new hall would "become for them the centre of national thought and Catholic activity", then reminding his listeners that the AOH was,

> cradled in the darkest days of Irish history, when Irish Catholics were almost beaten to the ground, when every effort was made to exterminate every vestige of their religion and to strangle their national life.

He then went on to refer to the Dublin Lockout and Strike, just then in the process of fizzling out, saying that his organisation had played a notable part "in combating the anti-Christian doctrine of Socialism – the Hibernians showed they were willing to stand by their priests and Church". And how exactly they had done this O'Brien explained in Athboy in March when he referred to the Hibernians' action "in preventing the deportation of Catholic families from their homes in Ireland".

Although rivals in certain respects the UIL and AOH shared a lot in common, most obviously allegiance to the Home Rule Party, and the pursuit of parliamentary independence. At the county convention of the AOH referred to earlier, the only business, apart from the election of officers, reported on 4 April in the *Meath Chronicle* was the almost inevitable expression of "our implicit confidence and trust in Mr. John E. Redmond, our matchless leader". Members of both organisations were instructed to draft their members into local corps of the Volunteers. It is then, perhaps, no coincidence that of the twenty eight places where there were UIL branches in 1914, only four of these, Girley-Cortown, Kilskyre, Killyon and Warrenstown, had no Volunteer corps by the time of the August Volunteer convention. In the case of the AOH, the figures are five out of twenty-five, with Breakey, Bellewstown, Meath Hill, Newcastle and again Kilskyre the exceptions. Indeed, in the case of these exceptions a corps often existed in an adjacent locality, for instance, Moynalty to Newcastle or Fordstown to Girley-Cortown.

The UIL and AOH each merited columns of their own in the local newspapers, almost always on the front page and consisting of branch notes, notices of dates of the next meetings, a brief account of activities and the perennial words of homage to Redmond and the Party.

Socialism, of whatever brand, elicited little sympathy amongst establishment opinion in early twentieth-century Meath. The opinions of the AOH, an organisation totally in support of the omnipotent Party, have just been quoted. Nor did the editorial writers think much of Karl Marx and his theories. In an angry editorial on 24 January 1914 entitled 'The End of Larkinism', the *Chronicle* hailed "the collapse of Socialism in Dublin [as] all but complete", giving it to be understood that the Lockout had happened because "organised despotism donned a democratic cloak. Hooligans and cornerboys whipped the workers into line", and concluded that socialism which had been "born in violence and maintained by violence [was] ending in violence".

In a sermon on the subject delivered in Mullingar Cathedral by Bishop Laurence Gaughran (bishop of Meath 1906–1928) late in January, His Lordship reflected that socialism had recently gained "some foothold in this country", then warned his congregation that this doctrine recognised "no God, no sin, no Hell, no Heaven", and

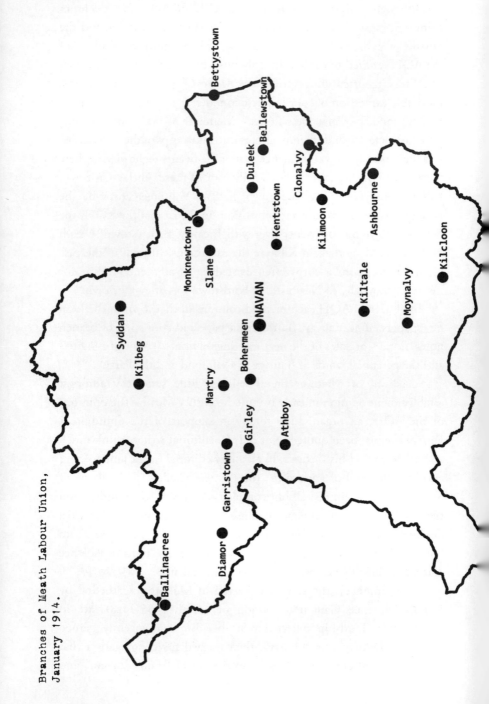

Branches of Meath Labour Union, January 1914.

Bettystown
Bellewstown
Duleek
Clonalvy
Kentstown
Kilmoon
Ashbourne
Monknewtown
Slane
Kilcloon
Kiltale
Moynalvy
NAVAN
Syddan
Bohermeen
Kilbeg
Martry
Girley
Athboy
Garristown
Diamor
Ballinacree

finished by praying that "this country might be protected and rendered strong against these dangers". This was fairly mild in comparison with the strictures of Bishop Nulty against Parnellism in 1892, but diocesan disapproval of left-wing ideas was made abundantly clear.

But if revolutionary socialism was unwanted in the county, organised labour fared a bit better. Next to the UIL and AOH, the Meath Labour Union was the third most prominent political organisation in the county at this time. At their annual convention in January 1914, the Union had delegates present from Martry, Bohermeen, Garristown, Kilmoon, Duleek, Clonalvy, Kentstown, Ashbourne, Kilcloon, Girley, Diamor, Ballinacree, Kiltale, Athboy, Syddan, Monknewtown, Kilbeg, Navan, Bettystown, Slane, Moynalvy and Bellewstown. The absence from this list of two of the county's three biggest centres of population (Navan, Kells and Trim), only emphasises the rural nature of the Union.

Not surprisingly then most of the employer-labour confrontations which took place in the county during this decade involved agricultural labourers in dispute with the farmers, although the years 1914 to 1916 were very quiet from this point of view. Of the leaders of the Meath Labour Union, two in particular deserve a special mention: James Harte was president of the MLU in the years after 1914. A Martry man, he was also very active in the GAA and was a member of Kells RDC. David Hall was destined to rise to a much higher political plateau, although he started from similar modest beginnings. Born in 1870 in Culmullin he made his living as an agricultural worker. The great upheavals of the years ahead saw him becoming chairman of Dunshaughlin RDC in 1920, a position which made him an ex-officio member of the county council. He was to serve a term as a Labour TD from September 1923 to June 1927, after which he did not stand again. Hall merits a mention in the *Magill Book of Irish Politics* (p 292), from which some of the foregoing biographical information has been obtained. The entry concludes by saying that, in April 1927, Hall, "acting on his own initiative, supported Dan Breen who had entered the Dáil to propose the removal of the Oath of Allegiance".

At their annual convention in January 1916 the MLU claimed to have a membership of over two thousand. Like the UIL and the AOH, it had its own column in the local newspapers on a regular basis, giving summary notes on branch meetings and activities. Although its main preoccupation was securing good wages and conditions for its members, the MLU also supported the Home Rule Party in its quest for Irish self-government. While not as zealous in their devotion to this cause as the other two organisations, nevertheless a meeting of the executive in August 1914, reported in the *Meath Chronicle* on 8 August 1914, passed the obligatory vote of congratulations to Redmond for his statement that "the coast of Ireland [would] be defended from foreign invasion by her armed sons", and a year later five of the Union's branches were represented at a major UIL-organised political rally in Navan.

Also represented at this gathering was the Irish National Foresters, the organisation which justifiably prides itself as being the forerunner of the present day social services and welfare programmes. At a time of often harrowing poverty and distress, when recourse to the local St. Vincent de Paul society, if such existed, was frequently the only hope for relief, the Foresters were providing protection for their members against sickness and other unwanted eventualities. Although a halting start had been made to the welfare state by the provision of old age pensions in 1908 and the National Insurance Act of 1911, these gave meagre enough benefits and the Foresters played a crucial role in supplementing whatever state aid accrued to its members.

Although the greatly expanding social services of the post-war world may have rendered some branches superfluous, many more went into liquidation and had their premises confiscated as a result of overspending by the organisation's executive committee in the 1920s. The Navan, or Dean Cogan, branch survived the time of the liquidation only because the deeds of its properties were lodged in a local bank. In the second decade of the century, however, the Foresters flourished also in Kells (Fr O'Growney branch), Trim and Oldcastle, although the only rural area with a branch was Rathmolyon which, as we have seen, was involved in the setting up of the local Volunteer corps there. There was also a rural branch just over the county boundary in Mullagh.

The Irish National Foresters were established in 1877. Its purpose is summed up in its motto 'Unity, Benevolence and Nationality'. Unity refers to the non-sectarian nature of the organisation, a factor which differentiated it from the AOH. This aspect is emphasised in the Chief

Ranger's ceremony book, a sort of official handbook, which stresses that the organisation is open to "all Irishmen irrespective of class or creed" and later, in the procedure for admittance of new members, the relevant passage exhorts the neophyte to respect all men "regardless of the altar at which they kneel". Benevolence refers, as the handbook puts it, to "protection and benefit in sickness, distress or death"; to this end every branch has an officer known as Woodward whose function it is to visit sick members and dispense their allowances and give a report on such matters at each meeting.

The forest is the metaphor by which the Foresters measure the terms of life; thus the branch chairman or president is titled the Chief Ranger, and his second in command is the sub-Chief Ranger while the Woodward, the officer who visits the sick members, means a person who guards the woods. Each branch also appoints Beadles whose role at meetings is "to guard the door against admission of unprivileged persons and disorderly members". A beadle was originally a parish officer with the power to punish petty offenders and the term seems to have come from Scotland. The sylvan image is maintained in the beautifully illustrated banner of the Navan branch. This banner depicts a figure, representing the Woodward, whose dress and appearance seems to have been taken straight out of the Robin Hood stories and who is shown bringing the fruits of the forest to a sick colleague.

The Navan branch was officially registered as a member branch on 3 March 1899. Its earliest meeting places were on Watergate Street and later on Church Hill. The INF national convention for 1910 was held in Navan in August; most of the business was conducted outdoors, as shown by a photograph that belonged to the Navan branch. This photograph is remarkable for its clarity, and it shows what the centre of the town looked like in the early years of the century. While the names on the shops and stores and other businesses may have changed the buildings themselves remain almost exactly the same today as they were over seventy years ago.

All of this is a long way removed from consideration of the goings on of 1914 and succeeding years, but we may return to this by reflecting on the third element in the Foresters' motto, that of nationality. This seems to have been dear to the organisation's founders who stated that the INF was based on the "broad and undying principles of Irish Nationality" and indeed the handbook concludes with the slogan 'God save Ireland', an aspiration associated with the Fenian Manchester Martyrs. When the Foresters were founded in 1877 the Home Rule movement was just beginning to gather the momentum that carried it through the exciting times of the following decade. Perhaps this explains the stress on Nationality in the handbook which was first issued in 1889. The INF was undoubtedly in sympathy with Redmond and his aims, but that is not to say that they were reneging on their avowedly non-political ethos, since at that time the dominance of the Home Rule Party over Irish political life was so overwhelming that the national interest became synonymous with the objectives of the party and their attainment.

Thus it is not surprising that the Rathmolyon Foresters were to the forefront in the establishment of their local Volunteer corps; that the meeting which founded the Volunteers in Navan held its initial meeting in the hall on Church Hill then rented by the INF; that at least one member, James McNamee, mentioned earlier as being on the first committee of this corps was also a prominent figure in the Dean Cogan (Navan) branch of the Foresters; or that the Navan and Oldcastle branches were represented at the UIL county rally in Navan in August 1915.

One of the most interesting developments in Meath in the second decade of the century was the growth of an organisation, mentioned already in passing, calling itself the Back to the Land movement. Land, of course, had been for a long time the perennial problem in Ireland and although the Wyndham Act of 1903 and an amendment in 1909 had done much towards providing a solution, there still remained in many parts of the country a land hunger that had not yet been sated. Meath was one such area, a fact made clear at a UIL branch meeting in Warrenstown in January 1914 when a speaker, in no uncertain terms, told his listeners that it was time "to compel ranch holders, graziers and land sharks to give up the land for division among the people."

The UIL had been established originally to hasten the redistribution of the landed estates and, although by now Home Rule was its primary objective, the League still maintained a strong commitment towards the landless tenants and farm workers. Back to the Land pursued its aim of land division with great vigour from its first appearance in the county in 1906. From its beginning the movement had very strong support in the editorial and news columns of the *Drogheda Independent* which reported extensively on its aims and activities. Surprisingly, Back to the Land merited hardly any mention at all in the *Meath Chronicle*. A typical editorial in the *Drogheda Independent* talked of Meath containing thousands of acres of untenanted land – and alongside the landless population.

This was rather a generalisation of the problem and it was much more convincingly stated by a Dublin Home Rule MP, John Nugent, when he addressed the annual convention of the county's AOH in April 1916. As reported in the *Meath Chronicle* of 1 April, Nugent began by pointing out that the county contained over 600,000 acres but supported a population of only 65,000; this gave it a density of population of only about nine per acre, in comparison, for instance, with neighbouring Louth which then had thirty two per acre. He went on to say that 120,000 acres in the county were let under the grazing system, and reasoned that if these ranches were to be divided into holdings of even twenty five acres then "those derelict lands" would be capable of supporting 4,800 families, which, at an average of five per family, would add another 24,000 to the county's population. Nugent concluded:

> was it any wonder that five workhouses had to be provided to contain the paupers, and that over £30,000 a year had to be found for the relief of the destitute poor?

Patrick White MP, a vigorous supporter of Back to the Land, stressed another aspect of the movement's aims, when he addressed a county meeting in the St. Vincent de Paul Hall in Kells in the same month. The population of Meath in 1841, he stated, had been over 180,000 but:

> 65,000 have passed away due to British misrule and unbridled landlordism while another 68,000 have left for foreign lands – the unscrupulous landlords have levelled homes so that cattle and sheep might graze there.

White declared that their aim must be "to undo this past evil and stay the tide of emigration."

The organisation had almost unanimous support amongst the then leaders of public opinion, both political and otherwise. We have seen how the AOH annual convention in 1916 provided a platform for Back to the Land. The Order was always represented at the movement's regular county meetings, usually held in Kells, while also invariably in attendance were delegates from the UIL and the Meath Labour Union. Local politicians made a point of being present, while clergy were also very much to the forefront; indeed the meetings in Kells were always chaired by Rev. Dr Dooley, VG, the local parish priest. Patrick White, as has been mentioned, was a committed supporter while David Sheehy put in occasional appearances, still attracted to a cause which he had first espoused a generation before in the Land League and Plan of Campaign days, a cause for which he had served a year and a half in prison.

But the real driving force behind the movement was another priest, Fr Robert Barry, parish priest of Oldcastle. Again and again, in the columns of the *Drogheda Independent* for these years Fr Barry's name appears in connection with Back to the Land activities, organising meetings, establishing new branches, addressing the county conventions and being a perpetual thorn in the side of local landlords, graziers or their representatives. This is evident from a meeting in Trim in March 1916, when a speaker stated that Fr Barry in Oldcastle had been directly responsible for the division of 2,300 acres and the placing of over a hundred families. And in March of the following year the *Drogheda Independent* reported that Fr Barry had harassed the Estate Commissioners into buying seven hundred acres of the Naper Estate in Oldcastle.

Apart from Oldcastle, there was a branch in Culmullin, which styled itself the Culmullin Vigilance Committee. This committee had as its guiding figure David Hall and its aim was the division of the local Culmullin and Creemore estates. In Nobber, the branch was led by a young doctor, P.J. Cusack, and its target was the Spiddal Farm, while in Dunshaughlin the land hungry were determined to divide the so called Bush Farm amongst themselves. The movement was also organised in the three main towns with Kells, as we have seen, very much the headquarters of county activities. These branches, and others, acted as watchdogs in their localities, waiting for farms or parts of estates to be put up for sale. What usually happened then is best illustrated from this example from Navan towards the end of 1917. In late September a branch meeting was held regarding the proposed sale of several thousand acres of the Fitzherbert Estate adjacent to the town. The branch members decided to call on Fitzherbert to sell to the Estate Commissioners for redistribution amongst the landless men of the district and also to appeal to local farmers and traders to abstain from bidding for the land.

On the following Sunday a meeting to muster support from amongst the public was held at Proudstown where over six hundred were reported to have attended. The following month, when the lands came up for auction, Back to the Land representatives were present at the courthouse in the town. Amongst them was Patrick White who said that he was in attendance in order "to protest against the attempts to revive landlordism and dual ownership"; he was prepared to bid for the ten lots at £10,000. This evoked no response from the sellers but when the auction got under way formally no bids were forthcoming from any quarter. The upshot was that Fitzherbert, his auctioneer and his solicitor were forced to leave the courthouse and the sale fell through.

These then were the personalities, branches and activities of the Back to the Land movement. One aspect of the organisation, an aspect which has already been alluded to in passing, needs to be highlighted. We have seen how the movement was strongly dependent on the support of the established political entities, particularly the UIL and the AOH In the case of at least one branch, the Navan one, this support actually involved total absorption of the Back to the Land membership into the local UIL. When the branch was formed in January 1916 the *Drogheda Independent* reported that the members have become a sub-branch of the UIL with its own chairman, secretary and committee. This bears out the statement made by David Fitzpatrick, namely, that "groups wishing to protect their own interests accepted that success was possible only within the Home Rule machine" (*Politics and Irish Life 1913–21*, p 100). This willingness to accept the suzerainty of Redmond, his party and the League may seem to have been a sensible policy, but as early as April 1915, even the staunchly nationalist *Independent* was bemoaning the "unwarranted apathy" of the UIL in Meath. And somebody else discerned at the time much the same as what Fitzpatrick, many years later, was referring to in the above quote. The *Meath Chronicle* was, by the end of 1915, beginning to distance itself from uncritical support of the Home Rule movement. A columnist who signed himself 'Tara', his real identity was probably Hugh Smith, later editor of the paper and, as we shall see, a prominent figure in the re-organisation of the Volunteers in the county after the 1916 Rising, was positively outspoken in his attacks on the Home Rulers. 'Tara' bluntly described the absorption of Navan Back to the Land into the local UIL as follows: "the UIL had officers but no members, while the Back to the Land had both and now the UIL have taken over their members". This policy of the Home Rule-UIL monster to bring within its grasp other organisations has been described by Fitzpatrick as illustrating "the techniques of the party vampire" (*Politics and Irish Life 1913–1921*, p 101), as though it were using the life-blood of such organisations to sustain itself. As early as the spring of 1914 the party had been casting longing eyes on the Volunteer movement and its rapidly growing tens of thousands. It was a longing which, when fulfilled, was ultimately to prove self-destructive for the all-embracing creature.

September 1914, the month after Slane Hill, saw further progress in the organisation of the Volunteer movement at a national level. In this scheme Meath became the kernel of the Tenth Brigade; all corps in the county were divided into six battalions; two of these were allotted to the Eleventh Brigade centred on Drogheda. The other four battalions with their bases in Navan, Kells, Trim and Dunshaughlin made up the bulk of the Tenth Brigade with headquarters in Navan.

September also was the month which brought a triumphal climax to a half-century of nationalist agitation and pressure when, on the eighteenth, the Home Rule Bill was granted Royal assent. The local press reported scenes of great euphoria and uninhibited celebrations, with bonfires, blazing tar barrels, lights left on in houses and shops, torchlight processions organised by the AOH and UIL, the public and communal singing of nationalistic songs and marches by Volunteer corps. When the bill passed into law in May of that year the *Meath Chronicle* reported in its 30 May issue, "an unprecedented display of practically unanimous enthusiasm on the part of the entire populace".

September was, however, to prove the best of times and worst of times and, for the Home Rulers, the bad was to outlive the good. The party's overtures to the Volunteers had been deflected by MacNeill and his committee until 9 June, when Redmond had presented them with an ultimatum to co-opt an equal number of his own nominated representatives. Reluctantly they had agreed. Then on 3 August, with the Great War in its early days, Redmond stated to the House of Commons that the defence of Ireland could safely be entrusted to the Irish Volunteers. Finally, on 20 September, just two days after the Bill had been granted Royal assent, the Irish leader, speaking in Woodenbridge, county Wicklow, urged the Volunteers not just to fight in defence of Ireland but to go "wherever the firing line extends". While the first two of the three just mentioned actions of Redmond may have caused some dissension in Volunteer ranks, it was the spontaneous address in Woodenbridge which was to have such far-reaching consequences.

Even before 20 September Meath had witnessed dissatisfaction with the direction the Volunteers were taking when the county Inspector-General Earl Fingal sent his resignation to headquarters. In his letter published in the *Meath Chronicle* of 5 September, 1914, Fingal gave two reasons for the withdrawal of his services. One was that his duties had never been defined and the other was that he believed the best policy was "to induce every man willing to serve to join Lord Kitchener's army". Ironically, then, Fingal's second reason for resignation was to become Volunteer policy within a matter of weeks. A columnist in the *Chronicle* of 12 September felt little regret at the departure of Fingal, stating that he had never been interested in the Volunteers' aim of securing and maintaining "the rights and liberties common to all the people of Ireland" but wanted to use the movement "solely as recruiting sergeant for the English army".

Whatever the truth of this charge, Fingal was soon followed out of the county Volunteer organisation by another member of the gentry class, Sir John Dillon, who in a letter to his local Skryne corps wrote that he was severing his connections because "due to recent events they (the Volunteers) were now a political body". Dillon was probably referring to Redmond's takeover of the Volunteer Committee in June and his reason for resigning – that "they were now a political body" – is interesting and brings us back to a point mentioned earlier, namely, where did the national aspect of the Home Rulers end and their political interests begin?

For most people in Meath, the reasons put forward by Fingal and Dillon for their opting out of the Volunteers probably carried little weight. Those disgruntled with the Irish leader felt this way for a reason totally opposite to what Fingal had said, that is, they felt the Volunteers should have no connection whatever with the war. But for the time being John Redmond still retained the support of both the County Board and the great majority of the corps. When the former met on the 7 October, they declared, as reported in the *Meath Chronicle* on 10 October, their "adhesion to Mr Redmond and the majority of the Provisional Committee of the Irish Volunteers ... and we request the various corps throughout the county to affiliate with the majority of the Provisional Committee under Mr Redmond's presidency". In Kells, according to the *Meath Chronicle* of 3 October, it was carried unanimously that "the members of the committee of the Kells INV corps repudiate the action of the Central Executive Committee ... and place on record our unswerving allegiance to John Redmond and the Irish Parliamentary Party".

Although definitive evidence is lacking, there is little doubt that the vast majority of the corps in the county harboured similar sentiments. It was to be almost six months before the first report of dissent from any corps appeared in either of the local newspapers while in the immediate aftermath of the crisis the *Volunteer Notes* column in the *Drogheda Independent* contained resolutions of support for Redmond from Dunshaughlin, Gormanston, Skryne, Fordstown, Bellewstown, Kentstown and Boardsmill. Indeed, in Boardsmill the corps was quite adamant in its support, for having first unanimously rejected the manifesto of what they termed the "Sinn Féin section of the Provisional Committee" this document was then, so the *Drogheda Independent* reports, publicly burned to cheering for Redmond and his party.

Behind the facade of solidarity with the leader, however, all was not well with the Volunteers. The very fact that the local papers carried motions of confidence in Redmond from only seven out of about sixty corps may indicate a growing apathy and disillusionment with the Irish leader. 'Tara', the *Meath Chronicle* columnist referred to earlier, was in no doubt about this. It was around this time he began his bitter and scathing attacks on the whole established Nationalist movement, Volunteers, United Irish League and the parliamentary party alike. As regards the Volunteers, he continually harped on the theme that they had now been reduced from a military to "a political organisation [fighting] with resolutions" and he urged all Volunteers to get a rifle which "will speak louder and more effectively than catch-cry phrases of adulation."

This was as early as September 1914, reported in the *Meath Chronicle* on 26 September, the month of the split in the Volunteers. But right through 1915 and into 1916 'Tara' relentlessly reiterated variations on this theme, referring to the organisation as "an impotent body" (March 1915), "the tool of Home Rule and the UIL" (June 1915), "sham Volunteers" (July 1915) and slyly asking in November 1915 why such Volunteers were so reluctant to join the British army, given the urgings of Redmond and the great recruiting drives going on in the county at the time. On a more specific level, in October 1914, the columnist alleged that the Volunteers in Navan had been three hundred strong "before Redmond had assumed the dictatorship, but now had only a score".

While, for obvious reasons, 'Tara' cannot be accepted as an objective commentator, there are certain indications which confirm the substance of his remarks regarding the demise of the Volunteers in the county. Best of all perhaps is the almost total disappearance from both local newspapers of the Volunteer columns which only shortly before had been so vibrant and enthusiastic in their accounts of meetings, drills and rifle practices. The sudden passing of these columns dates from October 1914 and henceforth they reappear only at very irregular intervals. There is no question here of deliberate exclusion of the organisation by the two papers: the *Drogheda Independent* was still, and was to remain to the very end, a staunch supporter of John Redmond; while the *Chronicle*, notwithstanding the partisan outbursts of 'Tara', maintained a moderate editorial line and still carried its column devoted to UIL (as well as AOH) activities. These columns, or their absence, may safely be taken as an accurate barometer of the state of the Volunteers, and the general disarray was reflected in an anonymous letter to the *Chronicle* of 19 December when the writer plaintively asked:

> The people of Meath are anxious to know what happened to the movement in this county and who is in charge? They are also anxious to know what became of the money collected for the purchase of rifles, or the money collected in aid of the Athboy Band?

The organisation's paralysis continued right through 1915. It can be seen at one level in an account in the *Meath Chronicle* on 30 January 1915 of a meeting of the Skryne corps. Three items of business were reported: the first was a motion condemning the Estate Commissioners for "bringing a man from Connaght to Sir John Dillon's farm at Cardiffstown, when there were young men in the vicinity quite capable of taking those lands and working them in a proper manner for the benefit of their neighbourhood"; the second was a request to the local clergy "to secure if possible the use of the schools for plays and concert to be staged by Kentstown Dramatic Class in aid of the Corps"; finally there was a condemnation of David Sheehy and a warning to electors "to beware when he seeks re-election" – this part of the report is very vague, and why Sheehy incurred the displeasure of the Skryne men is not stated. There are, then, references to neither drilling nor rifle practice; nor to Home Rule; indeed not even the obligatory homage to John Redmond. All this was a far cry from the Volunteers of just six months before. Of course, it is impossible to generalise on just one meeting of one corps, but there is further evidence to support the view that the Volunteers were by now rapidly in decline.

At an Easter rally called by Redmond for the Phoenix Park, it was reported that only three or four corps from Meath were in attendance. And at a county review held on the Hill of Tara in August – exactly a year after the outstandingly successful Slane review – only seven Meath corps were represented – Dunboyne, Dunshaughlin, Drumconrath, Kilmessan, Ratoath, Skryne and Robinstown. The *Chronicle* on 21 August 1915 noted that, despite reports of an attendance of between eight hundred and a thousand, the real figure was closer to three hundred and sixty-one, among them both MPs for the county; the same report also pointed out that "no town in Meath was represented".

The definitive evidence in support of the decline of the Meath Volunteers came at much the same time at the annual meeting of the County Board of the Irish Volunteers. Here the secretary reported that the number of corps affiliated and entitled to vote on that day was ten – Slane, Skryne, Drumconrath, Robinstown, Dunboyne, Kilmoon, Johnstown, Ratoath, Drumree and Killallon. As well as that, there were a further twelve corps registered with the Central Committee in Dublin. The total of twenty-two was only about one third of the number of corps which had met in Navan just a year before, and this drastic fall off resulted in instructions from the Inspector-General in Dublin to reduce the number of battalions from the original six to three. The corps were reorganised as follows:

First Battalion: Navan, Johnstown, Kentstown, Robinstown, Kells and Killallon.

Second Battalion: Kilbeg, Meath Hill, Duleek, Slane, Donore, Stackallen, Bellewstown and Drumconrath.

Third Battalion: Rathmore, Skryne, Dunshaughlin, Summerhill, Boardsmill, Ratoath, Kilmoon and Dunboyne.

More damning evidence came that same month, August 1915, at the UIL-organised convention held in Navan. This had been advertised and highlighted by both local newspapers for weeks in advance, and there was, as we shall see later, a not unimpressive turnout. But once again the Volunteers were poorly represented, with only seven corps in attendance – the same seven as at the Tara review except for Slane instead of Kilmessan.

The meteoric rise and fall of the organisation can be seen in microcosm in the fortunes of the Kells corps. A minute book of this corps has survived and covers the period in question. The book, in fact, is no more than a school copybook and the sketchy notes indicate an impatient minutes secretary, but there is enough there to confirm the general pattern established in respect to the county at large. The meetings were held in the St. Vincent de Paul Hall. The first entry is for 14 July 1914, and for the next few months these meetings were well attended; those present included several urban councillors such as John English, Patrick Collins, John Reilly and Nicholas Tully. At the meeting of 27 July it was decided to send a deputation to Rev. Dr Dooley to ask "how far he was willing to act with the committee in putting new life in the corps"; the next meeting was assured that Dr Dooley was "the heart and soul in the movement" and from then on meetings were invariably attended by a local curate, Fr McCann. Another who attended a number of meetings was the Marquis of Headfort, perhaps anxious to allay the report earlier in the year which implied that he had leanings towards the UVF; his opinions were usually solicited respectfully and he was treated with the expected deference, such as at the meeting on 10 August, which passed him a vote of thanks "for his kindliness in attending the meeting". At about this time also, the secretary was asked to write to the local branches of the AOH, GAA and INF asking "for their co-operation in the movement". The months from July to September show the Kells corps in fighting mood. At one stage there were three drill instructors, and at the meeting of 24 July a speaker stressed that "the best way to get men to attend drill is to get rifles for practice". A month later the secretary read a letter from the Birmingham Small Arms Company, stating that they were:

> unable to supply rifles but had handed the inquiry to the Messrs. Westley Richards and Co. who said that they were ready to supply Lee-Enfield military rifles at £5.5.0 each.

The secretary was ordered to procure six of these as well as six musketry instruction books. A meeting later in August showed how earnest the committee was in this matter when it was decided to write to Patrick White asking how John Redmond intended to distribute rifles "as we consider ourselves entitled to a certain percentage".

All of these features – strong clerical involvement, lukewarm gentry support, involvement of existing nationalist organisations, the early enthusiasm and impatience for procurement of rifles, and the presence of local politicians at the forefront – have been noted elsewhere. After those come other all too recognisable features. In late September the rot set in. The committee protested its "implicit confidence in the Irish party and its brilliant leader John Redmond". As though that were not enough, only a fortnight later, litany-like it put on record its "unswerving allegiance to John Redmond and the Irish Parliamentary Party", a resolution that has been quoted earlier in this section. By the end of 1914 membership and support were in rapid decline.

A special meeting held on 13 December was told that they needed "ten more members on the committee in order to fulfill the rules of headquarters in order to affiliate one company". And at the same time the depleted committee decided to abandon an idea, suggested in November, of holding a public meeting in the town for the purpose of re-organising the corps, although they had already invited down a speaker from headquarters and had five hundred handbills printed for distribution. It may be because the secretary just did not bother writing up the minutes any more or, as is more likely, because there were no meetings being held, but the next recorded entry is not until the following 23 February. And after that there is a huge gap until the final recorded meeting on 7 December 1916. Amongst the brief minutes for that occasion is the following:

> Mr Dillon wanted to know who gave authority to have the rifles sold and what became of the balance of the cash. The treasurer was asked for the bank book but had not it to put before the meeting.

There are strong echoes here of the forlorn rhetorical questions of the anonymous letter writer to the *Chronicle* almost exactly two years before.

Such then was the predicament of the Volunteers, but what of the foremost nationalist organisation, the United Irish League? According to 'Tara', in a column written in June 1915, most of the county's UIL branches "exist only on paper", and in the following paragraph he calls the League "a puissant body". During this year, 'Tara' launched a series of slashing attacks on the party in Westminster, with constant snide references to "the £400". This was the salary then paid to an MP, and the columnist continually accused the Irish party of selling their principles in order to retain this; but, as 'Tara' stated, the Irish people were beginning at last to see this and the decline of the League he attributed to this factor. Of course no one would expect 'Tara' to say anything good about any aspect or section of the Home Rule movement, but by 17 April 1915 even the *Drogheda Independent* was lamenting, as we have seen earlier, "the unwarranted apathy" of the UIL in Meath and expressing disquiet at "the number of unaffiliated branches".

Although certainly not afflicted by the paralysis that had immobilised the county's Volunteers, the League nevertheless had some cause for concern as to its own health. This is evident from the county convention – referred to on several occasions already – which the League organised and which met in the Catholic Young Men's Society Hall in Navan on 15 August 1915. The purpose of this convention, as advertised in the local press, was "to organise the National Movement in the County" and at the outset of proceedings this was repeated by a speaker who said that they were all present "to reorganise the branches of the UIL." Less than a year after Home Rule had been given the Royal Assent and placed on the statute book, the national organisation in Meath was in difficulty. Perhaps there was no contradiction here: after all with Home Rule granted had not the movement lost its *raison d'être*?

Whatever the reason for the fall off in support, the August convention tried to go some way to arrest that decline. It was an impressive gathering with the usual cross-section of representation. On the platform were the two MPs, several local councillors and about a dozen clergy (there were letters of apology for their absence from four other priests, one of them being Dr Dooley of Kells). Public bodies that sent delegations included Meath County Council, Navan and Kells UDCs, Navan RDC and the Navan Board of Guardians. The whole array of nationalist organisations within the county was also represented but, as stated earlier, only Navan and Oldcastle represented the INF. There were only seven Volunteer corps present and even the Labour Union was lukewarm in its support with delegates, coming from only five branches – Bellewstown, Bettystown, Dromone, Kentstown and Syddan. There was a better muster from the AOH, with eighteen of their branches being present; but this figure included only fifteen of the twenty five clubs which had been at the AOH county convention in April 1914; the other three at the Navan convention were Athboy, Rathcore and Oristown.

As to the UIL itself, the turnout of members must have been a disappointment, because of the twenty eight branches which have been listed as making up the League's strength in the county in January 1914, only thirteen were represented at the August 1915 convention; these were Rathkenny, Kells, Kilbeg, Slane, Oldcastle, Cortown-Girley, Oristown-Kilberry, Dunderry, Kilmessan, Warrenstown, Yellow Furze, Kilmoon and Rathmolyon. On the plus side, it must be stated, was the presence of new branches – Nobber, Moybolgue, Ardcath, Duleek, Athboy, Skryne and Garadice. While this gave a total of twenty, there is little doubt but that the stated purpose of the conference was fairly urgent. As reported in the *Meath Chronicle* on 4 September 1915, business was presided over by Rev. Fr Poland, Administrator of Navan parish, who explained the objectives of those present as twofold: the first is known, to reorganise the branches of the UIL in the county; the second is predictable, "to renew our confidence in John Redmond and the Irish Parliamentary Party", as Fr Poland put it.

Apart from resuscitating the UIL, Fr Poland told his listeners that they must work "to support in every parish in Meath the Irish National Volunteers since the war will end in a few months". The other wing of the Volunteers – those who had rejected Redmond's leadership – came in for much criticism: Fr Poland described them generously as "men who loved Ireland well but not wisely", although "there were some of them who have not done one hour's work in the national cause". Another speaker, John P. Timmon, a member of Navan UDC, condemned these same people for their "rotten dog-in-the-manger policy", while Ignatius Kelly, a national organiser for the UIL, averred that they were "traitors who would sell their country for an extra bullock".

The next couple of months saw a flurry of activity as the League tried to shake off its inertia. There were reports of the reorganisation of old branches, as at Navan and Trim, and the establishment of new ones, as at Batterstown, as well as meetings in areas such as Moynalty, Athboy and Yellow Furze to drum up support for existing branches. But this frantic outburst of organisation was short lived. To return to our barometer – the newspaper columns – to measure the level of support for the UIL, the readings show a sharp fall, and this decline continues until the end of 1915 and right into the pivotal year of 1916. What had once been a fixed weekly column with notes pertaining to an average of fifteen to twenty branches was, by the middle of 1916, appearing only at irregular intervals and greatly contracted in size.

As to the two MPs, the year 1915 brought them contrasting fortunes in their personal lives. White was married in July and the *Drogheda Independent* reported that he himself received great congratulations and his wife a warm address of welcome from the people of his native Clonalvy. Sheehy, however, had little cause for joy when, a few months earlier, in March, he appeared in a London bankruptcy court. The petitioner was a Mr. Blumberg of Piccadilly, to whom Sheehy owed £70. During the hearing Sheehy attributed the debt to losses incurred on the Stock Exchange as well as to betting on horses. The latter must, in fact, have made up the greater portion of his liabilities, for he admitted that since the previous 11 December he had lost no less than £400 on gambling on horses – an amount that was equal to his annual salary as an MP. At a general meeting of his creditors in April, the official receiver announced that he had put together a scheme for repayment of Sheehy's debts, and this was accepted. But clearly the member for Meath South had much more on his mind than the dire warnings which the Skryne Volunteers had meted out to him a couple of months earlier.

So far, much has been said about the county's various political and semi-political groupings, their activities and personalities. It may be timely now to look at the administrative and political structures then in existence. Whatever the shortcomings of British rule in Ireland in the early years of the century, the lack of representative institutions at local level could hardly be cited as one. In comparison with the present day, Meath enjoyed – some would say suffered from – what can only be described as a plethora of local democracy. Following the local government elections of 1914, an aggregate total of 433 members were sitting on no fewer than 17 elected bodies. The former figure may be distorted somewhat because, as we shall see, a significant amount of duplication existed, with members elected to one body being ex-officio members of another; and as well as that, there were about ten men who sat on three different councils. Even allowing for such discrepancies, however, the present day (1983) situation in the county of fifty-six members on four different councils pales in comparison with that of about seventy years ago – and this all the more when it is considered that the present population of over 90,000 far exceeds the 65,000 plus recorded in the 1911 census. The reputed 'jobs-for-the-boys' syndrome in Irish political life may well have its origins in these times, when the countrywide proliferation of elective councils created a whole host of local power bases and positions of prestige and a veritable army of men parading around with the letters 'Co. C', 'UDC', 'RDC' or 'PLG' after their names.

The aforementioned initials stand for the four different types of local bodies then in Meath. Three of these – the county council, the urban district councils and the rural district councils – had their origins in the Local Government (Ireland) Act of 1898. This act was part of an overall policy of reform by the Conservative Party, with the ultimate aim of 'killing Home Rule with kindness'. The electorate for these councils consisted of all those qualified to vote in parliamentary elections as well as similarly qualified women – who were not allowed to vote in the Westminster elections – and all peers; the qualification in question was based on property and wealth, and there was a complex system of indices to determine one's eligibility. Only those deemed entitled to vote were also eligible for election to a council; there were some exceptions to this, the most significant being that while women could stand for urban and rural councils, they were, for some unclear reason, excluded from membership of county councils until 1911. The Act stipulated that elections be held every three years; the general trend was for the urban elections to take place in January with the county and rural contests being held on the same date in June.

The new county council returned following the triennial elections on 15 June 1914 was made up of thirty one members. These fell into three categories. Two members were always co-opted at the inaugural meeting of a newly-elected county council; in 1914, one of these was Sir Nugent Everard, the Lord Lieutenant of the county, a man whom we have seen had been continuously a co-opted member since the very first council meeting in 1899; the other was P.J. Kennedy of Enfield, who had chaired this inaugural meeting and had held his seat ever since.

The second category were the ex-officio members; there were eight of these and they owed their positions to the fact that they were chairmen of the county's eight rural councils; the rural councils were, in a sense, sub-committees of the premier body, a fact which explains the presence of these eight men. The third and biggest category comprised those directly elected. For this purpose Meath was divided into twenty-one county electoral divisions, each returning one member. The divisions were Ardbraccan, Athboy, Ballyboggan, Bective, Crossakiel, Donaghpatrick, Drumconrath, Duleek, Dunboyne, Dunshaughlin, Enfield, Kells, Kildalkey, Moynalty, Navan, Nobber, Oldcastle, Slane, Stamullen, Tara and Trim.

Among those elected councillors were some mentioned already in this account: Matthew Gartland (Kells), James McGlew (Donaghpatrick), Patrick O'Growney (Athboy) and Patrick Boyle (Slane), all of whom were early activists in the Volunteer movement. For future reference, the name of Patrick Moore (Dunboyne) is worth noting: an individualist, and never far from controversy, Moore marked his debut on the council by opposing the co-option of P.J. Kennedy, an action for which he could not find a seconder. The chairman of the council was Thomas Halligan (Tara), who had held this position since 1908; while vice-chairman was Edward Kelly (Dunshaughlin), who had been in attendance at the first Council meeting in 1899 and had held his seat ever since.

Long service was, in fact, a feature of note, since no fewer than nine of the 1914 councillors had been present at the inaugural meeting fifteen years earlier. And to make a more recent comparison of the thirty-one men at the 1914 meeting under discussion, only five had not sat on the previous Council. One is also struck by the number of councillors with the letters JP (Justice of the Peace) after their names; there were eleven of these and when added to Everard, the Lord Lieutenant, and Kennedy, who was High Sheriff of the county, one is presented with a group of men committed to the preservation of law and order and to the maintenance of the status quo. It was this characteristic which more than any other marks the 1914 council out in stark contrast to the council that was to convene six years later.

The County Council had much the same functions as it has today: the council's sub committees included a Roads Committee, Finance

Committee (dealing with the collection of rates), the County Committee of Agriculture and the Joint Committee of Technical Instruction. Others related to particular problems of that time such as the T.B. Prevention Act Committee and the Diseases of Animals Act Committee. The council also appointed a number of its members to committees dealing with old age pensions, the Stoneyford District Drainage Scheme and Mullingar Asylum. There was even a Midwives Committee at that time.

As mentioned earlier, there were eight rural district councils in Meath. In determining the boundaries of these, the architects of the Local Government (Ireland) Act decided that they should be largely co-extensive with the Poor Law Unions which had been in existence since the 1830s. Meath had five such unions and hence the rural councils of Navan, Trim, Kells, Oldcastle and Dunshaughlin. However, the boundaries of the unions often transcended county boundaries; in such cases the arrangement was that the various parts of a union which extended over more than one county would each be given its own rural council within the confines of the particular counties. To clarify this point, take for example the Union of Ardee: most of the union was in county Louth but it overlapped into the north-east corner of Meath; so this section of Meath comprising only three electoral divisions – Drumconrath, Grangegeeth and Killary – had its own rural council, known as Ardee (Meath) RDC or Ardee No. 2 RDC. There were two other instances of this in Meath: the Drogheda (Meath) Council was made up of the electoral divisions of Ardcath, Duleek, Julianstown, Mellifont, St. Mary's and Stamullen; while in the extreme south-west corner of Meath was Edenderry No. 3. RDC, comprising Ardnamullan, Ballyboggan, Castlejordan, Castlerickard, Hill of Down and Killyon. Thus were the county's eight rural district councils.

For election purposes the council areas were, as we have seen, arranged into district electoral divisions. Each division returned two members – in exceptional cases this was three – and there was provision for each council to co-opt, if it desired, up to three extra members. The number of representatives on each rural council following the 1914 elections was as follows: Navan 27, Kells 50, Trim 40, Oldcastle 19, Dunshaughlin 24, Ardee (Meath) 6, Drogheda (Meath) 12 and Edenderry No. 3, 12.

The chairmen of each rural council were, as stated earlier, ex-officio members of the county council. Although statutory bodies in their own right, the rural councils were in reality offshoots of the county councils, on whom they depended for much of their revenue. Their functions can be seen from the five sections into which their minute books were divided: Finance, Health, Labourers, Burial Board and Miscellaneous. The councils' officers reported on a large variety of matters such as inspection of dairies, general sanitary conditions in the district, maintenance of roads, the building and letting of cottages, appointment of caretakers to burial grounds and so on.

Then, as now, there were three UDCs – in Navan, Kells and Trim. The fifteen members in Navan were elected every three years, or at least they were supposed to be, but the election in January 1914 was in fact the first since 1908. The chairman of Navan UDC in 1914 was John Spicer, who by this time had sat on this body and its predecessor, Navan Town Commissioners, for the previous thirty-five years; and its vice-chairman was John Timmon, whom we have met earlier as a prominent speaker at the UIL convention in August of this year.

Kells (fifteen members) and Trim (nine members) councils had a different electoral system than Navan. In each case one third of the council seats came up for election every year. This arrangement was provided for in the case of towns where such a set-up had existed previous to the 1898 Act. In 1914, the respective chairmen of Kells and Trim UDCs were Matthew Gartland and Francis O'Reilly, both of whom also sat on the county council. The responsibilities of the urban councils were similar to those of their rural counterparts – road (and street) maintenance, collection of rents and rates, preservation of public works and "their own proper business as sanitary authorities". (Amongst the functions laid down by the 1898 Act in relation to the latter were such intriguing matters as "nuisances, offensive trades and unsound meats", as well as the "sale of horseflesh"). The urban authorities also had duties in relation to electric lighting, technical instruction and "certain matters in relation to railway and canal traffic".

The fourth and final category in the local government system involved the Boards of Guardians, also known as the Poor Law Guardians. These dated back to 1838 when the act (officially entitled 'An Act for the more Effective Relief of the Destitute Poor of Ireland') which established the Irish workhouse network was passed into law at Westminster. This act divided the country into Unions, and we have seen how it was these unions that were the main determining factors in the rural district boundaries. In each union a workhouse was built and a Board of Guardians was established to govern each institution. Until 1898, these Boards were dominated by local landlords, property owners and Justices of the Peace. By the Local Government Act procedures, property qualifications and so on were much the same as those pertaining to the other councils.

There was, in actual fact, very little difference in personnel between the Guardians and the relevant rural councils. The Board of Guardians comprised the local rural councils as well as representatives elected from urban areas within a union, where such areas existed. Thus of the five Poor Law Boards in Meath, both Oldcastle (19) and Dunshaughlin (24) had exactly the same members as their rural councils. In Navan, Kells and Trim there was provision for the urban electorate to vote, respectively, six, four and three members on to the Guardians. When added to ex-officio rural councillors, this gave the Navan Guardians 33 members, Kells 54 and Trim 43. It can be seen now how a number of men could sit on three different local bodies, one example being the ubiquitous Gartland, who turns up as one of the elected urban representatives on the Kells Guardians. Despite the great changes in the election and composition of these boards, their functions, namely the administration of workhouses and hospitals and the relief of the poor, remained entirely the same. Meetings took place in the boardroom of the workhouse where rural council meetings were also held immediately before or afterwards.

Despite this complex network of local government structures and the great array of politicians that it engendered, and despite extensive – and sometimes blanket – coverage by the local press of the council's proceedings, there was much apathy surrounding the whole business of local administration in Meath. This apathy gripped both the electors and the elected. For instance, in the county council elections in June 1914, only nine of the twenty-one elective seats were contested. And the general indifference is even more clear cut in relation to the rural councils: for the Trim council there were elections necessary in only three out of eighteen divisions, and the relevant figures for the other councils were: Drogheda (Meath), two out of six; Kells, two out of twenty four; Oldcastle, two out of eight; Edenderry, one out of six; Ardee (Meath), one out of three; Dunshaughlin, one out of twelve; and Navan, also only one out of twelve. The situation in the urban areas was much brighter with, for instance, twenty seven candidates offering themselves for election to the fifteen seats in Navan, while in both Kells and Trim contests were needed to fill the seats following the annual retirement of one third of the councils in these places.

Even after the councils had been constituted, apathy – this time in the form of poor attendance – still prevailed. Once again, the urban councils are reasonably blameless. While the minute books show that cancellations of their meetings for want of a quorum were not unknown, by and large attendances were good, although an obvious advantage enjoyed by the urban councillors was proximity to their meeting places. The county council did not fare too badly either and in fact from its very first meeting in April 1899, no council meeting had ever had to be called off right up until January 1918.

A factor here may have been the custom then of publishing in the local newspapers every June the attendance record of each county councillor for the previous year. There were seven meetings annually and for the year ending 1 June 1914, the thirty one councillors between them had been present at a total of 136 meetings, which gives a respectable enough attendance rate of just over 60 per cent; the new council elected in this month managed between them 150 attendances for the following year, a very good rate of 70 per cent; but this was followed by a huge drop-off for the year ending 1 June 1916, with an aggregate total of only 100 meetings being attended by the thirty one members. On the whole, however, the county council performed well enough when one takes into account the long journey to Navan many members would have had to make at a time when transport for the vast majority was still by horse or, for those fortunate enough to possess one, a bicycle.

On the rural councils, however, poor attendance, non-attendance and indeed complete absenteeism were rife. In reading through the minute books for these councils, one observes how commonplace was the cancellation of meetings. Without going into specifics, the following comments taken from rough notes should illustrate this point: Dunshaughlin RDC, "attendance usually less than 50 per cent"; Trim RDC, ditto; Navan RDC, "frequent cancellation of meetings"; Kells RDC, "mediocre attendance, some cancellations". Farcical situations arose out of all this; for example, in March 1914, three men who, due to non-attendance, had been earlier disqualified from sitting on Dunshaughlin RDC were now co-opted back on to it on the pretext that "they had given satisfactory explanations"; while in June of the same year, no less than twelve men had to be co-opted on to the Kells council due to the non-acceptance of office by men deemed returned in the elections of that month.

Undoubtedly the biggest offender in all of this was Oldcastle RDC: the minute books show that for both August 1914 and August 1915 three successive meetings had to be called off and that for the whole of 1916 only about half the scheduled meetings took place. This was mild in comparison to what was to come, because, between mid-December 1916 and late May 1917, no meetings were held at all and from then until the end of that year meetings took place only at very irregular intervals.

At that time there was no inter-party rivalry or political differences on the councils. There was an obvious reason for this – the near monopoly of the Home Rule/UIL axis of council seats in nationalist Ireland. It has been pointed out earlier how public support for Home Rule was essential for any person seeking election to local bodies; and this had to be backed up by membership by the aspiring politician of a local UIL branch or, at least, an AOH club. In their reports of nominations to, and results of, local elections and of other political proceedings, the local newspapers never designated the councillors or guardians to a particular party or grouping: it was taken for granted that all were UIL men or, at least, nationalists or home rulers in a very broad sense.

The only chink in this monolithic structure in 1914 came just before election day when a meeting of the Executive Council of the MLU called on its members to vote for six particular candidates: four of these were running for the county council: the previously mentioned James Harte (in the Ardbraccan division), Thomas Rogers (Trim), Thomas Bowens (Tara) and Thomas Lynch (Moynalty), but of these only Lynch was successful. The other two, John Devine, seeking election to Trim

RDC, and William McKeever, to Ardee (Meath) RDC, also failed to secure election. But even this solitary non-UIL-sponsored candidate did nothing to break the monopoly since, as we have seen, the Labour Union was strongly supportive of the Home Rule Party. Indeed, at the time of the next general election four years hence, the county's leading Labour figure, James Harte, was to prove a staunch supporter of the Nationalist candidate in his constituency.

Reports of UIL meetings and rallies show councillors to the forefront in the proceedings, and we have seen the prominent part they played in the establishment of the county's Volunteer movement in 1914. We have also seen how all such gatherings were marked with the inevitable expressions or statements or resolutions of confidence in, or support of, or allegiance to, John Redmond and his party. The formal council meetings followed a similar pattern, and what follows is a litany-like selection of such declarations from the various bodies, a selection which should establish once and for all the vice-like grip and strangle hold which the Home Rule Party had on Irish nationalist political life in the early years of the century.

To start with the RDCs: in July 1913, P.J. Mulvany, chairman of Dunshaughlin RDC, proposed and it was unanimously adopted that they put on record their "feeling of satisfaction at the passing of the Third Reading of the Home Rule Bill", and also that they tender congratulations to Redmond and Prime Minister Asquith. The following year, in May, the council congratulated Redmond and stated that "they are proud to have lived to see that the hopes of all nationalist Ireland of the past century have been realized". In Trim, in October 1913, when the matter of a planned Home Rule demonstration to be held in Navan came up for discussion, it was ordered that the whole council should attend and not just a small number of selected delegates. And the following April, the council declared their confidence in Redmond and his party "for devotion to their country" and went on to state that "Redmond had upheld the cause of Ireland before the whole world".

In Navan in October 1914 the RDC was congratulating Redmond and his party "for putting Home Rule on the statute book" and, in reference to the brewing controversy of that time, they let it be known that "we have the fullest confidence in John Redmond as constitutional leader of the Irish Volunteers". Kells council, in July 1915, referred to Redmond as "the distinguished leader of the Irish Party". In April 1914 Drogheda (Meath) RDC unanimously adopted a resolution in which they fully placed their "confidence in our illustrious leader and his gallant party". In the same month in Ardee (Meath), the councillors recorded their "renewed confidence in the Irish Parliamentary Party under the able leadership of John Redmond" to whom they then expressed their "gratitude for his splendid services in the cause of Irish nationality".

Navan UDC at a meeting on 6 August 1914 congratulated Redmond on "his generous and statesmanlike utterance" when he pledged Irish support for the British war effort; and at the end of September, the Council's clerk was instructed to send congratulatory telegrams to both the Irish leader and the Prime Minister following the granting of Royal Assent to the Home Rule Bill. In May, Trim town council put on record their "desire to express our confidence in the wisdom and statesmanship of John Redmond and the Irish Party in carrying the Home Rule Bill to its final stages". (Following this, one council member, speaking with what was to prove greatly misplaced optimism, said that "this would be one of the last resolutions in relation to the party until the opening of the parliament in College Green"). In October, council chairman Francis O'Reilly referred to the split in the Volunteers, and it was unanimously agreed by the members that they "heartily approve of the manifesto issued by Mr. Redmond". As to the other urban council, Kells, in May 1914, chairman Gartland left no doubt as to his own loyalties and those of his council when he insisted that "the people of Kells are as good nationalists as anywhere in Ireland".

Indeed Gartland was not the only local politician presuming to speak on behalf of his whole community. In Trim a month later his words were echoed by Chairman O'Reilly, who averred that "it was a well known fact that the people of Trim have always shown sympathy with the Irish cause". The occasion of these words was an acrimonious debate between the chairman and another member, Thomas Rogers, mentioned earlier as one of the Labour Union-sponsored candidates in the county council elections of that year. At the Trim UDC meeting in May, Rogers had accused O'Reilly (who was not present) of never once having brought forward a resolution in support of Home Rule and furthermore that "he had never brought forward a resolution condemning Orangemen in Belfast for attacks on Catholics nor had he subscribed to the Home Rule fund for the relief of distressed Catholics". At the June meeting O'Reilly wasted no time in "heartily congratulating Redmond and the Irish Party for getting Home Rule through Parliament" while adding that there was "no need to act in a bigoted manner".

With that out of the way the two men launched themselves into an angry personal tirade against each other, with O'Reilly reminding his antagonist that "you are not in the slums now", and Rogers countering by asking if the chairman had "ever been at the funeral of a poor man" and stating cryptically that he (Rogers) had "never got Tories to sign his election papers". O'Reilly had the last word saying that he had been fifty one years in Trim and that he had been "one of the founder members of the Home Rule League there in 1873".

This exchange is cited only to emphasise that wherever a council's consensus on the question of Home Rule did come under strain it was usually due to councillors trying to outdo each other in their protestations of loyalty. Above the harmonious soundings of solidarity with the leader, the party and the cause there were audible only occasional and muted notes of dissent. But it is worth recalling just a few of these since they show that at least a few local politicians were already apprehensive for the future of the nationalist movement. For instance, in August 1914, in the immediate aftermath of the Bachelor's Walk killings of three civilians by British soldiers, a heated discussion erupted at a meeting of Dunshaughlin RDC in which one member, Martin O'Dwyer, insisted that it was "time for the party to speak out and to take no more platitudes or promises from English ministers"; and another – Patrick Moore, whom we have seen already to be no respecter of reputations – went beyond the limited horizons of the Home Rule vision when he said that there "would never be a day's peace in this country as long as the link which binds us to the accursed, galling chain is left unbroken".

A year later, in May 1915, this same council was the only one which expressed regret at the death of O'Donovan Rossa, and in a motion of sympathy recalled how he had "suffered so much for striving to redress the many grievances which Ireland was subjected to", and further decided that the council should be represented at his funeral and that "a fitting monument should be erected to perpetuate his memory". This seeming flirtation with republicanism may have been no more than the obligatory lip service accorded to dead patriots but it should be remembered that O'Donovan Rossa had been one of the most intransigent members of the most extreme republican organisation, the IRB, and that some of the policies that he had formulated in his lifetime were far removed from the constitutional niceties of the Home Rule movement.

Too much may be made of this particular episode, but other notes of skepticism were being sounded: for example, in January 1916 Christopher Owens – who was to remain a firm supporter of the Home Rule cause to the very end – prophetically told a meeting of Navan Board of Guardians that at the next general election "Home Rule will be thrown to blazes"; and, perhaps the shrewdest assessment of all had come as early as October 1914 – at the precise moment that the country was celebrating the attainment of self-government – when Francis Ledwidge, remembered today chiefly as a poet, coolly informed the meeting of Navan RDC that "as far as Home Rule is concerned it is uncertain when we can obtain it – we are just as far from Home Rule as ever".

2

April - May 1916:
The Republic Declared -
Action and Reaction

Men like Moore, Owens and Ledwidge were very much prophets crying in the wilderness whose voices were invariably drowned out by their fellow councillors. The councils reserved most of their opprobrium, however, for the advanced nationalist-republican groupings, almost always referred to by their opponents by the cover-all name of 'Sinn Féin'. In particular the Home Rulers aimed their bitterness at those Volunteers who in September 1914 had repudiated Redmond's leadership (this faction was henceforth known as the Irish Volunteers, the mainstream organisation under Redmond being referred to as the National Volunteers). At first, of course, the councils were enthusiastic in their support of the Volunteer movement. In May 1914 Navan UDC unanimously adopted a resolution from Limerick County Council, urging the formation of a Volunteer corps in every parish in Ireland. In June Kells UDC gave permission to their local corps to use the football park for drilling, and in the same month Navan RDC also adopted the Limerick motion. Even Oldcastle RDC, on one of those rare occasions when it did manage to muster a quorum, adopted a resolution forwarded from the Athboy Volunteers, urging that labourers be given a half day every Saturday to enable them to attend to their Volunteer activities.

After that came the split and the local bodies, of course, adhered faithfully to the Redmond line. In July 1915 it was to the local National Volunteers that Navan UDC gave permission to use Barrack Square for drilling purposes; while a few months earlier Navan RDC had rescinded a previous resolution giving a share of their advertisements and business to the newspaper of the Irish Volunteers; henceforth it would be given to the newspaper of the National Volunteers.

Sinn Féin, of course, had always been suspect in the eyes of the councils. Resolutions and motions sent by the organisation were always given the cold shoulder. For instance, in April 1914 a letter was sent to the various councils expressing Sinn Féin's anxiety at the proposed temporary exclusion of Ulster from the Home Rule settlement. Trim UDC chairman O'Reilly's attitude was that "resolutions like this one are more calculated to injure the peaceable solution of affairs than to assist", and it was marked 'read', a fate which also befell it at Navan UDC, Dunshaughlin PLU and Oldcastle RDC meetings. Then, at the end of 1914, Trim RDC passed a motion of thanks to Thomas Halligan, County Council chairman, for:

> condemning the so-called extreme nationalist Sinn Féiners who have never done anything for Ireland except bark and growl at our united Irish party and its illustrious leader.

Not that the county of Meath in these years presented much evidence of subversion or even disaffection among its populace. The occasional outbursts of dissatisfaction at council meetings were relatively mild, and there was only the odd disgruntled letter in the local newspapers, invariably from anonymous sources. The county, in fact, must have represented a model of good behaviour, to judge from this brief notice in the *Meath Chronicle* of 6 March, 1915:

At the Spring Assizes for county Meath at Trim Courthouse, Justice Boyd told the Grand Jury that there was nothing to go before them and he was presented by the High Sheriff with white gloves, symbolic of the crimeless state of the county.

As regards Sinn Féin, although it has been claimed that the organisation had its roots in this county in the very early years of the century (a matter that will be considered in the next chapter), it was not until well into 1917 that the first references to Sinn Féin clubs in Meath began to appear in the local newspapers. There were, however, companies of the breakaway Volunteers in existence well before Easter 1916. In March 1915, at a meeting of the Athboy corps of the National Volunteers, a heated debate ensued and, by a two-to-one majority it was resolved "to affiliate with the original committee with which we started since it is non-political". A couple of months later at a board meeting of the National Volunteers, the Athboy representative admitted that in his area "Sinn Féin was strong – I had to interview every Volunteer individually to secure his loyalty".

A notice in the *Chronicle* of 31 July 1915 announced the formation of an Irish Volunteer company in Kells; the notice was signed by the acting secretary, Hugh Smith, who was probably the 'Tara' of the *Meath Chronicle* columns. There was certainly a company in Dunboyne under Seán Boylan, who was destined to play a leading role in the political and military struggles of the years ahead. Another company was formed in Drumbaragh, but it amalgamated with Smith's Kells Company in October. The following month in nearby Carnaross, the Farrelly brothers formed the Volunteers in their parish and in a brief statement to the *Chronicle* of 27 November 1915 they stated that "the rights of Ireland could be defended not by paper resolutions or by mob oratory but by cold steel".

On the face of it, such bombast scarcely represented a threat to the established order of things. Certainly the opposition National Volunteer movement in the county did not think so, and at their County Board meeting held in mid-April 1916, one speaker referred dismissively to their rivals as "paper Volunteers that only exist in the columns of a newspaper". This comment was reportedly followed by laughter. It was to prove a hollow laughter: within a week these 'paper Volunteers' were to shake the British Empire to its very foundations.

It could be argued that the shoot-out between police and Volunteers just north of Ashbourne on 28 April 1916 has no place in an account of county Meath. The insurgents in question were not Meath men but rather the Fingal Volunteers drawn from the Swords-Lusk-Skerries areas. But this would ignore two fundamental facts: firstly, the scene of the fighting around Rath Cross is actually within the boundaries of Meath, and secondly, the police forces on duty that day were almost without exception drawn from barracks in Meath. And since this book is intended to be an account of the county in the broadest possible sense and not just of one section or faction therein, then the incident at Ashbourne deserves more than just a passing reference.

What follows is no more than a summary of the events of 28 April taken from an account written by one of the participants, Colonel Joseph Lawless, for the *Capuchin Annual* commemorative issue in 1966. Lawless, then a very young man, recalls that "early in Easter week we became aware that the rising was imminent", and how his father Frank, battalion quartermaster, had on Good Friday driven into Kimmage and brought back on a pony and trap "about twenty single barrelled shotguns, a quantity of buckshot ammunition, sixty pounds of gelignite, detonators and fuses". The Volunteers, the Fifth Battalion of the Dublin Brigade, mobilised on Easter Sunday, heard about the countermanding order and dispersed but with instructions from James Connolly to "hold everyone in readiness to act at any moment". When they convened again the following day they had fewer men in attendance, and for the next few days Lawless remembers that:

> the column, about forty-five strong, engaged in a series of lightning raids upon RIC barracks and communications in the area with the threefold purpose of collecting some much-needed arms, hampering enemy movements and drawing some enemy attentions away from the hard-pressed Volunteers fighting in the city.

Thus, in their tactics and targets, the Fingal Volunteers were very much out of tune with the military strategy then being employed in Dublin and instead they presaged the active service units and flying columns of the War of Independence. The battalion commandant was Thomas Ashe, a native of Kerry, who was by this time a national school teacher in Lusk. A Gaelic League activist and author of religious-political poetry in the style of Pearse, Ashe was to rise to national pre-eminence in September 1917 when he died from pneumonia arising out of forcible feeding during a short hunger strike in Mountjoy Jail. Another member of the column was Richard Mulcahy, a Waterford man who was to hold the position of Chief of Staff of the IRA during the War of Independence, and in a long political career was to serve as TD, Senator, Minister of Education in the first two inter-party governments and leader of Fine Gael from 1944 to 1959.

But to return to the events of Easter Week, Lawless relates how on the Thursday night they received information about the movement of "considerable bodies of troops from Athlone to Dublin"; they decided then that it was their job to cut the railway line, "the immediate objective being the Midland Great Western Railway line at Batterstown, twelve miles away". The men were then encamped at Borranstown, about three miles south of Garristown and just to the east of the main Dublin-Slane road. On moving out the next morning they soon came upon Ashbourne RIC barracks on this road just south of Rath Cross.

The column had been divided into four sections and two of these, acting as an advance guard, captured two constables, following which Ashe called on the police inside the barracks, about fifteen in number, to surrender. This merely provoked a fusillade of shots, and Ashe then set about deploying his four sections. Section one took up positions about one hundred yards from the barracks and began a continual firing on it; sections two and three were placed to the rear of the building and told to await further orders; while the fourth section was held well back in reserve. A Volunteer grenade thrown at the barracks fell short of its target but, according to Lawless:

> the noise of the explosion was all that was needed finally to break down the resistance for shortly afterwards a white flag or handkerchief fluttered from a window indicating willingness to surrender.

Location of RIC Barracks in 1916.

54

This was about a half hour since the first shots had been fired. It was not, however, to prove as simple as that for the Volunteers because, at precisely that moment, as Lawless puts it, "some twenty four motor cars laden with police reinforcements arrived on the roadside".

Navan barber Bobby Byrne recalled how, as a boy during Easter Week, he could distinctly hear the big guns in Dublin echoing in Navan. He also recalled the flurry of activity on that Friday morning as police reinforcements from all over Meath made their way into the town and how what few motor vehicles there were were hijacked or appropriated to be taken to Ashbourne. There were in Meath in 1916 thirty six RIC barracks, although the word 'barracks' should not here evoke the image of a sturdy and well-protected fortress; in fact, many of them were ordinary two-storey houses, and a few were mere huts. The locations of these posts were: Navan, Trim, Kells, Oldcastle, Athboy, Slane, Dunshaughlin, Nobber, Duleek, Dunboyne, Summerhill, Ballivor, Moynalty, Crossakiel, Carnaross, Bohermeen, Drumconrath, Longwood, Lismullin, Enfield, Kilmoon, Killyon, Carlanstown, Oristown, Kilmain-hamwood, Robinstown, Ballinabrackey, Moyglare, Stirrupstown, Georges Cross, Parsonstown, Julianstown, Gormanston, Ticroghan, Drumman and, of course, Ashbourne. It was from some of these barracks that the sixty to seventy policemen arriving in Ashbourne had been hastily drafted that morning.

The police party, led by County Inspector Alexander Gray and District Inspector Henry Smyth, an Englishman who had been based in Navan since 1912, threw the Volunteers into a sudden, but brief, panic. Sections two and three withdrew from their positions in some disarray but quickly regrouped to hear Mulcahy assure them that "the police had no chance of success and that we were going to rout or capture the entire force". Mulcahy then redeployed his men so that the third section as well as half of the second section were combined to carry the fight to the police; the other half of the second section led by Ashe was given instructions to cut off any attempt at enemy retreat, and they moved through the fields to take up positions about a quarter mile to the north of the police convoy.

Lawless was amongst this group and he describes a prolonged exchange of fire which ended only when the small group had used up all

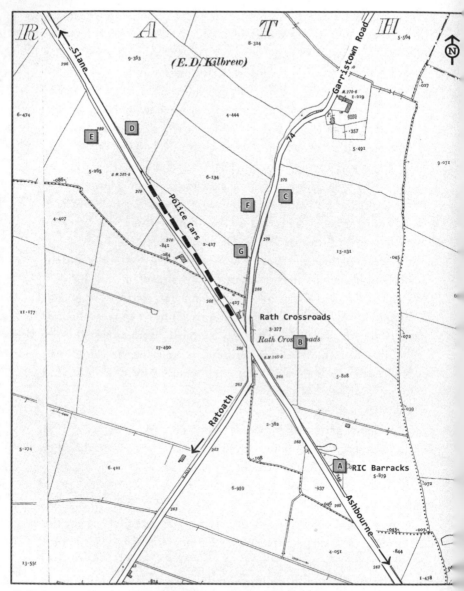

Rath Cross, Ashbourne, 28 April 1916

A. Position of Section One of Volunteers at start of fight.
B. Position of Sections Two and Three at start of fight.
C. Sections Two and Three retreat to this point after arrival of police.
D. Some of these men move to here to cut off any police retreat.
E. Belated arrival of Section Four - Volunteers exchange fire on each side by mistake.
F, G. Scene of heavy fighting along Garristown Road.

their ammunition, following which Ashe was ready to make 'the retreat which we thought was inevitable'. Ashe in fact had made his way back to Rath Cross where the rest of the Volunteers were engaged, but before he could give the order Mulcahy appeared and gave him the startling information that the force they had thought was the enemy and with whom they had exchanged shots was, in fact, their own fourth section which had belatedly arrived from the camp at Borranstown and were being conducted to their (Ashe's group) position by Mulcahy himself.

So the fight continued. Lawless recounted how he was confronted by an armed police constable and how he "should have been shot thrice over" but remarkably the policeman stood up with his hands over his head, indicating surrender, and he was soon followed by "eleven burly Royal Irish Constabulary men, a few of them wounded and all badly demoralised'. All had thrown away their rifles but handed over a plentiful supply of ammunition to their bemused captors. Shortly after this the remainder of the police reinforcements also gave themselves up on the main road on which Lawless remembered "were dead and wounded policemen and drivers, the remainder of the force climbing on to the road with their hands over their heads". Not surprisingly, the barracks garrison also surrendered and when they came out the rebels were amazed to see that:

> instead of the usual five or six men, this barracks had been re-
> inforced before our arrival and numbered fifteen under command
> of a district inspector.

Thus ended the fight at Ashbourne after about five and a half hours. The Volunteers' casualties were two killed and five wounded, the dead men being Thomas Rafferty and John Crenigan. On the other side both County Inspector Gray and District Inspector Smyth were killed in the action, as well as Sergeant John Shangher (Navan), Sergeant John Young (Killyon) and Constables James Hickey (Kells), Richard McHale (Crossakiel), James Gormley (Longwood) and James Clery (Moynalty). A chauffeur, Albert George Keep, in the employment of the Marquis of Conyngham, recruited to drive police to the scene, was also shot and later died of his injuries and, in all, up to twenty constables were wounded.

There were other Meath connections with the Rising. A large number of Volunteers mobilised on the Hill of Tara on Easter Sunday but on hearing of the countermanding order of MacNeill they dispersed and returned to their own localities. Undaunted, however, a group from Dunboyne tried to make their way to the city centre later in the week although this did not prove possible. A roll of honour, drawn up in the 1920s and listing those who participated in the fighting in Easter Week, was on public display in the National Museum: although the absence of the name of Seán Boylan from this roll represented a glaring omission. The full list as it appears for the Dunboyne contingent is: Peter Byrne, Aidan Crean, Peter Boylan, James Maguire, Giolla Criost O'Broin, Daniel Madden, Owen King, Francis Lowndes, Sean McGurl, Gearoid O'Broin, Margaret Crean, Liam O'Broin, Patrick Mullally, James Keating, Peter Keating and James Mullally.

From *The Last Post, Republican Dead 1913–1975*, is taken the following information:

> Allen, Thomas, Hill of Down, Co. Meath: mortally wounded at the Four Courts 29–4–16: buried near the Hill of Down, Kilglass, Co. Meath.

> McCormack, James, Julianstown, Co. Meath: killed in action near Liberty Hall, Dublin, 28–4–16: buried 1916 Plot, St Paul's, Glasnevin.

> Clarke, Phil, Slane, Co. Meath: killed in action at St. Stephen's Green, 25–4–16: buried in St. Brigid's, Glasnevin.

Another Meath man who was killed in the Rising was Seamus Fox, aged only sixteen. Fox was a native of Drumree where his father had owned the Spencer Arms Hotel until he sold it in 1915. The family then went to live in Dublin where father and son, both named P.J., joined James Connolly's Irish Citizen Army. Seamus was shot dead at St. Stephen's Green on the first day of the Rising while carrying a despatch from one garrison to another. He was later buried at Knockmark graveyard and in the late 1920s a memorial was erected in his honour.

In the immediate aftermath of the insurrection, local newspaper reports record about a dozen arrests of suspected participants or sympathisers. This is, of course, a paltry figure given the presence, as we have seen, of at least five Volunteer companies in the county and also given the fact that the Ashbourne conflict represented the heaviest fighting to have taken place anywhere in Ireland outside of Dublin. Most of those detained in Meath were released after a very short time, these included John Sweetman, the ex-MP whose letter to the *Meath Chronicle* in December 1913 had been the harbinger of the county's Volunteer movement.

Also freed after a week or so were two Oldcastle men, Charlie Fox, a merchant, and Michael Grace, an engineer. Their arrest was doubtless due to the administration's then obsession with the conviction that the Rising had been organised by Sinn Féin, to which both men had strong leanings, a fact that will become more apparent in the next chapter. Also detained were the four Boylan brothers, Seán, Peter, Joseph and Edward. Seán was certainly heavily involved, being a leading figure not only in the Volunteers but also in the IRB, who had planned, organised and led the Rising. Peter, as pointed out earlier, is included in the 1916 Roll of Honour. But the other two brothers had no connection whatever with the events of Easter Week, a fact underlined in a question tabled by William O'Brien (founder of the UIL in 1898 but for a long time at odds with Redmond and the Home Rule Party) in the House of Commons. Following this, both the 'innocent' brothers as well as Peter were set free. Seán Boylan was not as fortunate as he spent most of the next year in Wandsworth Prison and other internment camps in England and Wales.

Another of those arrested and a man whose trial gained widespread publicity was James Quigley, chairman of the committee which had established the Volunteers in Navan two years earlier. Quigley's case is interesting since it will be remembered that he held the position of County Surveyor, a position that made him one of the main officials in the employ of Meath County Council, a body which could be expected to have no sympathy with the rebel cause. The Council, as shall be seen later, put on record at their May meeting their "outrage at the recent deplorable outbreak in Dublin", but at the same meeting let it be known that they "refuse to believe that such a manly, generous-hearted official [Quigley] would have been party to the Ashbourne outrage".

Quigley's trial opened early in June at Richmond Hospital Barracks in Dublin, where it was charged that "he did convey information to a number of persons taking part in an armed rebellion and waging war against His Majesty the King". The defendant pleaded not guilty. The basis of the prosecution case was that the accused had been in the vicinity of Rath Cross on the date of the fighting and had been identified by a police witness as shaking hands with Thomas Ashe; also there had been found at his home a rifle, shotgun, explosives, ammunition and seditious literature.

In a long statement, Quigley outlined his connections with the Volunteer movement since it had been first established in Navan in April 1914. He maintained that he had often publicly "expressed his loyalty to King and Constitution", and as a young man had even tried to join the British Army. When the split in the Volunteer movement came in September 1914 he said that the Navan corps had voted four-to-one to remain loyal to Redmond's leadership but that "activities had died out when the War was well under way". As regards the Rising he insisted that "he had not hand, act or part in it", and that he had never at any time been a member of Sinn Féin. He had first heard of the insurrection while at Fairyhouse races on Easter Monday. Later that week, from Wednesday to Friday, his job had taken him to the general area between Slane and Kilmoon where he had to instruct gangers and supervise men on road building projects. While he admitted that he had witnessed the police arriving at Ashbourne he was adamant that he had never shaken the hand of Thomas Ashe. As regards the other charges, Quigley stated that the rifle, shotgun and ammunition were the property of the Irish National Volunteers and that they had been in his possession since the early days of that organisation; the explosives were for quarrying purposes related to his work; and the literature was merely a number of leaflets sent to him from Volunteer headquarters some time before.

A large number of witnesses spoke in support of Quigley. Amongst them were John Gallen, secretary to the Meath County Committee

April - May 1916

of Agriculture; P.J. McQuillan, first treasurer of the Meath Volunteer organisation, who told the court that the "Navan INV were against the principles of Sinn Féinism"; Patrick Boyle, the county councillor from Slane; and a number of gangers and roadworkers. Final witness for the defence was Patrick White who reminded his listeners that Ashbourne was only a short distance from his own native Clonalvy. Having deplored the outbreak of fighting and killing in his area, the MP then went on to vigorously defend Quigley by recalling his early involvement in the Volunteers and his part in organising the Slane review in August 1914. Since the Volunteer split White stressed that the defendant had remained loyal to Redmond's leadership saying that "he has always been a supporter of the Irish Parliamentary Party and has contributed to their fund".

A number of police who had been involved in the fight at Ashbourne then gave evidence against Quigley, but the prosecution case came over in an unconvincing manner and at the end of the two-day trial, the County Surveyor was found not guilty of all the charges against him. He was extremely lucky, to judge from the following extract taken from the aforementioned article written by Colonel Lawless about the Ashbourne incident:

> I noticed a motor cycle standing on the opposite side of the road, and then a man in civilian dress crouched near it in the hedge. I was about to fire on him when he saw me, and stood up with his hands raised. He said his name was Quigley, and that he had been trying to get in touch with us to warn us of the coming of the police convoy. I did not believe him, and perhaps because he was a very tall man, I thought he was connected with the police, but as there was a doubt in the matter I told him to leave his machine where it was and to clear off across the fields. I afterwards learned that Mr. Quigley was the County Surveyor of Meath, and a good nationalist and supporter of the Volunteer movement.

So while he may not have shaken the hand of Thomas Ashe and, while his attempt at 'conveying information' to the rebels came too late, Quigley could count himself a very fortunate man to have got away completely free, especially when one considers the exigencies of this time which saw some who were innocent of any involvement being sent away for long terms of imprisonment or, indeed, in a few cases, paying with their lives.

For over fifty years the 1916 Rising enjoyed a hallowed position amongst the shrines to Irish republicanism. To many it was (and still is) the high point of Irish history, an event for which everything else for over seven hundred years had been but preparing the way. But at the time it was a far different story. Those who may be regarded as the leaders and formulators of public opinion, politicians, clergy, journalists and so on, were certainly very vocal and outspoken in Meath at the time: vocal, that is, in suppression of the Rising and outspoken in their condemnation of the rebels and their cause.

Speaking at Mass in Navan on the Sunday after the surrender of the insurgents, Fr Poland bemoaned the fact that "in this church today rest the mortal remains of eight men who were healthy and stalwart just three days ago"; and then, in what was to prove a major misinterpretation, he gave as his opinion "that the annals of the happenings of Easter Week 1916 will form the darkest records in Irish history". And in a marked gesture of solidarity with the police Bishop Gaughran came to Navan to visit the wounded RIC men in the Infirmary there.

The two newspapers showed little sympathy with the Rising. The *Meath Chronicle* of 6 May was mild enough in its condemnation: the editorial column was headed 'A Tragic Blunder', and it went on to berate the foolhardiness of the Volunteers, although the writer concluded fairly enough that:

> this calamitous outbreak would not have occurred had the late Liberal government dealt in anything like a firm manner with the situation created in Ulster by Sir Edward Carson and his colleagues.

The tone of the *Drogheda Independent* was much more strident. The editorial for the issue of 29 April included the following:

> an armed conjunction of the Liberty Hall heroes, with some of the Sinn Féin Volunteers, has made an attempt at some kind of

miserable rising, something on the pattern of those exhibitions that have made Southern American states so ridiculous before the world ... the King's troops and the police force have now got the Larkinites and Sinn Féiners well in hand and the ridiculous rising is crushed and broken ....

This vitriolic attack continued the following week when the writer claimed that "the Rising's leaders were the victims of ill-balanced minds", and then went on to say though it was rather superfluous to do so: "we have not a shadow of sympathy with these men or their mad essay". The newspaper also greatly exaggerated the number of rebels involved at Ashbourne: first they numbered over four hundred, then about three hundred and, finally, between one hundred and thirty and four hundred. These distortions of the true figures were most unfair, especially since the Volunteer column at Ashbourne was definitely outnumbered and one finds it hard to believe that the newspaper's reporter could have been genuinely so far out in his estimations of the size of the column. The *Drogheda Independent* also included the following account of the scene in Navan as the dead and wounded police were brought by cars into the town that Friday night:

> windscreens riddled with bullets; mudguards and chassis dotted over with bullet marks; some cars arrived with punctured tyres and the sight of helpless bodies lying in the cars, with rough dressings around their wounds, exacted sympathy keen and deep from the relatives of those who had gone out in the morning of life to return motionless and dead.

The local councils were equally hostile. At their meeting of 29 May Meath County Council considered a resolution forwarded from Tullamore UDC to the effect 'that this council desires to record their outrage at the recent deplorable outbreak in Dublin which they believe to be greatly detrimental to the real industrial and political interests of Ireland and call on all nationalist Irishmen to support John Redmond's constitutional policy'. The adoption of this motion was proposed by P.J. Kennedy and seconded by Patrick Sheridan but there was some opposition to this and after a lengthy discussion an amendment was proposed by Patrick Moore and James Gammons as follows:

> that after the word 'policy' we add these words: "that we respectfully request the government to deal in a lenient manner with the prisoners now in custody who, through youth or ignorance, were the dupes of men who should have known better.

The motion was unanimously passed as amended.

Dunshaughlin RDC which will be remembered only a short time earlier as making republican-sounding noises, now hastily forgot these to put on record their "continued support of John Redmond" and their "greatest confidence in him". At their meeting on 9 May the councillors seemed to have been troubled by the prospect of a great number of malicious damages claims being lodged with them since the scene of the Ashbourne fight came within their jurisdiction. As to the Rising itself the councillors expressed their "abhorrence at the recent events in Dublin where so many innocent and inoffensive people lost their lives". (Almost four years later, however, there was to be an interesting sequel to this episode in the council's history).

Navan UDC unanimously passed a resolution recording their "heartfelt sympathy" to the relatives of the dead policemen and then went on to "deplore the recent disturbances that have led to such a terrible loss of life and property and caused such sorrow, misery and ruin". The strongest words of all came from Trim UDC where the chairman O'Reilly said of the Rising that "a more unfortunate occurrence had never taken place in the history of this country", and then lashed the participants as "ill-advised, uneducated, hot-headed young fellows led by scheming fanatics"; while Thomas Rogers, O'Reilly's bitter foe of two years before, bluntly and laconically described the Rising as 'cold-blooded murder'.

These then were the thoughts and attitudes of the county's leaders of public opinion. The Meath public at large seemed to have been in agreement. In the immediate aftermath of the Rising there was no gesture or statement recorded to indicate sympathy with the event. Quite the opposite, in fact, as both local newspapers remarked on the large attendances at the funerals of the dead policemen. And at the Navan Petty Sessions in May, the magistrates congratulated the people of the town on:

> their admirable demeanour on the night of 28 April ... we never doubted that their respectability and commonsense were such that their conduct could not have been excelled by any community in the Empire.

Even allowing for hyperbole there is no doubt that, thus far, the people of Meath were still loyal.

3

1914 - 1918:
Echoes of the Great War

At this stage I propose to digress from the narration of domestic political and military events to consider the impact on the county of the Great War. At the outset, it must be said that the people of Meath were kept very well informed about the war by their local newspapers. Both papers carried regular syndicated columns, often illustrated by maps, devoted to the progress of the war, while sometimes even the editorials passed over local and national occurrences to comment learnedly on the most recent twists in the conflict.

For the years 1914 to 1918 the most vivid reminder to the people of Meath that the war was having a direct effect on their lives was the continuous recruiting campaign being carried on from one end of the county to the other. The usual procedure was for the Central Recruiting Committee to get in touch with the local councils and request them to take the lead in this matter in their own areas. Most of the councils were circularised regarding this matter during 1915, and there was a wide variety of responses to the request. The most positive attitude, from the recruiting committee's point of view, came from the two Navan councils. In May 1915 Navan RDC resolved that the entire council would form itself into a recruiting committee for the area under its jurisdiction. The following month this committee appointed the following officials: chairman, Michael Johnstone (also chairman of the RDC) secretary, Charles Lacy (also clerk of the RDC) and treasurer, Thomas Macken. The following November, Navan UDC authorised John Timmon to form a similar committee for the town, the president of which was to be John Spicer, the council chairman.

In Trim there was less enthusiasm for the idea. While the UDC chairman Francis O'Reilly declared himself personally in favour, the rest of the members decided to take no action on the communication. And the RDC said that it "will give every assistance but we see no necessity for such a campaign". At about the same time, May 1915, Dunshaughlin RDC took a similar lukewarm attitude ordering that "no action be taken" on the matter. Oldcastle RDC went one step further in November when it ignored the circular and warned against "any likelihood of conscription or compulsion being enforced".

With or without local co-operation the recruiting campaign was carried on with vigour by a small group who travelled to the towns and villages of Meath in search of soldiers to fight for the empire. The two most prominent individuals in this enterprise were Sir Nugent Everard and John Timmon, and there is scarcely a report of a meeting that does not include either or both of these as speakers. These two men were backed by other local politicians, representatives of the gentry or upper classes, members of parliament, clergy and local businessmen.

The first big recruiting meeting held in January 1915 in the CYMS Hall in Navan included Lord Killeen and Stephen Gwynn MP as speakers, while in Kells the following month bank managers were prominent on the speakers' platform. Among the speakers at a meeting in Trim in August was none other than Pierce Mahony, the ex-Parnellite MP who had been one of the protagonists in the re-run election drama of over twenty years earlier, and was now drawn out of retirement to boost the recruiting drive. Among the army representatives who came to the county was the band of the Royal Irish Fusiliers which played at a meeting in Navan in May, and officers of the Leinster Regiment who made a lightning tour through Dunboyne, Ratoath, Ashbourne and Dunshaughlin in October.

In the early stages the drive for recruits was hampered by what the *Meath Chronicle* of 30 January 1915 reported as "the widespread distribution of anti-recruiting leaflets in Navan ... these obnoxious circulars being thrust under doors, into letter boxes and into open windows". The police were called on to investigate the campaign.

This proved no deterrent to the energetic Timmon who, a couple of months later, in October 1915, confidently told his listeners in Navan that he intended to erect a Celtic cross in the Market Square to commemorate those Navan men who would die in the war. Although Timmon received a number of contributions towards the cost of this Irish-style cenotaph, nothing ever came of his brainchild. Timmon may have been using this idea to revive a campaign that had barely got off the ground and that even at this early stage seemed to be stuttering to a full stop. A conference was held in Navan in March 1916 to review and re-organise strategy. Those present included Everard, Timmon, an assortment of local politicians, representatives of the RIC, members of the Tisdall family of Cortown and P.J. Cusack, the young doctor from Nobber who, we have seen, was active in the Back to the Land movement. The meeting was told that in 1914 their particular recruiting area had contained about 8,200 men suitable for service; up to January 1916 only about seven per cent of these had been enlisted leaving 7,639 recruitable men. Everard set a target of about 1,200 and it was decided that the county be divided into a number of districts, each with its own committee. These committees would be supplied with lists of the names and addresses of local men of military age who would then be approached and, in the event of refusal to enlist, would be asked their reasons for this refusal.

This new hard-sell approach was no more successful than the old methods. Accounts of recruiting meetings in the local newspapers almost always mention the paltry attendances and the consequent paucity of recruits. This was particularly so in rural areas but even in the urban areas the situation was little better. A meeting in Kells in July 1916, for instance, resulted in only one man joining up, while a report in the *Chronicle* of a typical meeting in the same year was headed "Poor

Turn-out in Drumconrath". It is estimated that up to twenty RIC men stationed in Meath during the war resigned their posts to go to the war. Another source of manpower was the local clergy. In April Bishop Gaughran authorised six of his priests to go to serve as army chaplains.

One would perhaps have expected the Irish National Volunteers in the county to join the British army in great numbers, but to judge from Tara's tauntings in the *Chronicle*, this was not the case. The columnist constantly alluded to their lack of enthusiasm for action in spite of Redmond's call on them to go "where the firing line extends". One exception to this was the captain of the Fordstown Volunteers, James Fox, who volunteered for duty, saying that he would bring ten men from his company with him. His company promptly congratulated him in the *Meath Chronicle* of 24 April, 1915 "on his manly and patriotic action in answering the call of the empire by joining the colours of the gallant Irish Guards," but none of his men could be persuaded to follow him.

In March 1917, Everard presided over a function where certificates were presented to the relatives of those in the Navan area who had volunteered for service. About eighty of these certificates were given out but by this time public opinion regarding the British connection was in the process of great change and an occasion such as this could do little to revive enthusiasm for a flagging cause. The death blow to this cause was to come a year later with the furore over the attempt to impose conscription, the dread eventuality which Oldcastle RDC had warned against over two years before. Everard's and Timmon's last public rally, a misnomer because of the sparseness of the attendance, came on Sunday 28 October 1918 when, along with Major Collins-Gerrard of Wilkinstown, they spoke in condemnation of the sinking of the *HMS Leinster* a fortnight earlier.

From 1914 to 1918 the local newspapers carried regular notices relating to those Meath men who did join the British army. In most cases such notices meant bad news, they were reports of the deaths of men in action. The following selection may be of some interest:

> Word reached Navan on Tuesday that Joseph Kerrigan, a
> private on the 1st Leinsters, and Thomas Heary, of Flower Hill,

a private in the Irish Guards, had been killed at the front on or
about 14th inst.
Meath Chronicle, 23 January 1915

William Fay, Garlow Cross, a member of the Leinster
Regiment, has been killed in action.
Drogheda Independent, 28 August 1915

News of the death of Private Murphy, Moat, Navan, has
reached his family. He had been dead since 12 May but his
parents had to wait nine months for the news.
Drogheda Independent, 15 January 1916

News has been received of the deaths of Lieutenant W.H.
Potterton, Royal Engineers, aged 24, and Lieutenant Purdon,
King's Royal Rifles Corps, aged 19. Both men were from the
Trim area.
Drogheda Independent, 10 August 1916

And one line in the *Drogheda Independent* of 11 August 1917 recorded
the fate of the best known Meath man to die in the war:

The poet Francis Ledwidge was killed in Flanders on 31 July, aged
26.

Ledwidge was in fact almost thirty years old at the time of his death
but even in this brief life span his interests and activities reflected in
microcosm the great hustle and bustle of these times. He had been a
founder of the Slane branch of the MLU in 1906, the second branch
to be set up in the county, and he had worked for a year as a full-time
official of the Union. A Gaelic Revival enthusiast, he had attempted to
have Irish classes begun in Slane but met with seeming indifference, and
even coolness, from the county's Gaelic League luminaries. For a man
of such energies it is not surprising to find him as secretary – founder
of his local Volunteer corps in 1914, and he was present at the great
Volunteer review in his village in August of that year.

Two months later, in October, came the turning points in his life and the decisions that were to lead him to an early grave. First of all, he was one of only six men in his corps who refused to accept Redmond's policies and continued leadership. As a result of this, political crossfire arose at the meetings of Navan RDC and Board of Guardians, to which he had been elected that year. It was at a meeting of the former that we have seen how he had cannily predicted that Ireland was "just as far from Home Rule as ever" and he was the only councillor to vote against a pro-Redmond motion. Later, at a meeting of the Guardians, he was accused of being pro-German in his outlook and sympathies. Five days later, on 24 October, came Ledwidge's second, and what was to prove fatal, decision: he enlisted in the Royal Inniskilling Fusiliers.

While this may seem contradictory, given his rejection of Redmond's policies, Ledwidge himself saw no inconsistency in his actions. He felt that the best way to combat the Germans was at the front, not "by passing resolutions at home". He was also convinced that the war would come to a quick end and that, when he returned home, his military training could be invaluable to a revitalised Volunteer movement. At their next meeting the Navan councillors and guardians must have felt quite sheepish as they thanked Ledwidge for "proving to us in the best possible way that he was not what we thought him, pro-German". One councillor gushed that he was "a real patriot, the Guardian Angel of Ireland's future", while another uttered the blandishment that "his name should be written in gold on a national album."

As for Ledwidge himself, he saw action at Gallipoli and then on the Western Front. He was killed by an exploding shell while road-laying in preparation for an assault during the third battle of Ypres. Buried in the Belgian village of Boesinghe, his beautiful and moving epitaph to Thomas McDonagh could be equally applicable to himself.

To return to the newspaper notices, occasionally they carried news of serious injuries rather than of death:

> Mr W[illiam] Bartley, a well-known Navan resident, is home from the front . . . He is almost recovered from the effects of a shell which killed his horse and seriously injured himself.
> *Meath Chronicle*, 20 February 1915

John Graham, Leinster Regiment, a native of Barrack Lane,
Navan, has been wounded at the Dardanelles.
Drogheda Independent, 28 August 1915

These extracts bring home the harsh realities of war and death and show
how ordinary Meath men died far from home in a cause for which most
of them probably had little enthusiasm. But there is a sense in which
the position was reversed in Meath, because the county played host to
hundreds of prisoners-of-war and refugees during these traumatic years.
From January 1915, the workhouse in Oldcastle was used as a detention
centre for several hundred – one account puts the figure at 450 –
German and Austrian nationals until they were moved to the Isle of
Man in June 1918 And Belgian refugees were housed in Dunshaughlin
workhouse and in Seneschalstown House during 1915 and 1916.

There is one final aspect of the echoes of the Great War worth
recalling. Remarkably, in the early part of 1918, the county began to feel
anxiety at a prospective food shortage, and on more than one occasion
the word 'famine' was used in the newspapers in relation to these fears.
While all this might now seem very alarmist it must have been very real
at the time because a hastily-improvised Food Supply Committee in
Navan within a few weeks had collected the then huge sum of £3,800
most of which was guaranteed by local businessmen such as John
Spicer and Clayton & Company, as well as by the big farmers in the
adjacent rural areas. Thankfully, the worst fears of the committee did
not materialize and, as 1918 and the Great War drew to a close, it was the
great flu epidemic of that year rather than famine which claimed many
victims in the county.

4

June 1916 - December 1918:
The Rise of Sinn Féin

Within a couple of months of the suppression of the Rising there was a small but perceptible shift in attitude on the part of some of the councils. In July Trim RDC passed a resolution of congratulations to "the Ulster Home Rule convention on their decision on temporary unity", and also reiterated their confidence in Redmond and the party. But there was an objection to this coming from Council Chairman Thaddeus Flynn who moved that the resolution not be adopted. Flynn could not get a seconder for his amendment and, while this incident might seem innocuous, it marks the first stirrings of dissent from this council. At their meeting on 8 June, Dunshaughlin RDC considered a rather long-winded four-part resolution which maintained their previously observed, strong anti-British stance and once again seemed to be making overtures towards the republicanism of the executed leaders. The resolution, proposed by Martin O'Dwyer and seconded by Michael Fitzsimons, read as follows:

(1) That we demand a measure of self-government for all of Ireland.

(2) That we condemn the government in shooting and sending away to penal servitude so many innocent men, thus outraging public opinion.

(3) That all those in prison should be brought to trial in public courts before the civil authorities and be given a chance to answer the charges against them.

(4) That we protest against the continuation of martial law and request that it be removed immediately.

While arguably there may be nothing controversial in all this, the interesting point comes in an amendment which ignored the motion completely and called on the council to leave "the settlement of the Home Rule problem in the hands of the leaders". When a vote was taken, however, the original resolution was adopted by eight votes to five. A week later a similar situation arose at a county council meeting. Following a discussion on Lloyd George's hastily conceived scheme to implement a measure of Home Rule that would involve partition of the country, it was proposed by P.J. Kennedy and seconded by Patrick Moore "that we condemn the proposals for a Home Rule settlement – repartition of Ireland – as published in the press, which in our opinion would only aggravate the state of affairs and further embitter relations with England". This was passed with only two members, Sir Nugent Everard and Trim man Francis O'Reilly, abstaining from voting and none at all voting against. Before now, the only opposition to the party had come from individual councillors who braved the wrath of their colleagues to put on record their concern at the direction that Redmond's policies were taking. But in these two cases we have whole councils, or at least majorities thereof, letting it be known, either explicitly or implicitly, that the days of unquestioned support of the Home Rule cause were numbered.

The case for claiming that certain aspects of the Sinn Féin movement may have their origin in the Oldcastle area has been made in *The Capuchin Annual*. In an article entitled 'The First Sinn Féin Paper' (*The Capuchin Annual* 1968, p 140–144), Niall Sheridan relates how his father Liam, of Drumlerry, was one of a small group of men who, from May 1902 until the autumn of 1903, were responsible for the publication of a newspaper called *Sinn Féin* (subtitled *The Oldcastle Monthly Review*). Sheridan recalled that:

> The new journal had been founded in Oldcastle, County Meath, on St. Patrick's Day, 1902, by a group of active Gaelic Leaguers. They gathered in the Naper Arms Hotel on that evening to entertain a young Dublin barrister, Patrick H. Pearse, already – at twenty two – a leader of the Irish-Ireland movement. His hosts were only a few years older. The group had a second purpose for their meeting – to choose a name for the new monthly paper which they had decided to launch.

Apart from Pearse and Sheridan, three other men were present. These were Paddy Bartley of Mountnugent, and Michael Grace and Charlie Fox, both Oldcastle men. We have seen in the previous chapter how Grace and Fox were, fourteen years later, to be arrested and detained for a short period in the round-ups after the Easter Rising. Grace is described in the article as an extremely able and intelligent civil engineer while Fox, "a leading Oldcastle merchant, was a man of sardonic wit and great personal charm ... he was undoubtedly responsible for the caustic anti-ascendancy quips with which the news items were peppered". The first issue of the paper appeared in May 1902 and its editorial unequivocally laid out its policies:

> We appear as a supporter of the movement that is at present being carried on by thinking men and women of Ireland to revive our ancient language, music and literature, our national sports and pastimes, our decaying industries and the cause of temperance .... a short chapter of Irish history will be one of our features, and we hope by this means to make the youth of this district acquainted with some of the bright and some of the dark passages in the lives of their forefathers which the National system of Education would hide from them ....

Among the contributors to the paper were Brian O'Higgins, a Kilskyre man who was later to play a role of some importance at a national level, and Seán MacNaMidhe, a pioneer of the Gaelic League in Meath. The paper also had its opponents, chief amongst them being Fr Robert Barry, the local parish priest who was later to become the driving force behind the county's Back to the Land movement. Niall Sheridan describes Fr Barry as:

> an honest, zealous man, who agitated effectively for land reform, but in politics was a die-hard conservative .... he could have little sympathy with a group of young men who brazenly preached sedition and regarded the Irish party as a putrefying corpse that should have been buried with Parnell.

As for the newspaper itself, it was financed by the four founders and about twenty advertisers, it sold at a penny, and at least thirteen issues appeared. Its demise came in the late summer or autumn of 1903 but this was due not "to clerical opposition or financial anemia .... the real cause was the lack of necessary organisation to ensure continuity".

The question may now be considered as to how authentic Niall Sheridan's claim is that the four men had "given Oldcastle a small niche in history and taught their readers the significance of those two Gaelic words which became the title deeds of a revolution". This may be examined from two viewpoints. Firstly the very name 'Sinn Féin' itself: according to Robert Kee in his *The Bold Fenian Men* (Volume Two of *The Green Flag*, Quartet Books, 1976, p. 156), "from May 1905 Griffith's new policy generally began to be called the 'Sinn Féin' rather than the 'Hungarian' policy". Arthur Griffith himself gave the credit for this to a young woman named Mary Butler who suggested it to him at the end of 1904. (The letter in which Griffith acknowledged this is actually quoted in full in *The Capuchin Annual* article. Griffith's newspaper was then called *The United Irishman,* but later wishing to change this he wrote to Paddy Bartley seeking permission to use the name of the then defunct Oldcastle journal. This was given and the first issue of Griffith's '*Sinn Féin*' appeared in March 1906.

On the face of it then, Griffith may have owed a debt to the Oldcastle people, but it should be remembered that, as Robert Kee again points out, the words 'Sinn Féin' "had long been fairly commonly used as a motto for Irish self-reliance and had in fact been the early motto of the Gaelic League." (*The Bold Fenian Men*, ps 156–7). This is noteworthy because Niall Sheridan states that his father "had been inspired to suggest 'Sinn Féin' through his reading of *An Claidheamh Soluis*". Thus, while the name 'Sinn Féin' was being employed in Oldcastle a few years before Griffith formally began to use it, it was not by any means indigenous to that area.

The other aspect worth considering is the ideology of the Oldcastle men as seen in the columns of their newspaper. Extracts from the first editorial have already been quoted and these bear a remarkable similarity to the policies adopted by Cumann na nGaedhael, an organisation founded by Arthur Griffith in September 1900 and very much the forcrunner of the Sinn Féin movement itself. In his book, Robert Kee has summarised these policies as follows:

(a)   diffusing a knowledge of Ireland's resources and supporting Irish industries;

(b)   the study and teaching of Irish history, language, music and art;

(c)   the encouragement of Irish national games and characteristics;

(d)   the discountenancing of everything leading to the Anglicisation of Ireland.

(*The Bold Fenian Men*, Quartet Books, p 150).

While those objectives were very laudable, the last of them often gave rise to a very narrow view of nationalism and a tendency to castigate everything that was not purely Gaelic and/or Catholic as 'West Britonism'. The Oldcastle journal was marked by this characteristic and the issue of July 1902 berated John Timmon for organising a cricket team in Navan and asked how many hurling teams had he begun in his town; and later in the same column, the writer chided a dance band in Navan for playing foreign tunes and wondered did the conductor not know any Irish tunes. The *Sinn Féin* newspaper also carried on a virulent anti-alcohol campaign – Michael Grace was vice-president of the local Pioneer Total Abstinence Society – and it linked "decay of our race and drink" as the "two evils that stare us in the face".

Whatever about the narrowness of such attitudes, and it must be remembered that they were in line with the then mood of the Irish-Ireland movement, it is still of great significance that, for over a year, a newspaper carrying policies far in advance of the dominant Home Rule movement was being published and read in the north of the county. Oldcastle may not have been the birthplace of the Sinn Féin movement but in the early years of the century its local newspaper was educating people in the principles and ideas that were to take over fifteen more years to become the common currency of Irish nationalism.

From the suppression of the Rising in April and May until the end of the year 1916 Meath remained quiet. The only indication of an exception to this came in July, when a number of young men were charged with unlawful assembly at Summerhill on the night of 30 April and also with the robbery of musical instruments belonging to the local Irish National Volunteers. Whether this had a political motive or whether it was mere blackguardism is not very clear from the newspaper report but either way it was fairly harmless.

The first few months of 1917 also passed off peacefully but it was the surprise by-election victory in South Longford of the imprisoned Joseph McGuinness at the end of May which seems to have been the catalyst that sparked off a whole series of reactions, culminating in the ultimate dominance by Sinn Féin of the county's political scene. The by-election saw the inscrutable Dunshaughlin council back to its familiar ways: a two-part resolution, introduced by Martin O'Dwyer and Michael Fitzsimons, included a formal protest against any suggested partition of the country and went on to congratulate the electorate of South Longford and to call on the government to release McGuinness "whose election represents the true nationalist feeling of the country". The resolution was passed but at the next meeting a number of the members, including chairman P.J. Mulvany (later a Farmers Party TD from 1923 to 1927), objected to the second part and claimed that it had been passed at the end of the meeting when a large number of councillors had already left. A motion was tabled calling for the original resolution to be rescinded and this was carried by eleven votes to three. While the minute books of the other bodies contain no debate on, or reference to, the South Longford by-election, it did have some effect outside the council chambers.

At the end of May eight men "of a very respectable class", as the *Meath Chronicle* of 26 May described them, were charged with unlawful assembly at Athboy on the night of the by-election victory. The court was told how a crowd of two hundred had gathered around the police barracks shouting slogans such as 'Up The Rebels' and 'To Hell With The King', and had refused to disperse despite several warnings. Three of the men, the county councillor Patrick O'Growney, Thomas McGuinness and Seán O'Grady, were given a month's hard labour; another three, Joseph Martin, Bernard McConnell and Patrick Carey were given fourteen days of the same punishment; and the other two, Seán McGurl and Nicholas Byrne, were discharged. Of course, this case in itself did not represent a major upheaval in the established order but there were other indications of disaffection setting in.

It was from about this time onwards that the *Meath Chronicle* began to give widespread publicity and column space to the activities of republican-style organisations and, as a converse to this, the domineering position formerly enjoyed by the forces of moderate nationalism (UIL, AOH, and INV) now was coming to an end. There were new columns given over to Sinn Féin and Cumann na mBan, much more attention paid to the Gaelic League, reports of National Aid Concerts and a series of explanatory articles on Sinn Féin policies. Even the conservative *Drogheda Independent* recognised the stirrings of change. "What has become of the proverbial political sanity of our people?" its editorial writer of 14 July had cried despairingly following the by-election victory of Sinn Féin, yet from July onwards it opened its columns to this very organisation.

Sinn Féin certainly began to get itself organised in the second half of the year. At a meeting of clubs in Kells on 1 July a North Meath Executive was formed. Clubs represented were Navan, Kells, Oldcastle, Newcastle, Carnaross, Kilskyre, Crossakiel, Drumbaragh, Ballinacree, Moynalty and Clongill. The officers appointed are of interest: John Sweetman was president, Michael Grace was chairman while the secretary was Pádraig de Búrca of Kells who was also closely connected with the county's revitalised Volunteer movement.

South Meath was slower to organise but an executive was formed on 18 November. The clubs present at this meeting included Trim, Athboy, Dunshaughlin, Summerhill, Rathmore, Kildalkey, Kilmore, Castlejordan, Ballivor and Clonard. Martin O'Dwyer of Dunshaughlin was appointed president, vice-presidents were Bob Allen of Trim and Bernard McConnell of Athboy; treasurers were Bernard O'Reilly and Seán O'Higgins; secretaries were Eamon Cullen and Séamus O'Higgins. As with de Búrca in North Meath the last two named were soon to be important figures in the new Volunteers.

The rise of Sinn Féin continued unabated right through 1918 so that by the end of that year local newspaper sources indicate the presence of clubs in Ardamagh, Moybolgue, Martry, Loughan, Kilmainhamwood, Kilbeg, Bohermeen, Girley, Rathkenny, Ballinlough, Drumconrath, Fordstown, Meath Hill, Slane and Stackallen in the North Meath Executive area; and in Duleek, Boardsmill, Dunboyne, Kilmessan and Enfield in the South Meath area. This represents a total of forty-two Sinn Féin clubs in the county by the time of the general election in December 1918.

The aims and policies of Sinn Féin were, and continued to be, a matter of some confusion. At a meeting in Navan in October the ex-parliamentarian Sweetman tried to clarify this. He reminded his listeners that in 1899 the very first meeting of Meath County Council, at which he had been present, had passed a resolution that had been on the orders of the council ever since. This stated that:

> this council reasserts the claim of Ireland to her inalienable right to native self-government … we hold that no body of men are competent to make laws for Ireland, only an Irish parliament and we will do all in our power to regain this, the undoubted right of every nation.

Although, Sweetman claimed "few County Council members now act in accordance with this resolution", it was still on the books and it had now become Sinn Féin policy. This probably did little to clarify the confusion since a phrase such as 'native self-government' could be open to more than one meaning and could certainly be claimed by the home rulers as their own ultimate goal.

Sinn Féin Cumainn, December 1918.

Meath Hill

Drumconrath

Kilmainhamwood

Moybolgue

Ardamagh

Newcastle

Kilbeg

Moynalty

Loughan

Rathkenny

Clongill

Slane

Stackallen

NAVAN

Bohermeen

Martry

Carnaross

KELLS

Drumbaragh

Fordstown

Rathmore

Skryne

Kilmessan

Dunshaughlin

Summerhill

Kilmore

Dunboyne

Girley

Athboy

TRIM

Kildalkey

Ballivor

Boardsmill

Enfield

Kilskyre

Crossakiel

Ballinlough

OLDCASTLE

Clonard

Castlejordan

Ballinacree

Duleek

By the middle of 1917 Patrick White MP was undergoing an examination of his political conscience, and a letter to the *Freeman's Journal* on 3 July marked his final break from Redmond's party. In this he described Lloyd George's forthcoming all-party convention as "the latest British farce" and called on all Irishmen "to repudiate all association with the proposed sham convention", as well as urging Redmond and John Dillon to withdraw from involvement in it. The *Freeman's Journal* noted testily that:

> this letter will not surprise those acquainted with White's public record and still less those familiar with his conception of party loyalty as displayed during recent months.

The writer concluded that White had "now decided to transfer his services to the ranks of Sinn Féin". P.J. Burke, secretary of the North Meath Sinn Féin Executive was sceptical about this, and, in a letter to the *Drogheda Independent,* he viewed White's action as "a continuity of his 'Stand-in-the-ditch' policy since the spread of Sinn Féin in his constituency". White shared this dilemma with a number of his MP colleagues. Having bailed out of the sinking ship of Home Rule he found nothing waiting for him save the cruel sea of political anonymity. He struggled on for another year and in June 1918 publicly supported the candidature of Arthur Griffith in the East Cavan by-election, saying that "every vote for Griffith is a vote for Ireland to be free while every vote for his opponent is a vote for slavery". At this time also White's former colleague David Sheehy said that "the Irish party had not shed many tears over the departure of White", and then ridiculed the latter's evocation of Parnell and Davitt in his support with the comment that "Davitt had utter contempt for him".

With the Home Rule party disowning him, with criticism of his "desertion" coming from the local councils, with continual calls from the *Drogheda Independent* for his resignation, and with seemingly little welcome for him from the Sinn Féin ranks in Meath, White's political career soon fizzled out. He re-emerged just once in an attempted comeback in the general election of August 1923 when the political landscape of post-revolutionary Ireland must have seemed a world apart to the ex-Home Rule MP. White polled 183 first preference votes out of almost 25,000 votes cast.

Meath's reorganised Volunteer movement made its first public appearance at a rally in Kells on Saint Patrick's Day 1918 "to proclaim Ireland's right to sovereign independence". The companies which participated in this rally were from Oldcastle, Athboy, Navan, Trim, Kells, Drumconrath, Stonefield, Carnaross, Loughan and Ballinlough. Ironically on this very day in Mullingar Cathedral Bishop Gaughran delivered a hard-hitting sermon reported in the *Drogheda Independent* on 23 March 1918 in which he appealed "to the young men of this country and diocese to be on their guard against the agents of secret societies". This was an obvious reference to the Volunteers, and the bishop went on to say how he still remembered:

> the troubles of 1867 ... the huge holocaust ... when men were sacrificed on the evidence of numerous informers ... it makes my heart sick to think over the scenes of those bygone days.

We will see in the next chapter how, from the end of 1916 onwards, the moribund Volunteer movement had been revitalised in preparation for the coming troubles of the years 1919–21.

There were hints in 1918 of the imminent unrest, beginning with the arrest late in March of a Dublin man, Eamonn Fleming. Fleming was described as a Sinn Féin organiser, but it was actually Volunteer companies that he had been sent from Dublin to organise in this county, and it was on a charge of illegal drilling that he was tried in camera in Athboy. During this trial a crowd gathered round the police barracks and had to be baton charged by the local RIC. Fleming was taken to Trim where the trial was hastily rearranged and he was sentenced to nine months imprisonment. Meanwhile, six of his would-be rescuers were arrested in the Athboy area and charged with riotous conduct and assaults on police constables. Of these, Patrick Butterfield, John McGovern and Daniel McGovern junior were sentenced to two months in jail, while Daniel McGovern senior, William Moore and John McKenna were discharged with warnings as to their future behaviour. A few months later, in July, Patrick Morris, Joseph Lynch and Leo

McKenna were charged with having taken part in an unlawful assembly in Kells. The unlawful assembly in question was, in fact, a lecture on the policies of Sinn Féin. The three men were tried at Georges Cross court where the magistrate was told that they belonged to both Sinn Féin and the Irish Volunteers; they refused to recognise the court and were each given a month in Mountjoy Jail.

It was only in the previous month that the great and sustained outcry against the British government's proposal to impose conscription on Ireland had finally ended with the scheme being shelved. More than anything else it was this issue which undermined British credibility and drove the Irish people towards Sinn Féin. Even the conservative councils came out strongly against the idea, following the lead of the MPs in Westminster. The county council pledged itself "to abide by and carry out the decisions and directions of the Irish hierarchy and leaders of the Irish nation". The Dunshaughlin councillors expressed their concern at the proposal, and saw it as "another of the many blunders made by English statesmen when dealing with the affairs of this country". Navan UDC stated that if the idea were put into operation "the result would be disastrous to both Ireland and England". While the extremely cautious Kells UDC (reluctant to allow the local Sinn Féin club to use a hall under their jurisdiction a few months earlier, and the only council in Meath to adjourn their March meeting out of respect to the late John Redmond) now, at their meeting on 15 April, unanimously voted against conscription.

Amongst the council members there were only two exceptions to this united front. One was John Law, a Protestant, of Ardbraccan House, Navan, who had been co-opted on to the county council in May 1917 to fill a vacancy (incidentally, in the vote for co-option he had defeated Labour Union President James Harte). Law had dissented against the conscription motion and even the usually moderate *Drogheda Independent* was moved to call him 'a Protestant Unionist' and to remind its readers that since Law had been co-opted rather than elected on to the Council his views represented himself alone. Lest anyone might be in any doubt about this matter, the people of the electoral area which he purported to represent, namely Ardbraccan, held a meeting at Bohermeen on Sunday 28 April at which his views were denounced and Law was called on to resign from the council.

The case of Michael Connolly of Dunshaughlin RDC is less clear. At a meeting of Dunshaughlin Board of Guardians in late April, a *Meath Chronicle* reporter present claimed that Connolly had come out in favour of conscription and quoted him as saying that "they will not take fellows off the farms; there are plenty of idlers such as bank clerks, drapers etc". The following week, on 11 May, in a letter which was published in the *Meath Chronicle* but not in the *Drogheda Independent*, Connolly indignantly dismissed the report as "a garbled account of a private and jocose conversation" which had taken place between the end of the Guardians' meeting while awaiting a quorum for the RDC. His real views, he claimed, were embodied in the resolution passed at this latter meeting which has been referred to earlier.

The pressure against conscription was sustained throughout April, May and June. Public meetings were held in all the towns, the biggest one being at Navan on 14 April at the very outset of the campaign. The two main speakers here (it attracted a crowd of up to six thousand) were John Sweetman and James Kelly, a Duleek-born accountant who was then chairman of the Navan Board of Guardians and later was to serve as a Fianna Fáil TD from 1937 to 1943. Catholic clergy were also to the forefront with Fr Poland (by now parish priest of Rathkenny) and Fr Cooney (the new Administrator in Navan) taking their places on the platform for this meeting. A few days later, at yet another meeting in the town, the decision was taken on the urgings of the local priests to publicly burn copies of newspapers such as the *Irish Times* and the *Evening Mail*, which were favourable towards conscription. Yet another priest, Fr O'Farrell PP Carnaross, showed no inhibitions when he turned a gathering in June into a recruiting platform for Sinn Féin and the Irish Volunteers, telling his listeners that of the four to five hundred men of military age in the town, fewer than one hundred were in the local Volunteer company. The campaign also included an anti-conscription pledge taken in every parish in the county on Sunday 21 April, and a one-day strike organised by the Labour movement two days later, while a so-called Defence Fund was established in the county at the end of the month. The money collected was not needed as Lloyd George backed down on his proposal in June.

There was some unrest amongst the ranks of the Meath Labour Union during this summer of 1918. At a rally held on the Fair Green, Navan, at the end of June, the members put their employers on notice that they were seeking a minimum wage of thirty shillings per week, with three pounds harvest bonus to be paid to agricultural workers. The members of the Meath Farmers Union were given only a week to agree to this and, when this was not forthcoming, the farm workers in the Dunshaughlin area went out on strike. The stoppage was, however, short lived, Labour leaders James Harte and David Hall met a farmers' delegation led by Arthur McCann of Ardsallagh and an agreement was reached on a weekly wage of 25/6. This led to disgruntlement on both sides and a number of farmers, notably county councillor P.J. Kennedy, withdrew from the Farmers Union in protest against what they regarded as too excessive a wage. Some of the labourers were unhappy too, but for the opposite reason, and Hall's own branch in Culmullin voted in August to disaffiliate from the MLU, later followed by a number of others. These now formulated a wage demand of 33/6 per week. There are some indications that these breakaway branches may have joined a rival labour organisation later that year when Thomas Johnson, later leader of the Labour Party in the Dáil in the 1920s, and Cathal O'Shannon spoke at a public meeting in Trim. Both men were prominent in the ITGWU.

On the political front the Labour Union were now faced with the dilemma as to whether they should or should not run a candidate in the general election which would be held before the year's end. Twenty branches were represented at an executive meeting in Navan at the end of September when William O'Brien, general secretary of the ITGWU, was also in attendance. After a long discussion they decided not to put forward a distinctive Labour candidate in the election. They would concentrate on the local government contests and, as regards the general election they would remain neutral, not even issuing a recommendation to their member as to how to vote. In the coming campaign Labour Union members were to be involved in both camps, so that the days of their unquestioned acceptance of the Home Rule position on national matters had come to an end.

As early as September Sinn Féin had selected their candidates for both of the Meath constituencies. At a meeting of the south Meath executive in Kilmessan the delegates had chosen Eamon Duggan, a choice which, the *Drogheda Independent* reported, was "not universally popular among Sinn Féiners". It is difficult to understand this since Duggan was a man of impressive credentials. Born in 1874 in Longwood he had qualified as a solicitor in 1914 and had built up a large practice. Although living in Dublin by this time he had kept in touch with his native county and, in 1915, he took up the case of tenants on an estate near Longwood. These tenants, apparently, did not have the benefits of the land acts or land courts but after much negotiation and correspondence Duggan had persuaded the estate owners to sell to their tenants on satisfactory terms. It was around this time that he had joined the First Dublin Battalion of the Irish Volunteers and he soon rose to the position of Adjutant Officer. He was 'out' during Easter Week when his company fought out of the North Dublin Union.

Amongst his companions there was another Meath man, Thomas Allen, who was killed in the fighting. After the Rising had been suppressed a number of British officers who had been held captive by Duggan's garrison praised the manner in which they had been treated. This was of little consolation to Duggan who now followed a path that became familiar to many of his fellow rebels. He was court-martialled in Mountjoy Jail and sentenced to three years penal servitude, of this he served fourteen months, mostly in English jails such as Portland, Lewes and Maidstone, before his release in June 1917.

On his return he came to prominence in September when he acted as solicitor for the next-of-kin at the inquest of Thomas Ashe. Looking forward beyond 1918, Duggan was to establish himself as a significant figure. He was for a time Director of Intelligence of the IRA until his arrest late in 1920. Freed at the time of the Truce, he was appointed Chief Liaison Officer of the IRA. for the period of that Truce. The role for which he is most remembered is, of course, as a signatory of the Treaty on 6 December 1921. He was to hold the position of Minister for Home Affairs in Michael Collins's Provisional Government, and, with the establishment of the Free State he acted as a Parliamentary Secretary from 1924 to 1932. He remained as a Cumann na nGaedheal TD for Meath until 1933 and thereafter served as a Senator until his death in 1936.

The man Sinn Féin selected to contest the Meath North constituency was Brian O'Higgins, the Kilskyre-born writer who had contributed to the Oldcastle *Sinn Féin* newspaper. Born in 1882, O'Higgins moved to Dublin in 1900 where he was to spend most of the rest of his long life. Deeply involved in the Irish-Ireland movement of these years he was a Gaelic League organiser and teacher of Irish in the Meath-Cavan border area for a couple of years. An early member of the Sinn Féin organisation he wrote literature and propaganda for a wide variety of nationalist and republican organs in the years up to 1916, even starting his own newspaper called *Irish Fun* in October 1915. He was in the GPO during Easter Week and was interned in Frongoch Camp until February 1917. On his return to Ireland he took a position as resident secretary of O'Curry College, Carrigaholt, county Clare, an Irish college under the auspices of the Gaelic League. In May 1918, however, O'Higgins was arrested again in connection with the so-called 'German plot' of that time.

It was while languishing in Birmingham Jail that he was selected to stand in his native constituency. There was, however, a problem since the Sinn Féiners of West Clare had also chosen him as their candidate, and it was for this constituency that he was to be returned unopposed to the First Dáil, although still in prison when this met. The rest of his career may be quickly summarised. He played an important role in the setting up and operation of the Sinn Féin arbitration courts which were to supplant the British legal system in 1920–21. He acted as Leas Ceann Comhairle of the Dáil from August 1921 until he resigned in February 1922 following the vote on the Treaty of which he was a strong opponent. Arrested during the Civil War he spent thirty-five days on a hunger-strike which ended only when he fell unconscious. He refused to join Fianna Fáil in 1926 and became a leader of the soon to be depleted Sinn Féin. From 1932 until 1962 he was mainly associated with the publication of the *Wolfe Tone Annual*, an intransigent republican publication. Brian O'Higgins died in March 1963.

But to return to the events of 1918, a new candidate was needed for the Meath North constituency since O'Higgins had been 'claimed' by West Clare. For this purpose a special meeting of the Sinn Féin executive was held in Kells Town Hall on Friday, 12 October. The delegates were addressed by the Sinn Féin priest, Fr Michael O'Flanagan, and the candidate selected unanimously, on the proposal of Pádraig de Búrca and

Michael Grace, was Liam Mellows, an English-born socialist then resident in New York. For a man who was to turn out to be an uncompromising freedom fighter, Mellows ironically had been born at Hortshead Military Barracks in Lancashire in 1892. Three generations of his family had served in the British army but his father returned with his family to Ireland in 1895 and most of Mellows's childhood was spent in Wexford. Prominent in the Irish Volunteers he took the anti-Redmond side, and, after a spell in prison in England he returned to organise the movement in South Galway. At Easter 1916 he led some sporadic fighting in that area and then went on the run, finally turning up in New York at the end of that year.

It was during his time there that Mellows first became aware of, and then a convinced disciple of, the socialism of James Connolly. Mellows was not to return to Ireland until October 1920 when he was soon appointed to the post of IRA Director of Purchases, a euphemism for the importation of guns, ammunition and explosives. Following the Treaty he became known as one of its most truculent opponents and was one of the leaders of the Army Executive based in the Four Courts. Mellows's brief but stormy career came to a sudden end when the Free State authorities ordered his execution, along with three of his comrades, on 8 December 1922.

It was another month before the Home Rulers got around to selecting their candidates. On Sunday 10 November about forty delegates, representing the "Nationalists of North Meath" as the *Drogheda Independent* of 16 November put it, convened at the premises of the INF in Navan to select a pledge-bound candidate in place of Patrick White. The organisations and bodies present were as typical a cross section as would be found at a Home Rule rally or convention in these years but the volume of support had dwindled greatly. There were only seven UIL branches with delegations, namely: Nobber, Rathkenny, Ballinlough, Kilbeg, Yellow Furze, Slane and Oristown-Kilberry. AOH clubs in attendance were Ardamagh, Meath Hill, Navan, Kilbeg, Kilmainhamwood and Nobber, and only one branch of the Irish National Foresters, Navan, in whose premises the convention was being held. The local bodies who sent members were Navan and Kells RDCs and the county council. Ignoring a nomination for a Dublin man the delegates unanimously selected P. J. Cusack, the Nobber-based doctor who had been prominent in the Back to the Land movement as well as being involved in the recruiting campaign.

Nine days later the nationalists of south Meath came together at the courthouse in Dunshaughlin to perform a similar function. Once again their ranks were fairly depleted. There were only four UIL branches: Skryne, Donore, Duleek and Dunshaughlin; and only three AOH clubs: Ballivor, Trim and Athboy. The report in the *Drogheda Independent* of 23 November mentions representation from certain areas without specifically stating that this involved an UIL or AOH branch; these areas included Ashbourne, Boardsmill, Ratoath, Danestown, Kentstown and Curraha, and the representation was probably no more than a few individuals from each area who took it upon themselves to come to the convention. Certainly the paucity of official delegates and the attendance of unofficial ones indicated a very haphazard and extremely lackadaisical approach to what was to be, perhaps, the most important election ever in Irish history.

None of the local councils in south Meath was represented either, although county council chairman Thomas Halligan did participate as a delegate from his local UIL branch in Skryne. Also present was the sitting MP David Sheehy who at the outset let it be known that he had no intention of running in this election. Perhaps this was due to his age, he was seventy-five, or perhaps because he saw little prospect of success. Whatever the reason Sheehy sounded a very weary man as he brought an end to a long career during which he mournfully told his listeners, "that he had made many enemies and lost many friends". (A passing mention in James Joyce's *Ulysses*, published in 1922, ensured Sheehy a certain status and prestige. He lived until 1932).

To return to the 1918 convention, and with Sheehy's bowing out, the whole business degenerated into farce. The delegates selected the High Sheriff of Dublin, Lorcan Sherlock, as their candidate. A wire was sent to him to see if he would accept but the reply was negative. The meeting then adjourned and reconvened a week later in Kilmessan. A candidate had still not been found and the only decision reached was to seek a recommendation from John Dillon. It was not until 1 December that a candidate was found in the person of Thomas O'Donoghue, a Kerry-born, Dublin-based solicitor and a complete unknown to the people of Meath.

The last three months of 1918 saw the great flu epidemic raging through the county. The number of obituary notices in the local newspapers for this period was greatly increased with the cause of death given as the seemingly endemic flu. In the Navan area it was reported that close on five hundred were affected. Schools were closed and extra clergy had to be brought in to do the work of three of the town's five priests who had been afflicted. On the last day in October the local fever and workhouse hospitals had 135 patients, compared to 77 for the same date in 1917; while in Trim, on one day alone, Tuesday 19 October, four people died from the sickness.

It was against this background that the election drama was played out. Consistent with the trends of the previous two years the two local newspapers found themselves on opposing sides, but the emotions generated by the contest often saw them take up extreme positions. For instance, an editorial in the *Drogheda Independent* in December warned, with, as it turned out, a certain degree of foresight, that:

> Sinn Féin would try again by armed force to establish an independent republic – "and that the logical sequence of Sinn Féin's programme was immediate disappointment and ultimate disaster" – they would be crushed under the juggernaut of English domination.

The *Meath Chronicle* of 2 November 1918, on the other hand, was stressing:

> on how every individual in the Sinn Féin movement works, between then and now depends the future of Ireland, not perhaps for years but for generations.

It expressed contempt for the home rulers, describing John Dillon's attitude as a "hopeless, forlorn leader grasping at a last straw". The *Meath Chronicle* of 23 November 1918 wrote that his party even with "the alleged support of the Liberals (…)" failed to secure even the smallest ameliorative measure for Irish grievances", and yet now, "they insult the intelligence of the electorate by asking a mandate to return with the remnant of that party to fight a coalition government". The choice, so the editorial writer concluded, was between:

a renegade, disreputable party who have sought to defile the honour of the nation, who have played into the hands of English ministers (…) or a party independent and self-reliant (…) who will work in Ireland to bring about the freedom of their country.

The strident tones of those comments, plus the fact that the *Chronicle* was printing election literature for Sinn Féin, landed it in trouble with the authorities. In early December a party of police and military raided the works in Navan and Kells and dismantled the printing machinery, so that, for first time since its inception in 1897 the paper failed to appear as usual on the following Saturday. But it was back to normal on election day, Saturday 14 December, when the front page carried a photograph, very rare in those days, and a detailed biography of Eamon Duggan. (Mellows had been accorded similar generous treatment in the issue of 30 November).

Nor did the clergy approach the election united behind one candidate. The conventions which had met to appoint the Home Rule candidates had included a sprinkling of priests while the nomination papers lodged on behalf of Liam Mellows included the names of six priests. Amongst them was Fr O'Farrell, parish priest of Carnaross, who had used the anti-conscription meeting in Navan in June to recruit for the Irish Volunteers and Sinn Féin and who was by this time president of the North Meath Comhairle Ceantair (Executive) of the latter organisation. The home rulers still maintained the support of the majority of Meath's political leaders, amongst them Harte of the Labour Union and Joseph Madden, president of the county's AOH. They also enjoyed the backing of most of the local councillors who were willing to get embroiled in the campaign including Thomas Halligan (County Council); P. J. Mulvany (Dunshaughlin RDC); Matthew Gartland (Kells UDC); John Spicer (Navan UDC); John Clarke (Kells RDC) and James Gammons (Ardee No. 2 RDC), all of whom carried the prestige value of being chairmen of their respective councils. Against this, the only representative who for certain declared himself for Sinn Féin, and who worked and spoke on behalf of that party was the Dunshaughlin and county councillor, Patrick Moore. It may be pointed out, however, that the patronage of elected representatives had by this time become of dubious value, as the local government elections (already postponed in 1917 and 1918, and to be postponed again in 1919) of January and June 1920 were soon to prove.

As for the campaign itself, the *Drogheda Independent* of 23 November reported that it got under way in the middle of November with both sides holding meetings at the Hill of Slane (the Sinn Féin gathering was addressed by Sean T. O'Kelly and Harry Boland). This at the outset gave a certain finesse and dignity to the proceedings but over the next month the campaign, in north Meath at least, was to degenerate into a rough and tumble affair. In Kells where both parties were holding public meetings, the home rulers were subjected to such disruption that both Pádraig de Búrca and Eamon Duggan felt obliged to appeal to those present to allow the Nationalist meeting to continue, Duggan saying that this was "no time for stone throwing or name calling".

Similar hostility was shown to Dr Cusack in Carnaross. Perhaps it was not a good idea to venture here since the political faith of its parish priest made the area sacrosanct for republicanism. In fact, Fr O'Farrell gallantly asked the crowd to allow Cusack to speak and afterwards to permit him to leave when a number of the more optimistic local Sinn Féiners were hoping he would remain to listen to the speeches of their side.

Rathkenny was the scene of a further mêlée on Sunday, 1 December. The *Drogheda Independent* of 7 December reported:

> Dr Cusack was pulled from the platform and Mr Monaghan (a supporter) was struck a severe blow which broke the cartilage of his nose.

Even the *Meath Chronicle* of 8 December 1918 acknowledged this, reporting that:

> a man was observed on the footboard of [Cusack's] car speaking in a highly excited tone and flourishing his fists in Dr Cusack's face ... Mr Michael Monaghan received a nasty cut about the face as the result ... of a blow of a stick ... the Rev. J.J. Poland, PP, arrived on the scene and prevented what might have resulted in a very serious conflict.

The biggest fracas of all took place in Navan on that same day, probably after Cusack and his party had fought their way out of Rathkenny. If so, it was very much a case of jumping from the frying pan into the fire since, once again, a Nationalist meeting had to be prematurely abandoned due, according to the *Drogheda Independent*, "to a terrific din kept up by a section of the crowd". In anticipation of trouble the Navan priests had appealed at that morning's masses for freedom of speech and, once again, a prominent Sinn Féiner, Seán MacNaMidhe, asked for a fair hearing to be given to Cusack. Both appeals were in vain.

Former Senator Pat Fitzsimons clearly recalled that Sunday. A horse-drawn brake serving as a platform was situated directly in front of Crinion's Hotel on the Market Square. When Christopher Owens, a member of Navan RDC, rose to address the hostile crowd, Pat remembered that his opening words were "fellow Irishmen and fellow idiots". This hastened the end of the meeting as a group of men made repeated attempts to overturn the brake and, as the *Drogheda Independent* put it, "Owens laid round him with a stick". Having failed to overturn the platform someone then simply released the brakes so that the brake, speakers and all, went free-wheeling down the hill before coming to a halt at Everard's business premises.

On election day, 14 December, the *Drogheda Independent* claimed that "personation was rife and many nationalists found that on entering the polling booth their vote was gone". Of course, this newspaper was certainly not an unbiased commentator and indeed there probably has never been an election without such allegations, but it is of interest that more than one of those spoken to recalled airily how they had voted five or six times on that day. Personation was a fairly tame matter after the mêlées of the previous weeks but the day itself did not pass without incident. In Kells a group of soldiers turned with fixed bayonets on a jeering crowd and a single rifle shot was fired to scatter them.

This election was the first to be contested in both Meath constituencies since 1900. For a mid-winter's day the poll for North Meath was a remarkably high 80 per cent, with the absent Mellows having an easy victory by 6,982 votes to Cusack's 3,758. This result was quite pre-dictable and on election day even the *Drogheda Independent* reporter was admitting that the Home Ruler would gain a majority only in the Slane-Wilkinstown-Drumconrath-Nobber districts, the area which he served as a doctor. Cusack's defeat was attributed by the Meath Chronicle of 4 January 1919 to "the poor ramshackle organisation at his disposal".

In South Meath Thomas O'Donoghue must have felt much the same way. On a much lower poll of 62 per cent, Eamon Duggan trounced him by 6,371 to 2,680 votes. O'Donoghue was gracious in defeat and, after the count had been completed in Trim courthouse, speaking without rancour, he remarked on the "good feeling which prevailed between both parties". The *Drogheda Independent* also accepted defeat without bitterness as it grudgingly conceded that "today Irish policy is undoubtedly that of Sinn Féin" and sportingly reported that, "never before was a successful candidate (Duggan) accorded such a princely reception despite the drizzling rain of a cold mid-winter night".

As for the *Chronicle*, on 4 January 1919 it commented predictably that a "Republican party (…) replaces the old decadent parliamentarians", and that the electorate had stated "its belief in the ideals of the men who fought for an Irish Republic in Easter Week." Of course, this newspaper had not shown the same enthusiasm for these ideals in May 1916 when it will be recalled that its editorial had decried the rising as a "tragic blunder – Ireland will now deplore the folly of these men".

The Sinn Féin victory was greeted and celebrated all over the county. Houses left their lights on, there were torchlight processions often led by pipers' bands and always followed by fighting speeches and bonfires and tar barrels blazed in every area. There was much waving of tricolours and singing of republican songs and there were many victory dances and céilís. Amidst the great euphoria of election night in Kells a speaker in Newmarket Street recalled for his listeners how Parnell had come to Navan in March 1891, just seven months before his death and at the height of his desperate struggle for political survival, and had addressed his audience as "men of royal Meath" but added with typical ambiguity that someone in the future "might have the privilege of addressing you as men of republican Meath".

Now, according to the speaker in Newmarket Street, this time had come to pass. This speaker, incidentally, was Pádraig de Búrca who was secretary of Sinn Féin's North Meath Executive. Perhaps of equal significance was his position by this time as Commandant of the Fourth Battalion of the Meath Brigade of the Irish Volunteers, soon to be also known as the IRA.

5

January 1919 - July 1921:
The Troubles (1): The Military Struggle

In the previous chapter passing reference was made to the revived Irish National Volunteer movement in the county and to the first signs of unrest between 1916 and 1918. This chapter deals in great detail with this revival and attempts to chronicle the military campaign against British rule in the three years after 1918. In so far as can be ascertained the only previous attempt to do this was by Séamus Finn, a leading Volunteer figure in the county, whose *History of the Meath Brigade of the IRA* was serialised in Garrett Fox's column in the *Meath Chronicle* between 15 May 1971 and 9 September 1972. It should perhaps be pointed out that accounts of these years – and this applies not only to Meath but also to the country as a whole – are often coloured by later events, namely, the split over the Treaty and the Civil War of 1922–23, as well as subsequent political developments. Thus, in recounting certain incidents, credit due in some cases may be exaggerated and in other instances omitted altogether.

Séamus Finn was born in 1896, the son of a draper in Athboy. The foreword to his serialised history in the *Meath Chronicle* stated that he meant it "only as a straightforward reminiscence of what actually happened ... it is not a complete history but covers all of the large work that fell to our lads to do". Finn's account begins in the immediate aftermath of the 1916 Rising. He recounts how the Irish Volunteers who mobilised on the Hill of Tara on Easter Sunday were sent home and how this led to "much resentment and disappointment", feelings which he encountered as he travelled the county over the next year in an attempt to revitalise the demoralised spirit.

This campaign of revitalization began following a Gaelic League class in Athboy: present were Patrick O'Growney, Bernard McConnell, Seán O'Grady, Pat Carey, Patrick and George Butterfield, Michael Hoey and Liam Doyle, as well as Finn himself. Several of these men have been mentioned in the last chapter as having been arrested and imprisoned arising out of mild disturbances that were to occur in the area in 1917 and 1918. It was decided at this meeting that Finn and O'Grady, an insurance agent born in Clare, should make contact with other parts of the county. In Drumbaragh Finn had talks with Hugh Smith, the virulently anti-British *Meath Chronicle* columnist; Pádraig de Búrca, the Kells schoolteacher soon to be a leading figure in Meath's Sinn Féin organisation; Seán Hayes, Michael Sweeney and Philip Tevlin. Meanwhile O'Grady got in touch with a fellow Clare man, Con McMahon, also an insurance salesman based in Navan. A number of meetings were held at Larry Clarke's in Brews Hill; amongst those others present, Finn recalls, were Pat Loughran, Joe Woods, Tom Gavigan and Michael Gaynor.

At a funeral in Dublin in August 1916 Finn met Bob Price, a man of some standing in what remained of the shattered Volunteers movement. Price urged him to set up some sort of a county authority to co-ordinate the activities of the various disparate units in existence, as well as to set up new ones. A further meeting held at Larry Clarke's appointed Con McMahon as chairman, with Finn as secretary/adjutant – a rather skeletal structure.

Coming into 1917 Finn claims that Sinn Féin cumainn "became the main base for Volunteer activities" and that "where there were

Irish classes and hurling clubs it was easy to get men to join the Irish Volunteers". At this stage he mentions companies he organised such as Ballinlough (where John Keogh was the leading figure), Bohermeen (John Newman), Longwood (the Giles brothers) and Summerhill (Éamon Cullen, later to be an Assistant Commissioner of the Garda Síochana). He recalls a meeting with the men of Trim who let him know of their deep disillusionment with the let-down of the previous year: those present included Harry and Pat O'Hagan, Séamus and Seán O'Higgins, Mick Hynes, Joe Lalor, Pat Duigenan and Pat Mooney.

In all of this there may be a danger of Finn overstating his role. Finn's role was perhaps more as a co-ordinator than as a founder; there were men in each area willing to take the initiative in setting up companies. Take, for instance, Trim: Joe Lalor, mentioned above, had two brothers in the Volunteers, George and Paddy. Their involvement continued a republican tradition in the family as their father, a tailor, had been in the Fenians. Paddy recalled that the first meeting of the Trim Company had been held in November 1916 at the water reservoir at Effernock, about a mile outside the town at which eleven men were present. This eleven also formed the nucleus of a Sinn Féin club, "but these constitutionalists soon distanced themselves from the Volunteers." The first company captain was Séamus O'Higgins, a publican and auctioneer, who was later succeeded by Mick Hynes, a shop assistant.

In the north Meath area a major driving force was Séamus Cogan, a farmer's son from Stonefield, just out of his teenage years. Peter O'Connell recalled how, in the spring of 1917, while cutting turf one day he was approached by Cogan, who was, incidentally, his first cousin, and "he informed me that he was about to form a company of Irish Volunteers in Stonefield." Peter O'Connell himself was then just seventeen years old, having been born in Fartagh, Virginia, in 1900. As with Paddy Lalor, his father had been a Fenian who had been 'out' in 1867. Peter, a man with a remarkable memory and a great feeling for the history of his native north Meath, had stories about the activities of the great Fenian leaders James Stephens and Thomas Clarke Luby in the Moynalty-Mullagh area during the 1860s. He remembered how, as a very young boy, his father showed him where he had hidden his blunderbuss following the ill-fated 1867 rebellion. Peter spent two years at the Masters, later the Christian Brother's, school in Kells where Pádraig de Búrca was one of his teachers. In his statement to the Military History Bureau he recounts some of his memories of the war years:

> I remember recruiting meetings being held and men going off to join the British Army, and soldiers coming home on leave. The recruiting meetings were addressed by members of the Irish Parliamentary Party and officers of the British forces. At one such meeting, held at Carnaross and which was to have been addressed by a Colonel Farrell of Moynalty, there was no audience other than the RIC and their sympathisers.

He remembered a corps of the Irish Volunteers in the area and its split in 1914. Then came the Rising: fourteen local men were present at the Hill of Tara on Easter Sunday but were sent home, following which "there was little Volunteer activity in Carnaross and much discussion as to the merits and demerits of the rebellion". A few days after Cogan's initial approach to him in the spring of 1917, "about ten or twelve of us met at a barn in Stonefield and lined up for our first parade." Thus was born the Stonefield company, a company which it will be seen was to prove itself unique amongst all those in the county. There was drilling, instruction in semaphore signalling and the first tentative steps to securing weapons: a rifle was obtained from "a man in Tandera named Tobin who had a Lee-Enfield rifle which had been left in his custody by a relative who had taken part in the rebellion ... we soon learned the mechanism of the rifle, how to load and unload, and had practice in bayonet charging". Trim and Stonefield were two of the earliest companies to be organised, but these were still early days (1917), and the beginnings of units elsewhere in the county shall be considered later.

What follows next is a digression from the story of the Irish Volunteers but it is a subject deserving of a brief consideration. The influence of the Gaelic League and GAA in creating the Irish-Ireland climate prevalent in the early years of this century is now universally acknowledged by historians. These two organisations acted as de-Anglicising forces, making Irishmen more conscious of their separateness as a nation. In this respect the quote from Séamus Finn's memoirs, given in the last

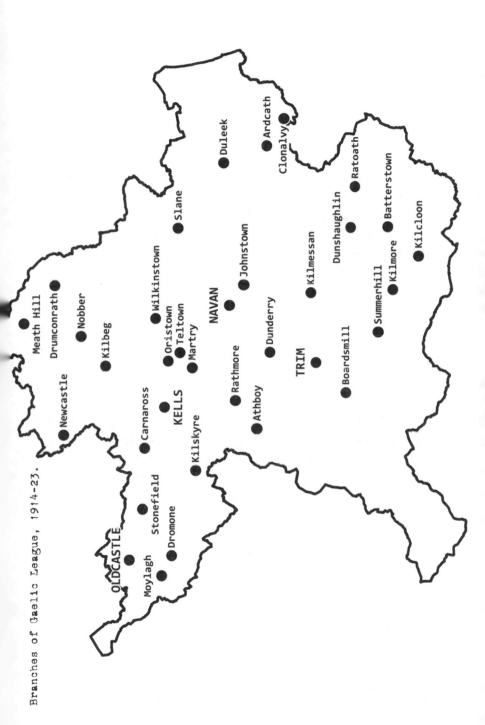

Branches of Gaelic League, 1914-23.

section, that "where there were Irish classes and hurling clubs it was easy to get men to join the Irish Volunteers" is of some interest. It is not intended here to give a history of either of these organisations in Meath but merely to point out where branches or clubs existed between the years 1913 to 1923.

Although the Irish language in the county had largely died out by the turn of the century, Peter O'Connell recalled that "we had several Gaelic speakers in the townland when I was a boy." Indeed the national secretary of the Gaelic League, Professor Agnes O'Farrelly, was a native of this area and often visited Peter's house, where both of his parents were Gaelic speakers. The old custom of 'making a céilí' – visiting someone's home and speaking in Irish – was commonplace at the time. The Gaelic League's main contribution to Irish life at this time was largely social and concerts, céilís and outdoor entertainments called 'aeríochts' are to be seen advertised in the columns of the local press.

In October 1917 there were branches of the Gaelic League in Navan, Trim, Kells, Athboy, Dunshaughlin, Summerhill, Kilmore, Stonefield, Carnaross, Oristown and Kilskyre. Over the next five years organisation seems to have been very haphazard. The local newspapers often refer to the number of branches which were affiliated to the county committee as distinct from those affiliated to headquarters in Dublin and others who were affiliated with neither. Apart from that, lists of branches often indicate much fluctuation, with some old branches disappearing, new ones appearing and the old ones reappearing a few years later. For the record and for what it is worth, apart from those mentioned above, there were, at one time or another in these years, Gaelic League clubs in the following places: Teltown, Ratoath, Boardsmill, Newcastle, Batterstown, Slane, Drumone, Martry, Johnstown, Dunderry, Wilkinstown, Kilmessan, Oldcastle, Moylough, Kilcloon, Clonalvy, Duleek, Drumconrath, Nobber, Kilbeg, Rathmore, Ardcath and Meath Hill. This gives an impressive total of thirty-four with representation spread evenly over every part of the county.

Although proclaimed in 1918, at the time of the so-called 'German plot', the Gaelic League's activities in Meath do not seem to have suffered much interference from the authorities. In fact, the only really noteworthy incident was the banning of a Gaelic League concert scheduled to take place in Dunshaughlin workhouse on Easter Sunday 1920. Apparently, the ban on the concert was not announced until the previous day after all the arrangements had been finalised. The *Meath Chronicle* of 26 April 1919 reported as follows:

> "Two wagon loads of military, numbering about 30 ... arrived in the village on Saturday and occupied the barrack square ... District Inspector Foy took over complete possession of the Workhouse buildings ... The gates were locked and D.I. Foy ... informed them of the fact that the concert had been proclaimed."

That night a crowd of two hundred not very loyal subjects turned up at the workhouse led by a number of priests, but after making a token protest and singing 'The Soldiers Song', they dispersed peacefully. The concert was in fact held a fortnight later, much to the delight of a columnist in the *Chronicle* who, with great satisfaction, was able to report that amongst the items presented, "there was nothing of the Vulgar Jazz, the indecent Gorilla Trot or the objectionable Kangaroo Hop – the latest innovations from British music halls."

A ban on all public assembly in the county in April 1921, at the height of the Troubles, applied to Gaelic League-organised social activities, but long before this, as we shall see, on at least two significant occasions in 1917 aeríochts had been used as a cover for Volunteer organisational activities.

Amongst those veterans spoken to there was near unanimity about the overlapping membership of their Volunteer Company with the local GAA clubs. "We were all playing football at the time, even while we were on the run," Jack Lynch said, referring to the Carnaross Volunteers. For the period in question, the first annual convention of the Meath GAA was held in March 1914. At this the secretary gave the number of clubs in the county as forty-six. A report of the convention in the *Meath Chronicle* of 14 March 1916 named and graded the clubs as follows: there were in fact only six senior clubs, namely, Navan Harps, Donore, Carnaross, Kells Stars, Commons and Bohermeen; the intermediate clubs made up the bulk of the membership, there being 29 of them: Ballinacree, Ballinlough, Oldcastle, Moylough, Athboy,

GAA Clubs, 1914.

106

Trim, Rathcormick, Dunshaughlin, Kilcloon, Enfield, Garlow Cross, Summerhill, Bogganstown, Kilmore, Rathmolyon, Skryne, Curraha, Slane, Lougher, Martry, Kilbeg, Duleek, Rathkenny, Grangegeeth, Ross, Drumconrath, Kilmainhamwood, Navan Harps and Navan Emmets. Unfortunately, the report does not list the other clubs comprising, presumably, the junior grade, but a scanning of the sketchy and intermittent fixture lists appearing in the *Chronicle* over the next year indicates that there were clubs in Rodanstown, Longwood, Ratoath, Dunboyne and Kilskyre.

Despite the strong republican character of the Association, the county board in Meath seems to have distanced itself from direct political involvement in these years. Newspaper reports of conventions and meetings record numerous resolutions supportive of the national struggle and condemnatory of British administration, but only on one occasion did the Board touch directly upon a subject that could be described as politically sensitive. This was at the annual convention in March 1919 when a resolution was introduced calling for the banning of all members of the RIC from entry to GAA grounds. The delegates were almost evenly divided on the issue, with those against raising the problem that many GAA members had brothers and even fathers in the police force. Besides, they inquired, who was actually going to enforce the ban, to physically turn away the police from the grounds? It was decided to refer the motion to the adjourned convention and to take soundings from the clubs in the interim: the adjourned convention probably got the county board out of a prickly situation when it defeated the motion by the very narrow margin of twenty two votes to twenty.

The frequently common membership of GAA clubs and Volunteer companies can be seen in the list of delegates given as attending monthly and annual meetings of the county board of the Association. A full list of these would be too numerous to give but amongst those already mentioned in this account are Pádraig de Búrca (Kells Stars), Seán O'Grady (Athboy) and John Newman (Bohermeen). Bohermeen were in fact the kingpins of Meath football in the early years of the century and in 1914 Newman himself had captained them to their sixth senior championship in succession, a record which still stands. Advanced nationalists and republicans were also strongly in evidence amongst the officers of the county board. Both de Búrca and Seán MacNaMidhe of Navan, a leading figure in Sinn Féin, held the position of chairman at various times between 1914 and 1919, while the secretaryship was held by Larry Clarke of Navan and later by Paddy Giles of Longwood. When Pádraig de Búrca resigned as chairman in August 1919, the position passed to the man who had been instrumental in introducing the anti-RIC motion mentioned earlier: this was the delegate from Dunboyne, Seán Boylan, a man who was by this stage better known in the county as Commanding Officer of the Meath Brigade of the Irish Republican Army.

"A relentless worker", is how Peter O'Connell described Seán Boylan; "during the troubled times he often left us here in Carnaross after a battalion meeting and at three in the morning would be setting out to cycle to Dublin." More than one person referred to Boylan as "Mick Collins's right-hand man". Of course, the vast range of Collins's activities probably acquired him a whole army of right-hand men, but there is little doubt that Boylan was the most influential and significant figure in the republican movement in Meath in these years. Apart from his leading role in the GAA and the Volunteers he was to become, from the summer of 1920 onwards, a member of both Dunshaughlin RDC and Meath County Council while also being deeply involved in the ultra-secret Irish Republican Brotherhood.

Born in 1882 Boylan worked in his family's market gardening business in the Dunboyne area but from an early age was involved in political activities. His son, also Seán, recalled that his father had been present at the unveiling of the Parnell Monument in O'Connell Street very early in the century while he also led a group of Dunboyne hurlers in the cortège of the funeral of O'Donovan Rossa in August 1915.

There is some confusion regarding Seán Boylan's role during Easter Week. He was certainly present at the Hill of Tara where he had the unpleasant task of telling the men to disperse. Amongst those mobilised there was a group of men from Carnaross Company who travelled in three cars and brought a football with them to allay any suspicions. This story was related by Jack Lynch, two of whose brothers were in the 'football party', although Jack himself was too young and was not to join the company until the following year; but he remembered that when "they reached Tara they were told to await further orders but were disappointed when Seán Boylan of Dunboyne told them that the fight was called off and to return home". This was Easter Sunday.

The following day when the rebellion belatedly got under way Boylan hastily organised a group of Volunteers in his own area. Peter and Nick Moran were not then part of the movement – again because, like Jack Lynch, they were too young at the time – but they did recall that on Easter Monday about ten to twelve men left the village and made their way to Powerstown House in Mulhuddart. Amongst those present, they remembered, were Sean himself, his brother Joe, Peter Lee, Jim Mullally, Frank Lowndes and Kit Lynam. But the small group got no further, as the outskirts of Dublin were cordoned off and they seem to have played little, if any, part in the fighting.

In the previous chapter reference has been made to the Roll of Honour which commemorates the part of the Dunboyne people in the Rising. The authenticity of this list of names may be open to question especially since the name of Seán Boylan himself does not appear on it. What is certain, however, was that Boylan and three of his brothers were arrested in the aftermath of the suppression of the insurrection. We have seen that two of them, Edward and Peter, had no connection whatsoever with the Rising and were soon released. But Seán was to spend about a year interned first in Wandsworth and then in Frongoch, the main camp used for the rebels. It was probably here that he first met Michael Collins.

On his release, probably about Easter 1917, Boylan at once resumed his organisational activities. In his statement to the Bureau of Military History, he related that he "got most of the Dunboyne Volunteers together again. A few of the original members dropped out. We had now about twelve active men". For the purpose of boosting membership, Boylan thought up an ambitious scheme:

> I organised an aeríocht, which was held in one of the fields of our farm, in the month of September 1917 .... Michael Collins and William T. Cosgrave attended and addressed those of the locality to join the Volunteers, with the result that we received several new members.

Boylan's activities took him further afield: "From then to the end of the year I travelled all over Meath and organised new companies in nearly every town and parish". In this respect, he seems to have complemented the role of Séamus Finn and indeed when the various companies were first established in a formal structure both these men were in leading positions. It is difficult to pinpoint exactly when this took place: Finn placed it in August 1917 while Boylan recalled it as having occurred early in 1918. Both men, however, were agreed on one point, that the county convention which established the Volunteers on a proper basis was held at Dunderry, where once again an aeríocht was used as cover for the illegal activities.

At this it was decided that the entire county plus the Delvin area of county Westmeath would form the Brigade area. The Dunderry meeting distributed the companies amongst six battalions and appointed staff at both brigade and battalion level. The brigade staff elected was:

O/C: Seán Boylan
Vice O/C: Seán Hayes
Adjutant: Séamus Finn
Quartermaster: Séamus O'Higgins
Director of Engineering: Eamon Cullen

The companies and officers of each battalion were as follows:

First Dunboyne Battalion:
Dunboyne, Kilcloon, Kilmore, Kilbride, Summerhill
O/C: Barney Dunne
Vice O/C: Frank Carolan
Adjutant: David Hall
Quartermaster: W. O'Toole
Intelligence Officer: Bernard O'Reilly
Transport: James Maguire

Second Trim Battalion:
Trim, Boardsmill, Ballivor, Longwood, Enfield, Dunderry
O/C: Mick Hynes

Vice O/C: Paddy Mooney
Adjutant: Seán O'Higgins
Quartermaster: Patrick Duigenan

Third Athboy Battalion:
Athboy, Kildalkey, Delvin, Archerstown, Fordstown
O/C: Michael Fox
Vice O/C: Patrick Corrigan
Adjutant: Larry Ginnell
Quartermaster: Patrick Carthy
Engineer: Joseph Martin

Fourth Kells Battalion:
Kells, Moynalty, Loughan, Kilbeg, Newcastle
O/C: Patrick Farrelly
Vice O/C: Thomas Reilly
Adjutant: M. Cahill
Quartermaster: Michael Govern

Fifth Oldcastle Battalion:
Oldcastle, Ballinlough, Ballinacree, Carnaross, Stonefield,
Moylough
O/C: Séamus Cogan
Vice O/C: Seán Farrelly
Quartermaster: Phil Tevlin
Engineer: Matt Tevlin

Sixth Navan Battalion:
Navan, Yellow Furze, Kilberry, Johnstown, Clongill,
Bohermeen, Commons
O/C: Patrick Loughran
Vice O/C: Arthur Levins
Adjutant: Ciarán O'Connell
Engineer: Joe Hughes

It should be borne in mind that the above information relates to a specific time, either August 1917 or early 1918, and that this was still up to two years before the first real stirrings of unrest appeared in the county. Two points must be made: firstly, since it was still early days, the process of forming companies continued and, as shall be seen, this was still going on as late as 1920. Secondly, there were constant changes amongst the personnel making up the brigade and battalion staffs due to arrests, men leaving the county and even deaths. It would be impossible to list all these changes up to the year 1921 and indeed it is difficult enough to locate exactly where companies were in existence although in both cases this will be attempted.

The company in Kilbride had its unofficial headquarters at the Mannings' house. Jack Manning was the company captain for most of the period of the Troubles. His younger brother, Tom, recalled joining the movement in September 1918. About a year before he had been told he was too young, but when he approached Seán Boylan one night after a mission in Dunboyne he was accepted and at once was given his first assignment: to carry a despatch to Dunshaughlin. Tom, then aged nineteen, put the piece of paper in his shoe and survived a not very thorough search by police outside Dunshaughlin workhouse. He was to act as a despatch rider on numerous occasions over the next three years and escaped from several tight corners, none tighter than at Lagore, between Ratoath and Dunshaughlin, early in 1921. "I had to get into a fox covert and crawl clear, with bullets whizzing all round me ... it was the nearest I ever came to death", he recalled. At its height the Kilbride Company had thirty-two men.

At the other end of the county, in Oldcastle, Owen Clarke traced the beginnings of the Volunteers there. Owen himself was born in Belturbet, county Cavan in 1898 and came to Oldcastle in October 1916 to work as a shop assistant in Charlie Fox's stores. This was the same Charlie Fox who had been among the group of men who had begun the Sinn Féin newspaper back in 1902. By all accounts he was quite a character: although a fervent republican, he did not allow this to interfere in any way with either his personal life or his business pursuits. He married a widow whose first husband had served in the British Army in India. When Charlie provided clothing from his drapery to help in the escape of two German nationals interned in Oldcastle workhouse, used as a detention centre for German and Austrian nationals resident in Ireland during World War I, he was arrested but soon released due to, it is thought in the area, his wife's influence in the Viceregal Lodge.

Fox also opened a cinema in Oldcastle during these years mainly to cater for the tastes of British soldiers based there. "There were two houses every evening", said Owen Clarke, "one for the soldiers and the other for the townspeople". But to return to Owen's story, he remembered how the company had been organised by two Dublin men, Harry Murray and John Kavanagh. These had come to stay in Fox's after the Rising in which they had participated, and after which they had spent some months interned. The first captain of the company was a tailor's assistant named Tommy Harpur. At one time they had twenty to twenty-five members. Later Owen Clarke himself became captain. Ironically back in 1914 he had tried to join the British Army but had been turned away because of his youth.

Although not mentioned in the list of companies given earlier, James O'Connell recalled joining his local unit in Skryne "sometime in 1917". James – known as 'The Yank' because he was born in New York in 1901 and spent the first ten years of his life there – remembered that it was a very small company with never more than a dozen men. He felt that this was due to the great number of Skryne men then employed on the estates of landlords and gentry in the area. "These men were unwilling to risk losing their jobs; remember that the land stewards knew everything that happened and their influence was feared", said James. The first captain of the Skryne Company was a man named Dolan. James recalled drilling in various locations, usually disused farmhouses, and also himself giving lectures on engineering from literature that he had got from headquarters in Dublin.

Matt Wallace joined an 'unlisted' company in Kiltale towards the end of 1917. At this time he was living in Batterstown and working on the roads for Meath County Council. It was a ganger who asked him to join the company; Matt needed little persuasion as his older brother Tom was already a member.

It was under similar circumstances that Willie Coogan joined the company in Bohermeen. He was then working on the roads and one of his fellow workers approached him and asked him to join up. He recalled that the men used to meet and drill at Gibney's shed just off the New Line. Another Volunteer in this company was Johnny Bennett of Ardbraccan. At the age of fourteen Johnny began to learn the trade of a stonecutter. He spent most of the years 1917 to 1919 working in Tullamore and was recruited into the Volunteers there by some of his workmates. He recalled one blazing Sunday afternoon in mid-summer being sent on a forced march from Tullamore to Moate and back again. The march was led by the now legendary Ernie O'Malley. On his return to Ardbraccan Johnny joined the company in Bohermeen but left again in 1920 to spend six months working in Belfast. He had vivid memories of the sectarian hatred there and the 'No Pope' slogans splashed across the walls. Later, both Willie and Johnny transferred to a company formed in Martry: the captain was John Murtagh, while Johnny became second lieutenant and Willie was appointed quartermaster.

Let us return now to 1918. Most of the noteworthy events of this year, and there were few enough of them, have already been touched on in the previous chapter. Reported in the *Meath Chronicle* of 23 March 1918 was a rally of Volunteer companies in Kells on St. Patrick's Day "to proclaim Ireland's right to sovereign independence". Ten companies were in attendance at this gathering. This represented a small enough turnout but it is of significance in that it was one of only two occasions in the post-Rising period that the Meath Volunteers paraded publicly and openly. This was in marked contrast to the early days of the Volunteer movement – 1914 to 1916 – when public rallies and demonstrations were used to whip up support and enthusiasm for the Home Rule cause. The re-organised, or 'new', Volunteer movement was now a secretive affair and was also soon to be made illegal.

It may also be pointed out at this stage that the post-1916 organisation had lost much of the 'respectability' that had characterised the earlier movement. The gentry class, the local politicians and the clergy were little in evidence, and we have seen Bishop Gaughran's warning to the young men "of this county and diocese to be on their guard against the agents of secret societies." The 'new' Volunteers were drawn generally from the lower classes. This conclusion is drawn from conversations with those surviving veterans of the Troubles. In the rural areas most Volunteers were the sons of small farmers or were farm labourers, or worked on the roads. In the towns the companies were dominated by tradesmen and assistants in shops, public houses and draperies. Age-wise, the organisation was by now dominated by the youth, those in their late teens and their twenties with only the occasional man over thirty. The months from April to June 1918 were dominated by the conscription crisis. The campaign in Meath of opposition to conscription has already been described. In so far as it affected the Volunteer movement there is general agreement that it provided a boost in recruitment. This is stated by both Séamus Finn and Seán Boylan, although the latter enters a note of caution:

> The Volunteers took a very active part in this campaign and during the period several new recruits joined the various companies. Here in Dunboyne I would say that our strength went up to about forty. When it was all over, a lot of our new men left, which reduced our strength to twenty-four.

In his own area in north Meath, Peter O'Connell recalled the great activities of these months:

> A branch of the Sinn Féin organisation had been established in the area by this time. They organised protest meetings at all the church gates. At all those meetings they had the full support of the Volunteers. Among the speakers on the platforms whom I remember were: Pádraig de Búrca, Fr O'Farrell of Carnaross and a Fr Gaffney at Virginia. During this period several schools and colleges in the country were closed down and the students came home. Several of those students joined the Volunteer companies in the surrounding areas. We had many new recruits in the Stonefield Company most of whom, with few exceptions, remained loyal to the end. The strength of the company at the time was twenty-five and remained at that strength from then on.

The Volunteers were also involved in the vital East Cavan by-election in July of this year. The southern part of this constituency extended into north Meath and the Sinn Féin candidate, Arthur Griffith, made his headquarters at Fox's in Oldcastle. Seán Boylan stated that on his instructions:

> the Volunteers of north Meath went to the East Cavan area where they canvassed and worked for the success of Arthur Griffith. In several instances they had to protect the speakers on behalf of Arthur Griffith from very hostile mobs composed of Hibernians, who were the main support of the nationalist candidate; Orangemen; and members of the Ulster, or Carson, Volunteers, who all continued to break up or prohibit Sinn Féin meetings.

Peter O'Connell was one of those Volunteers sent to East Cavan who "took an active part in the work of canvassing, organising Sinn Féin meetings and all the usual work attached to an election. The Hibernians, Unionists and pro-British element ... were our main opposition." Griffith, incidentally, won this election by about 1,000 votes.

Five months later the Volunteers were back again at the same work, this time in connection with the general election. They carried out the functions of canvassing and supplying personation agents and policing the polling booths on election day. The enthusiasm of some Volunteers however carried them far beyond the bounds of legality, and several of those spoken to airily recalled that they voted on several occasions on that day, and this even though they were under the voting age. One of them, who asked not to be named, jokingly related his memories of that day:

> I must have voted thirty times at various polling booths in our area. But I was not by any means the only one to do so and even the officials were in on it. From mid-day onwards I used to be greeted with a friendly smile by the presiding officer at a particular booth and his poll clerk would laughingly ask: 'Whose name is it this time?'

21 January 1919 is the date generally given as the starting point of the War of Independence or 'the Troubles'. On this date the first Dáil met in Dublin while, more ominously, down in Tipperary, a small group of

Volunteers, led by Dan Breen, ambushed and killed two RIC men. It was, however, to be almost the end of the year before the first serious shooting began in Meath.

Before this, in August 1918, came the first action by the county's Volunteers, specifically the Navan Company, to gain headlines in the local newspapers. This action, however, had little if anything to do with the anti-British struggle and at the time only those 'in the know' would have suspected that the Volunteers were responsible. The background to this incident was a bitter labour dispute mainly in the southern part of the county where the ITGWU-led agricultural labourers had gone on strike against the Meath Farmers Union. This had begun early in July, and the details need not concern us here except to say that by the middle of August matters were coming to a head. It was at this point that the Union-organiser for Meath, a northerner named Eamonn Rooney, approached the officers of the Navan Company. He told them that he had information that the employers who, according to Séamus Finn, were of "strong pro-British tendencies", had asked for a large number of military to be sent to the county to protect their interests: could the Volunteers help the workers to prevent this? One man who remembered this meeting with Rooney recalled that there was a great reluctance on their part to get involved.

Rooney must have been persuasive, however, because on the night of Saturday 16 August, about six Volunteers made their way to the railway line at Farganstown, about two miles outside Navan. One of those was a man who worked on the railways. At a point about twelve feet above the surrounding countryside, a twenty foot long rail was removed from the track and thrown into an adjoining field. The party of men had arranged to have a warning message left at the house of the stationmaster in Navan in order to have the passenger train stopped in case it were to pass before the train carrying the military. As it turned out neither of these arrived on the scene first but rather a goods train travelling from Drogheda to Navan. The *Meath Chronicle* of 23 August 1919 described the ensuing destruction thus: "wagon piled on wagon, huge wheels and irons twisted into unrecognisable shapes, train wreckage everywhere." Fortunately, none of the three men employed on the train was seriously injured, but this was of little consolation to the Volunteers whom

Séamus Finn describes as "very annoyed" by the whole affair.

Meanwhile, the job of organising continued. Eamonn Fleming, whom we have seen had been arrested in March 1918, was replaced by Paddy Garrett, sent from headquarters to move around the various companies in Meath, giving instruction in the use of firearms and supervising drilling. Paddy Lalor had vague memories of Garrett as a Dubliner who had fought in the British Army in both the Boer War and World War I.

Up to the end of 1919 the police in general adopted a 'softly, softly' approach to the Volunteers. Finn states that they often approached parents, employers and priests to get them to use their influence to dissuade young men from Volunteer activities. But they seldom interfered directly. Indeed, in September 1920, after the taking of Trim Barracks, Paddy Lalor recalled taking a quick read through police day books relating to the years 1918–1919. Several of the entries referred to his own family, and they read to the effect: "Kept the house of Lalors, prominent republican family, in Castle Street, under observation for two hours." But there was never any attempt to arrest, or even to interfere with, Paddy or either of his brothers, and up until the latter part of 1919 they never felt in any danger.

This low profile policy began to change in September 1919 when a series of police raids on the homes of Sinn Féin and Volunteer members took place in several parts of the county. The *Drogheda Independent* described the result as "insignificant", and indeed most of those detained were released almost at once. One exception, however, was Séamus O'Higgins, the Brigade Quartermaster. At a court martial at Ship Street Barracks in Dublin, O'Higgins was charged with unlawful possession of an automatic pistol, ammunition and seditious documents. He refused to recognise the court but it is doubtful if this made any difference as he was sentenced to a year's imprisonment with hard labour.

A similar sentence was handed down in November to Matt Tevlin, captain of the Carnaross Company, on a similar charge. But the following month both men were freed under the provisions of the so-called Cat and Mouse Act. This act had been passed earlier in the decade to get the then government out of their dilemma in dealing with the hunger-striking tactics of the suffragettes. The idea was that the hunger-striker would be freed from prison when he/she entered into a very weakened condition but that he/she would return when his/her health had returned to normal. But there was to be no returning for either O'Higgins or Tevlin, who spent twenty one days on hunger strike in Mountjoy. The *Drogheda Independent* of 27 December reported phlegmatically in late December that "we are informed that both men are being searched for in vain by the authorities."

Shortly before this the leaders of the Meath Volunteers addressed themselves to what was a perennial problem, not just in their county but all over Ireland – the shortage of weapons. This was to remain a difficulty right up to the Truce, but it was to be alleviated somewhat by widespread raids on houses throughout 1920 where it was known that there were guns. However, in the autumn of 1919 plans were drawn up with the dual purpose of obtaining weapons as well as striking at the British administration in the county. Seán Boylan put it thus:

> In the months of September and October 1919 special meetings of the Brigade staff were held to formulate plans for attacks on RIC barracks situated in the area. By the end of October plans were ready to attack the barracks at Bohermeen, Summerhill, Ballivor and Lismullin (or Dillon's Bridge).

The attacks on the first two named failed to materialise "due to a misunderstanding as to the time and place certain officers were to be met", says Boylan. In the case of Ballivor and Lismullin, the raid was fixed for the night of 31 October – Hallowe'en. Séamus Finn says that on the day before, himself, Boylan, Pat Loughran and Paddy Mooney went to Dublin to finalise plans at headquarters with Michael Collins, Dick McKee and Gearóid O'Sullivan. Here weapons and ammunition were distributed. On the following night the relative peace in county Meath was abruptly ended when an RIC sergeant was seriously wounded in Lismullin, while in Ballivor a constable was shot dead. The war had claimed its first victims in the county.

In researching this account, one was struck by the amount of adverse criticism of the town and people of Navan regarding their contribution to the national struggle in these years. "A garrison town", was one

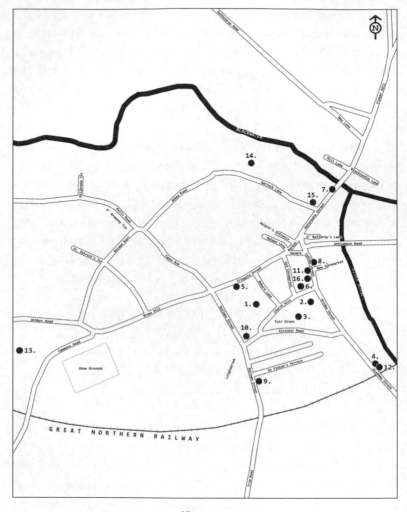

Navan

Places mentioned in the text:

1. Catholic Church
2. Church of Ireland
3. Banba Hall
4. St. Vincent de Paul Hall – frequent venue of Sinn Fein Courts
5. Catholic Young Mens Society Hall
6. Foresters Hall
7. AOH Hall
8. Courthouse
9. Technical School
10. Flat House Pub
11. Picture Palace Cinema
12. Home of Postmaster Hodgett

British Forces

13. Workhouse – occupied by military, 1920–21
14. Military Barracks
15. RIC Barracks
16. Temporary barracks used by Auxiliaries

description; "the company there played no part whatever in the fight" said another, while a third was adamant that "there was a spy on every corner." The basis of such comments, that Navan was somehow pro-British, lies perhaps in the fact that in 1920–21 Navan UDC was the only one of all the councils in Meath to retain its links with the British Local Government Board rather than transfer its allegiances to the Dáil's Department of Local Government. This facet of the story belongs to a different chapter and will be dealt with later, but it is certainly a very shaky foundation on which to build a theory of Navan people as Empire lovers.

Deposited in the County Archive in Navan is a copybook listing members of 'An Uaimh Company, IRA, 1916–23'. There are about seventy names given as well as about twenty names of members of the local Fianna Éireann, the youth branch of the Volunteers. This copybook also contains sketchy notes of certain incidents in the area in which the company was involved. A second list obtained from the same source may, however, be more accurate. This has about fifty names and probably relates only to the period up to 11 July 1921, the date of the Truce, following which there was a great influx of new members to the IRA countrywide. These latecomers, referred to by Ernie O'Malley as "trucileers", were usually regarded with great contempt by the pre-Truce men who saw them as jumping on the bandwagon after the fighting had been done and the danger past. Anyway, the point is that there was in Navan quite a large Volunteer company as well as a Fianna Éireann group. As to whether this company played its proper role in the fight for freedom is open to debate, but it must be remembered that, in common with other companies, it was hampered by shortages of weapons and ammunition. Which takes us back to Hallowe'en 1919 and Lismullin RIC barracks.

Pat Fitzsimons, later to be a long-serving member of both Navan UDC and Meath County Council as well as serving as a senator from 1948 to 1973, was one of the group of twenty-six Navan and Commons Volunteers who cycled the five miles out to Lismullin on that Friday night. Pat was originally from the Virginia area and was working in Mullagh where he joined the Volunteers early in 1918, after hearing a speech by Pádraig de Búrca. Later that year he came to work as a barman in a public house in Navan and joined the local company there. Afterwards, towards the end of 1920, he was to rise to the rank of Battalion O/C. Also present that night was Patsy Bennett, an Ardbraccan man and a brother of Johnny. Patsy joined the Navan Company in 1918 but left in 1919 to join the much smaller unit nearby in the Commons. "The leadership there was much better", he said frankly, in reference to Paddy Stapleton. Later on this company of about a dozen men formed the nucleus of the Ardbraccan Company.

Although the company captain in Navan at this time was Joe Woods, a Louth-born draper's assistant, the most important figure was Pat Loughran, who had been chosen as Battalion O/C at the Dunderry aeríocht and was to hold this position until his arrest late in 1920. Pat was from the Robinstown-Dunderry area and had worked in a Dublin drapery until his return to Navan in 1916. He had joined the Volunteers in Dublin where his Battalion O/C had been William T. Cosgrave.

The barracks at Lismullin was a one-storey building situated on the main Navan-Dublin road. Behind it was the estate of Sir John Dillon while in front stood the Hill of Tara. The barracks was manned by a Sergeant Matthews and Constables Griffith and Shea. Just after ten o'clock on the night in question there was a loud knocking on the door. "We sent up James Boylan and another man and they gave a password which we had learned was used by those friendly to the police in order to secure admission", said Pat Fitzsimons. But the ruse did not work and the police fired a number of shots through the door. This was the prelude to a half-hour exchange of fire. Although Sergeant Matthews was wounded in the head and the police were completely outnumbered, their rifles were far too powerful for the few shotguns that the raiders had between them. The Navan men returned to where they had left their bicycles and, between walking and cycling, they made their way home via a circuitous route. "At one point we had to wade through the Boyne so that by the time I reached home at two in the morning I was soaked to the skin", Pat Fitzsimons laughingly recalled.

For the record the men who were involved in this abortive raid were: Pat Loughran, Joe Woods, Pat Fitzsimons, Joe Bailey, James Boylan, Tom Gavigan, James Hilliard, Michael Gaynor, Michael McKeon, John Boland, James Gorman, James Lynch, Patrick Keating, James Mackey,

Thomas Kinsella, Matt Loughran and William Loughran of the Navan Company; and Paddy Stapleton, Patsy Bennett, James Byrne, Richard Byrne, Pat Watters, Loughlin O'Rourke, Patrick Boyle, Michael Hyland and Thomas Walsh of the Commons company. The source for this list of names is the copybook referred to earlier.

The raid on the barracks in Ballivor on the same night was also a joint effort by two companies, this time Trim and Longwood. "Up to this we had only one rifle in the company", said Paddy Lalor,

> This was given to us in 1917 by Jimmy Mooney when he came home from the war front where he was fighting with the British Army. He ran the risk of being court-martialled and locked up for returning without it.

It was, incidentally, a brother of this Jimmy Mooney who led the group of Volunteers in the attack in Ballivor; this was Paddy Mooney. Paddy had been chosen as Vice O/C of the Trim Battalion at the Dunderry convention mentioned earlier.

At about ten o'clock that night Mooney, Pat Fay and Stephen Sherry approached the front door of the barracks which was situated in the centre of the village. As in Lismullin, after knocking on the door, they gave a password used by those on good terms with the police. "They also gave the name of a local farmer, saying that he had come in to report a cattle drive which was quite common in the area at the time", said Paddy Lalor, who was one of the raiding party. This time the trick worked and a Constable Agar opened the door. Apparently he tried to close it again when he saw the three men outside but it was too late and in the ensuing mêlée the constable was shot through the heart and died at once. Constable William Agar, aged thirty-five and a native of Carlow, was the tenth policeman killed that year.

Meanwhile the rest of the group, there were fourteen in all, rushed the barracks from both front and rear. The station was manned by a sergeant and two constables (excluding Agar) but they were locked inside the day-room by the Volunteers. Others of the raiders quickly gathered a revolver, five rifles, revolver pouches and a large amount of ammunition and made a hasty getaway in the direction of Kildalkey.

This is the substance of the reports which appeared in the two local newspapers the following week. However, Paddy Lalor is emphatic that the sergeant named McDermott was not present when his station came under attack. Paddy even caustically recalled that on the following morning the headlines in the *Daily Sketch* read to the effect: "Heavy rebel fighting in South Meath. Gallant old sergeant defends his lonely country barracks" and that a photograph showed a grim sergeant standing determinedly outside the front of the buildings. "The whole thing was a cover-up to save his skin and his pension", said Paddy.

Séamus Finn lists the following men as having participated in this operation: Paddy Mooney, Pat Fay, Stephen Sherry, Joe Lalor, Paddy Lalor, Michael Giles, John Mooney, Pat Duigenan, Harry O'Hagan and Joe Kelly of Trim company; and Pat Giles, Larry Giles, Michael Fagan and a man named McEvoy from Longwood.

No one was ever convicted of involvement in either the Ballivor or Lismullin raids although in the case of the latter the police did make an early arrest and a draper's assistant, Tom Gavigan, was sent to Mountjoy Jail. It seems that in the rush back to Navan Gavigan had left his bicycle behind and his name was found on the bicycle pump. On 10 November he appeared in Navan before Resident Magistrate Reilly who ordered that he be detained for a further eight days. He reappeared in court on 18 November on the charge "that he did unlawfully and feloniously discharge loaded firearms with intent to kill Sergeant Matthews and did grievously wound him". Fortunately for himself however, Gavigan was set free as District Inspector Rodwell admitted to the RM that he had not been able "to get sufficient evidence to justify asking for another remand".

The morning after the Ballivor escapade Paddy Lalor and five or six others were arrested in Trim and taken in for questioning. But they were soon released. Paddy is convinced that the police deliberately made a sham of the investigation, and concluded:

> the interrogation was a mockery and did not follow the usual
> procedures; I got the impression that the police wanted to avoid
> at all costs anything that might aggravate the situation in the
> area, such as the detention and conviction of any of us. Life for

them had been quiet up to then and they probably wanted to keep it that way.

Raids, attacks and other incidents involving physical force were by now becoming quite commonplace in Ireland. Robert Kee has written about them that "such deeds, since sanctified into deeds of heroism, struck very many Irishmen at the time quite otherwise. This was long before any Irishman had been killed in a reprisal and no Black and Tan had yet set foot in Ireland." Even a summary glance through the recorded reactions of Meath opinion in the wake of Ballivor and Lismullin serves to confirm the accuracy of Kee's comment (*The Green Flag: a history of Irish nationalism*, p 658).

An editorial in the *Drogheda Independent* of 23 August 1919 – which, remember, had only recently and reluctantly abandoned its conservative stance in support of Home Rule – first observed that "one of the most peaceable and law-abiding counties in Ireland." But now this had changed and the writer went on to say that:

> It is to be hoped that the perpetrators of this murderous outrage … will be made ameniable, and that the fair fame of the hitherto crimeless district of Meath will not be further smirched by anything of a like nature.

The *Meath Chronicle* was no less vociferous in its condemnation, although the wording was less emotive. In the issue of 20 September 1919 it had warned its readers "not to play into the hands of the enemy by deeds of violence or crime … Ireland must continue to act constitutionally." Now in the 8 November 1919 issue the *Chronicle* expressed deep sympathy with the wife of the dead man; they had only been married for six months, and stressed that:

> a just cause, as ours is, does not require to be buttressed by crime or bloodshed. Meath repudiates responsibility for these outrages and every decent citizen has a duty to denounce them.

There was also strong condemnation from the local councils. A member of Navan RDC asked indignantly:

> do these pagans – I do not believe they are Irishmen – know
> that where they committed these outrages is within two or three
> hundred perches of the place where St. Patrick first preached
> Christianity at Tara?

And the November meeting of the county council adopted a resolution
which denounced "murders and outrages … engineered by the dangerous
pests of society." Nor was there support from amongst the general public
for the Volunteers' action. In Ballivor at the inquest a jury of local people
was appointed to assess the verdict of the coroner. Following the verdict
of wilful murder the foreman spoke in praise of the police "who were
always popular with the public and did their duty impartially." Another
speaker gave as his opinion that "those responsible for these crimes were
not advancing the position of our unfortunate country one iota."

Finally, the attitude of the Catholic clergy remains to be considered.
In both parishes where the attacks had occurred the parish priests
strongly attacked those responsible while emphasising, with some
justification, that no one locally had "hand, act or part in the affair."
But this, and all that has gone before, was mild in comparison with
the scathing attack delivered by Bishop Gaughran at early Mass in
Mullingar Cathedral on the Sunday following the raids.

At this point it may be worth noting the bishop's observations on
a number of issues during the period under review. Take, for instance,
his statement printed on the front page of the *Meath Chronicle* of 11
September 1915 praising the work of the so-called Dublin Vigilance
Committee in inspecting theatres, music halls, and picture houses:

> It is of the utmost importance to supervise these, especially the
> picture houses … they are now in every small town and sure to
> degenerate and do incalculable harm.

There were three picture houses in the county – the Picture Palace in
Navan, the Picture Theatre in Kells and Charlie Fox's Electric Cinema
in Oldcastle.

The bishop's Lenten Pastoral Letter, delivered to his flock in March 1919, and printed in the *Chronicle* on 8 March, addressed itself to the evils of idleness:

> There are hundreds of men idle in the towns of England, Scotland and Ireland not because no man will hire them but because they can get substantial sums without working.

In the immediate post-war depression and army demobilisation it would be very difficult to sustain this argument, but the bishop went on to criticise "legislation which puts a premium on idleness."

On a political level the bishop's vehement opposition to socialism, expressed in the immediate aftermath of the 1913–14 Dublin Lock Out, has been recorded at an early stage in this account. We have also recorded the bishop's stern strictures to the young men of his diocese in regard to membership of secret societies. Imagine, then, His Lordship's response, reported in the *Meath Chronicle* of 8 November 1919, to the killing in Ballivor carried out by the society to which he was obviously referring. Little restraint was exercised as he invoked the curse of God on those involved: "the society engaged in this diabolical work", he raged,

> brings God's curse not only on the perpetrators of such foul deeds but also on all who actively co-operate with them. Murder is a usurpation of God's authority, it is a grave injustice to God and this is the reason why God so emphatically declared that He Himself will strictly avenge it .... what benefit can come to the country from crimes that are representing Irishmen to be as savage and uncultured as the bushmen of the forest.

After that litany of condemnation, it comes as little surprise to hear Séamus Finn conceding gloomily, as 1919 turned into 1920, that:

> there were murmurings among the rank and file .... the people too did not take kindly to extreme measures and it was difficult to get around on Volunteer work.

The provision of arms and ammunition continued to be a problem. In the introduction to his *History of the Meath Brigade*, Séamus Finn states that:

> at no time were we in Meath in possession of sufficient arms, ammunition or other war materials to engage any large sized force of the enemy ... I have known men go into ambush positions with shotguns and cartridges packed with buckshot and crude, home-made grenades.

In his account also Finn, at one point, in an evocation of 1798, describes how a number of blacksmiths "converted steel springs of carts, traps and motors to pikes." This was all very rudimentary and scarcely had the furore over the Ballivor-Lismullin attacks died down than the Volunteers began to renew their raids on houses in search of weaponry.

The local newspapers record numerous raids for the early part of 1920. Indeed, the series had begun on St Stephen's night, 1919, when six men got away with just one gun from the home of Laurence McKenna of Gainstown, Navan. A bigger haul was obtained from the stately home of Mrs Chayters of Smithstown, Dunshaughlin, when it was reported that nine masked men forced an entrance through a back door and took off with two shotguns, a rifle and ammunition. On 20 February in the same area, a revolver, a shotgun and ammunition were removed from the home of the local politician P.J. Mulvany. A week earlier at Rathvale, Athboy, the residence of R.H. Wallace, a racehorse owner and trainer, had been relieved of two shotguns and a much coveted rifle.

There are other instances of such raids recorded for the Bective and Kilmainhamwood areas, but these were not always the walkover they sound. For example, in March, a man named Nulty of Farganstown, Navan, was quoted in the *Drogheda Independent* of 20 March that, when a midnight visitor came looking for his shotgun, he "struck and beat him, cutting his face and knocking out four of his teeth" before setting him to flight.

In the months of August and September there was another spate of gun raids. Seán Boylan stated that:

> In the early autumn of 1920, on instructions from GHQ, I had

all arms in civilian hands collected throughout the brigade area. In most cases the arms were surrendered voluntarily, but in other cases the Volunteers collecting the arms were met with armed opposition. In the Dunboyne Battalion area, Captain Sam Watt of the British Army, who lived at Hilltown, Clonee, opened fire on the Volunteers as they surrounded his house, but John Connell, the officer in charge of the raiding party, prevailed on the captain to surrender. The Volunteers then seized a couple of shotguns and a revolver. The arms generally were shotguns, a few revolvers and a few miniature rifles.

It was about this time also that extensive raids took place in the Fifth Oldcastle Battalion area. Peter O'Connell recalled that "we secured about twenty shotguns and three rifles .... the rifles were got in a raid on the home of a retired British Army officer, Archdall of Maperath House." But it was only after a half hour of gun fighting that these were given up, according to Jack Lynch, who was present that night along with most of the Carnaross Company. It was probably around this time too that Patsy Bennett and Larry Collins, also of the Commons Company, walked the railway line to Navan, coming out at the top of Flowerhill, where they then coolly proceeded to the house of the RIC District Inspector and came away with two guns.

At the end of September there seems to have been one last frantic push by the Volunteers, a push that was anticipated and countered by the authorities. The *Drogheda Independent* referred to the race for guns between the two sides, and said that practically every home which was still suspected of containing guns was visited by one or the other. This gave rise to much humour at the time, but other cases proved to be without humour. When six intruders broke into Reginald Radcliffe's house at Hurdlestown, Kells on 11 August and began to search for weapons, Mr Radcliffe suffered heart failure and died instantly. The intruders, it was reported in the *Meath Chronicle* on 14 August 1920, continued with the raid and got away with four rifles.

Despite all this activity shortage of weapons was to remain a chronic problem for the Volunteers. In his three years in the Navan Company Bobby Byrne only once handled a gun when he fired three shots from a

German Mauser. And he recalled an occasion towards the end of 1920 when himself and Mick Hilliard one night went to enforce the Belfast Boycott by removing Northern-made goods from the depots at Navan railway station: "we had no guns but were very resourceful in those days," Bobby said. "I poked a fountain pen into the ribs of the night watchman and in the darkness he took it for granted that it was a gun!" But even at a more serious level on the occasion of the biggest ambush planned in the county in these years by the Volunteers, that at Sylvan Park, Kells on 1 April 1921, one of those who participated, Charlie Conaty of the Stonefield Company, recalled that when he was given a rifle that day, it was only the second time he had ever fired one, the first time having been just two nights earlier.

In the months following the attacks on Ballivor and Lismullin barracks the RIC began a gradual retreat from their smaller rural outposts into the towns. "Between November 1919 and Easter Sunday 1920", stated Seán Boylan,

> Ballivor, Summerhill, Bohermeen, Lismullin, Georges Cross, Mullagh, Moynalty, Drumconrath, Carnaross, Stirrupstown and about ten other RIC barracks were evacuated and their garrisons transferred into the larger towns such as Navan, Trim, Kells and Oldcastle.

Séamus Finn elaborated on this and went so far as to say that by the middle of 1920, "the only places where the police still remained outside the towns were in Longwood and Crossakiel". Crossakiel was later burned on 10 August, although Longwood station survived more than one attack and was to remain open right up to the Truce. "On instructions from GHQ", stated Seán Boylan, "all of these barracks were burned down after they were evacuated." Most of these burnings were carried out on the night of Easter Sunday, 3 April, when the stations at Ballivor, Carnaross, Stirrupstown, Ashbourne, Kilmoon, Summerhill, Killyon, Crossmacar and Lisclogher were completely gutted. In some cases, as at Bohermeen, Georges Cross and Lismullin, it took a second visit before the work was completed. This outbreak of pyromania continued into May when the barracks in Mullagh and Moynalty went up in flames, although the raiding party which set fire to the station at Drumconrath on 25 May seems to have expended most of its energy in putting out the blaze when it spread to a hotel adjacent to the barracks.

Barracks were not, however, the only targets. In the middle of May the tax offices at Kilbeg and Oldcastle were raided and documents, ledgers and files were taken out and burned. Charlie Conaty took part in the Oldcastle operation. Born in September 1901 Charlie was reared in Ballyhist, Carnaross where he attended national school until the age of fifteen. He was subsequently employed as an assistant land steward on the estate of Sir Nugent Everard who owned about five hundred acres of land in the area. In May 1919 he joined the Stonefield Company and became first lieutenant in the spring of 1920. Peter O'Connell was also present on the occasion of the raid on the income tax office in Oldcastle. He recalls the night thus:

> Members of Stonefield Company mobilised at the graveyard in Oldcastle. We numbered seven and were in the charge of Séamus Cogan. Our objective was to raid the income tax office in the town. At the graveyard we were met by Tommy Harpur of the Oldcastle Company. He informed us that he had cut barbed wire which surrounded the office and had opened a door leading from the street into the backyard of the building. We placed two men on the Main Street convenient to the door leading to the building where they had a good view of the RIC barracks across the road.

What happened next was decidedly civilised:

> When all was ready we knocked on the back door. The officer in charge, named O'Brien, lived on the premises. He put his head out of a window and said, "I will come down". When he did so we explained our business. He put on the lights and showed us his office. He wished us luck and went back to bed.

The documents were collected, taken away and burned. The entire operation could hardly be described as arduous, "but", according to

Peter O'Connell, "it was one of our first assignments and it was useful for breaking us in."

A fortnight later the Stonefield men were back again, and this time they burned the workhouse in Oldcastle to the ground. This was the building that had been used as an internment camp during the First World War and information had been received that it was to be reoccupied by British military.

It was around this time and in the same general area that a sinister development occurred. The *Meath Chronicle* carried a report of it in the 12 June 1920 issue. On 5 June a young man named Bernard Dunne from Carnaross was cycling home from Kells at about six o'clock in the evening. About a mile from his home he noticed a Ford car approaching him at a slow pace; "there were three men in the car", he told a *Chronicle* reporter, "and it forced me into the ditch." Following this Dunne saw one of the men lean out of a rear window with a gun in his hand. He fired three shots at Dunne from a range of three feet. One of the bullets wounded him on the left arm but remarkably he had enough strength to cycle back to Kells where he was treated by Doctor Brangan. Dunne was in no doubt but that his assailants were police from Kells barracks and that their motive was undoubtedly that Dunne was at that time vice-captain of the Carnaross Volunteer Company. "Bernard was always in and out of Kells on his bicycle", remembered Jack Lynch. "His movements were being watched. He knew who his attackers were. He was badly wounded and took no further part in our activities."

Generally speaking, however, the police were still seemingly turning a blind eye to Volunteer activities. Indeed, for the first half of 1920 and over the whole county only one Volunteer of any prominence was arrested. This was Leo McKenna, a member of the Navan Company, who was later to hold the position of acting quartermaster of the Sixth Navan Battalion. In the previous chapter we have seen that the same man had been sentenced in July 1918 to a month's imprisonment on a charge of "taking part in an unlawful assembly." Now in April McKenna was arrested at his place of work, a hardware store in Navan, and sent for his second sojourn in Mountjoy. But this was to prove as short-lived as his first and he was released on 6 May following a hunger-strike and the pressure of public opinion. This shall be considered in more detail later on in this account, but it is to the north Meath area that our focus now returns and to the death in action of one of the county's most prominent Volunteers, and a battalion commandant to boot.

Since the evacuation and burning of the small rural police barracks in the first half of 1920 the Volunteers themselves had set up their own police force which, however rudimentary, was to prove quite effective. The work of these police shall be dealt with in the next chapter, but for present purposes it is enough to know that it was this type of work which formed the background to the killing of Séamus Cogan in Oldcastle on the morning of 22 July 1920.

On the previous night Cogan and a number of Volunteers from the Oldcastle area had been drilling in Ballinvally, following which Cogan brought some of them around on police work. They commandeered a motor-car from a large farmer and former county councillor named Patrick Sheridan, mentioned in the first chapter of this book, and were taking a prisoner convicted of cattle stealing to what was known as "an unknown destination", that is, a place of detention, in this case Tully Mills, on the Mountnugent Road. This information was given by Owen Clarke, and he continued as follows:

> There were seven in all in the car that night; Jimmy O'Neill was driving while Cogan and myself were also in the front seat; in the back were Harry Sheridan, Tommy Gavin, Tom Lynch and our prisoner. On the Main Street in Oldcastle we saw in front of us a group of soldiers who had come from Cavan but had lost their way and were looking for directions. Of course we only found that out later and when an officer called on us to halt, Cogan gave orders to Jimmy O'Neill to keep driving.

As to what happened next, or, more precisely, who shot first, there are various versions and to this day even Owen Clarke is unsure but what is certain is that there was a short exchange of gunfire. "Almost at once", continued Owen,

> Cogan was shot through the head and fell across into my lap. We could see at once that he was dead. In the back seat Harry

Sheridan had been shot in the hip while Jimmy O'Neill, our driver, was wounded in one hand and was to lose two fingers. He managed to keep driving for a short distance outside the town but then the car went out of control and it overturned into a field. We took out the body and carried it to a nearby hayshed and hid it there and it was not found by the police until two days later.

Owen himself managed to make his way back to Fox's where he was staying. It was by now about three o'clock in the morning and the night's events had clearly left him distraught. "I got into bed", he said,

not even thinking of getting rid of my blood-soaked clothes. But Charlie Fox came into the room knowing full well what had happened and took away the clothes and dumped them into a pump hole. He also took away my .35 revolver. Later, when the police arrived, I managed to bluff them that I had been in all night.

But he was not to remain free for very long. The new commandant, John Keogh of Ballinlough, ordered Owen and the others who had been in the car that night to go on the run and they used to sleep out in hay barns at night. About a month later, however, Owen went back to Fox's to serve at a special mass organized by Mrs Fox. Here he was arrested, as were both Jimmy O'Neill and Tommy Gavin subsequently.

Following the discovery by the authorities of Cogan's body an inquest was held at Kells workhouse. Cogan's body was then handed over to his relatives and on the following Sunday the funeral took place to a newly acquired republican plot in Ballinlough graveyard. The Volunteers made elaborate preparations for the funeral. "I made Conaty's of Ballyhist my headquarters and from there I sent out orders for every company to mobilise for the funeral," wrote Séamus Finn. "It was the biggest funeral cortège ever seen in county Meath and was over four miles long," stated Seán Boylan. It certainly must have been an impressive feat of organisation. The *Meath Chronicle*, in its report of 31 July 1920, estimated the crowd at between 12,000 and 15,000, including up to 1,000 Volunteers marching in military formation, as well as about two hundred motor vehicles, a huge number to be seen at any one place in those days. The cortège, according to Finn, consisted of a small advance guard of cyclists, the main body of Volunteers, members of other republican-leaning organisations such as the GAA, the Gaelic League and Sinn Féin and then the general public. Cogan, appropriately, was given a republican-style funeral: "in order to render military honours to Commandant Cogan," stated Seán Boylan,

> I had all the roads leading to the graveyard effectively blocked by cars, so that the military in the vicinity could not approach the graveyard. When three volleys had been fired over his grave we dispersed. The military did not interfere.

Séamus Cogan, aged only twenty-three, was a great loss. "He was one of our best officers," wrote Boylan, "and I felt his loss keenly." Séamus Finn expressed similar sentiments but also pondered the whole futility of the incident leading to his death: "such work should have been done by subordinate officers and Volunteers, and not by a Battalion Commandant," he concluded pertinently.

Notwithstanding the vicious attack on Bernard Dunne in Carnaross and the killing of Séamus Cogan, the county remained relatively quiet throughout the summer. But a sure sign that all was not normal, and that perhaps the authorities were anticipating more trouble, came when additional numbers of British military were drafted into the county in June and July. On Thursday, 10 June, about one hundred men of the First Battalion Cameronians occupied a portion of Navan workhouse. Old and sick inmates had to be moved out to accommodate the military, and the building soon took on the aspect of a fortress, with barbed wire entanglements all around it. These men were additions to the long-established battalion of the Leinster Regiment which had for years been stationed in the old military barracks on Abbey Road. About a month later, on 16 July, a company of the South Wales Borderers arrived in Kells and was billeted in the fever hospital which then stood at the top of Carrick Street as the road leads out to Virginia. Later they moved into the workhouse, now long destroyed, which stood at the edge of the town on the road to Moynalty. On the following Sunday, at the various masses, the priests warned their congregations against any interference with the military. In particular, young girls were warned not to associate with them.

A similar warning delivered by the Navan clergy to their parishioners was ignored by at least two girls with uncomfortable, if scarcely tragic, consequences. A hair-cropping suffered by the two girls hardly represented a major blow to British morale but it is of some interest if only that such tactics were used extensively elsewhere in the country by Volunteers to punish women who were seen in the company of police or military. The incident happened on 31 July on the Moat Road where the two girls were walking with their soldier boyfriends. The two soldiers were ordered away by a group of three men who then took the girls separately and cropped their hair. A few days later two young local men named Dalton and Kane were arrested and charged with assault. They were soon released only to be re-arrested almost immediately, this time on a charge of possession of firearms. At their trial the two men produced a host of witnesses in their defense, but all to no avail as they were both sentenced to a year in prison. Of the two men, Dalton certainly was a member of the Volunteers, being associated with the Commons, and later the Ardbraccan Company.

Navan barber Bobby Byrne did not mind at all admitting that it was scissors from his father's establishment that was used in the above described incident. "The next day police visited the shop and examined all our scissors and other equipment," said Bobby. "One of the girls was blonde and maybe they were looking for traces of this but we had everything well wiped clean by then!" Bobby's father had founded the establishment in 1902. As a young man Bobby recalled being involved in the Pioneers and also being influenced greatly by the Gaelic League and contemporary Irish literature. Along with his neighbour in Market Square, Tom Reilly, Bobby joined the local group of the Fianna and later was sworn into the Volunteers after a drilling session in Balreask, just outside the town. Once he was sent with a despatch to Bellinter: "I was to give it to the Quinns," said Bobby,

> They were known as experimenters in bomb making. I remember
> that as I approached the house there was a loud explosion and

when I reached it there were rocks, stones and all kinds of rubble sitting on the roof of the house!

Later, as the Troubles reached their height, Black and Tans and military frequently came in for haircuts to him. "I can still remember their Webley revolvers sitting on the seats. In the company we sometimes discussed plans to take the revolvers but nothing ever came of it."

In his statement to the Bureau of Military History, Seán Boylan recounted being present "at a meeting of all brigade officers in the country in August 1920, held at the Gaelic League rooms in Parnell Square ... each officer was asked for details as to the operations carried out in his area and also those contemplated. The officers from GHQ present included Dick Mulcahy, Gearóid O'Sullivan, Diarmuid O'Hegarty and Mick Collins. When my turn came, I said we intended to attack Trim RIC barracks. Mick Collins remarked: "It's a very big job." I replied: "We will take it." He said: "When will you take it?" I said: "Sunday week." This rather dramatised exchange formed the background to what was the biggest and most successful operation carried out by the Meath Volunteers – the capture and burning of Trim barracks on Sunday, 26 September 1920.

In what is a fundamentally sound, if sometimes over-dramatised account, of this operation, written in the 1940s for a compilation book titled *With the IRA in the Fight for Freedom*, Séamus Finn starts by describing the barracks as:

> a miniature fortress of stone walls and barred windows, that stood in the centre of a plot of ground two acres in extent on the south side of the Fair Green ... facing to the east it stood 150 yards back from the Summerhill Road, and was surrounded by a wall fifteen feet high. Strong iron gates barred the approach.

Boylan gave the garrison strength at the time as about twenty-four, and this approximates to Finn's figures of "twenty-five constables, two sergeants, one head constable and one district inspector." The local newspaper reports following the raid gave the police strength at a much lower ten to twelve men, but it is almost certain that Finn's and Boylan's figures are the more accurate, given the closing of rural barracks and the drift of police into the towns since the beginning of the year.

The Volunteers had a contact on the inside. Said Finn:

> We were afforded very fortunate assistance by an ex-RIC sergeant named T.J. McElligott ... this man gave us the names of constables who were reliable from our point of view, and one of these in turn gave us valuable information regarding the layout of the barracks itself and the movements of its garrison.

The man Finn is referring to here is undoubtedly Pat Meehan, who had resigned from the force shortly before this but was later to become a superintendent in the Gardaí. One thing that the Volunteers did learn was that the district inspector was to be absent during a certain weekend and it was this which decided the date of the attack for Sunday, 26 September. This involved a change in Boylan's original scheduled date which was early September.

The movements of the police were observed on a number of Sundays and it was noted, wrote Finn:

> that the bigger portion of the garrison left the barracks at 7.55a.m. each Sunday morning for eight o'clock mass ... one sergeant, and occasionally the head constable, would remain behind. In all we estimated that the manpower of the garrison at that time each Sunday morning would be about eight men.

Numbers of meetings to draw up plans were held at O'Hagan's, on Market Street, in Trim. This was the headquarters of both the Sinn Féin and Volunteer organisations in the town. Seán Boylan estimated that up to one hundred and fifty men were involved in the plans, but only about forty of these actually participated directly in the raid in Trim. The rest were engaged in the blocking of roads, and Boylan recalled that:

> all roads within a radius of eight miles were blocked with the exception of one, the Trim-Summerhill-Athboy to Kildalkey road, which was left open as a way of retreat.

The tree felling operation probably extended even further than this as Johnny Bennett and Willie Coogan recalled blocking roads very early on that Sunday morning at Charlesfort Cross in Cortown, at least ten miles from Trim. "We got saws and hatchets and other tools from McCabes and we worked in the dark to cut off the route where the three roads meet", said Johnny.

Plans were finalised on the previous Friday. It was decided to divide the men into three sections. Séamus Finn remembered it thus:

> Section Number One consisted of Mick Hynes and Paddy Mooney who were in actual charge of the attack; Lieutenants Mick Giles and Harry O'Hagan; Volunteers Joe Lalor, Pat Fay, Stephen Sherry and Joe Kelly from the Trim Company; Volunteers C. Caffrey, P. Quinn and J. O'Brien from the Kilmessan company and Captain Paddy Giles and Volunteer Larry Giles from Longwood company. All belonged to the Second Battalion. Section Number Two were Paddy Lalor, Pat Duigenan, Sean O'Higgins, Pat O'Hagan, J. Healy, Joe Nolan, Phil Doggett, Pat Hynes, P. O'Hara, Matty Matthews and Luke Sherry. Section Number Three were Pat Proctor, J. Andrews, P. Andrews, Dick Harmon, C. Reid and M. Plunkett. The Brigade Adjutant [this was Finn himself] and Volunteer Mick Gaynor were to cover the front of the barracks with rifles once the attack began.

Each of these sections had a specific task, Finn continued:

> The men of Number One Section were all armed with revolvers … their instructions were to climb the wall at the point selected, rush the back door of the barracks directly opposite that point and so gain admittance and, if possible, to overpower and capture the police. Number Two Section was to follow closely upon the heels of Number One … and then to gather up and remove all arms, ammunition, grenades and other war materials that the barracks contained. Number Three Section was set the task of bringing along the tins of oil and petrol with which the building

was to be set afire. Its task was to sprinkle the building liberally with both oil and petrol and then touch off fires where they were likely to do most harm in the shortest possible time.

There was also a fourth group involved and their job was to round up the seven or eight RIC men as they came out of Mass. Seán Boylan himself led this section and with him was James O'Connell:

> I remember leaving Skryne the previous night and going to Dunboyne where I met up with Paddy Kenny of Dunshaughlin, Barney Dunne, Christy Ennis and Kit Lynam of the Dunboyne Company. After we made our way to Trim we took positions outside the church and as the police came out after mass we detained them there. One of them managed to slip away and hide inside the church in a confessional but he was spotted by Tom Wallace, a brother of Matt, who went in after him and got him out again.

Others in this group included Vice O/C Frank Carolan, James Maguire and M. Phoenix, all from the Dunboyne area.

Meanwhile back at the barracks the plans were working, as Finn put it, "like magic." The men had been astir since half-six in the morning and the action began as soon as the small group of police had left for Mass. Then, stated Boylan, "Mick Hynes and his men left their positions and, one after another, climbed across a wicket gate set in a wall on the south side of the barracks." This particular point was chosen, apparently, because it was directly opposite to the office of the district inspector who was away and hence the men would not be observed entering the grounds. Boylan continues:

> When all had silently crossed to the other side of the wall they approached towards an open side door of the barracks. As they did so, a dog barked and gave the alarm. Most of the Volunteers, however, succeeded in getting through the door where they were confronted by Head Constable White with revolver drawn.

His was the only resistance encountered but he was shot through the lung and after that the rest of the police surrendered at once. Paddy Lalor, who was that day in charge of the second section, had great admiration for the head constable: "he was the only one with a bit of fight in him but later we heard that he was demoted in rank for losing his barracks." Lalor contrasted his behaviour with that of the sergeant in Ballivor a year earlier, who was not even at his station when it came under attack and yet ended up on the front page of a national newspaper the following morning.

By this time Paddy's second section was inside the building and they rushed upstairs to the room where they knew the arms and ammunition were kept. Paddy recalled that when they had broken down the door they found inside a terror-stricken Englishman who put up his hands begging for mercy and continually yelled that he had just been recruited and had "not come to Ireland for the shooting"! Section Two quickly gathered up all the weaponry which the *Meath Chronicle* of 2 October 1920 reported to consist of twenty shotguns, twenty rifles, six revolvers, a box of grenades and some bayonets and ammunition. These were taken out to the motor car driven by Nicholas Gaynor of Ballinlough and were taken away to be dumped.

By then the third section was about its work of demolition. Finn explains how first they gallantly:

helped the captured police remove their personal belongings and those of their friends at Mass and then set fire to the barracks which soon was a blazing holocaust and before noon was no more than a smouldering ruin.

The Volunteers' chivalry even extended as far as taking the wounded head constable to a local doctor for treatment. As for themselves, says Finn, "we did not require attention, for our men had carried out their morning's work without suffering as much as a scratch." Everyone got home safely too. James O'Connell got a lift in a car leaving Trim but they found that some of their own men had prematurely blown up a bridge on the Summerhill road and so had to go by a different route back to Dunboyne. "From there", said Jimmy, "I cycled back to Skryne and was home by midday. The idea was to get back before being spotted as missing by the local police."

All in all then the raid itself was an unqualified success but the aftermath was not for, as Séamus Finn wrote, "events did not work out so happily in Trim." In the weeks leading up to the operation, the planners had more than once discussed ways and means of protecting:

> our well-wishers and friends in Trim against possible reprisals on the part of the enemy. We surmised that the homes of our most prominent local supporters, the O'Higgins family, the O'Hagans, Mooneys, Allens and Plunketts of Navan Gate might be attacked by the police.

Arrangements had in fact been made to protect these and other houses but, for reasons that will become clear, these measures were not implemented. It was probably the sacking of Balbriggan only nine days earlier by a large force of Black and Tans which had prompted the Meath men to consider such precautions. But now it was the turn of Trim to experience the full fury of a backlash by British forces with which unruliness and indiscipline had, by this stage, become synonymous all over Ireland.

The reprisals began at four in the afternoon when four lorry loads of police and military drove into the town. Paddy Lalor described them as "a frightening sight, shouting and yelling, with different types of headgear and uniform, some Tans, some Auxiliaries, some police and some military." On the Fair Green between the Wellington Monument and the gutted barracks a group of men and boys were playing hurling until their game was abruptly ended as the supposed forces of law and order, without warning, began to fire indiscriminately into them. Two people were wounded, James Kelly of Laracor and George Griffin, aged only sixteen, of Carberrystown. Both men, and all others present who were later interviewed by the local press, insisted that no provocation whatever had been offered to the intruders. This act, however, was to prove but a curtain raiser to a drama of vandalism and thuggery that was played out in the early hours of Monday morning.

Before this, however, a number of prominent townspeople, including

Rev. Michael Woods PP, had approached some British army officers and had obtained an assurance that there would be no further reprisals. One of these people, a solicitor named O'Reilly, later told a *Meath Chronicle* reporter that a Major Dudley had told him that they had no orders to fire. The delegation for their part promised to ensure that the people would remain indoors during the night.

As for the Volunteers, it seems that quite a number of them had reconvened at O'Hagan's by nine o'clock that night. They had returned to provide protection in the event of further enemy retaliation. Finn picks up the story from here:

> The townsmen met our officers and men when they arrived to take up positions from which they could prevent reprisals, and told them that such precautions were no longer necessary. Our men were actually hampered when making preliminary arrangements to occupy their positions and consequently they had no choice but to withdraw ... at an inquiry later held at headquarters in Dublin the officers constituting the court declared that in view of the interference of the townspeople of Trim in the matter, little or no responsibility rested with our men for their failure to guard against the possibility of British reprisals in Trim.

Thus when the second and more violent wave of British retaliation struck the town at two o'clock the following morning there was no resistance to its impact.

Paddy Lalor had returned home that morning after the raid had been successfully completed. Fortunately for him, however, his father had sent him away. "They'll make sausages out of you", were the words Paddy remembered his father using to him. "I went to the Boyne Cottages beside the river to stay with a man called Pat McGrew. I had often stayed with him before", said Paddy. Out of sheer exhaustion he slept right through the night of terror. It was ironic then that it was Paddy's family, particularly his father, who were subjected to the British forces' particular brand of viciousness. Even over sixty years later it still pained Paddy to think of the treatment meted out to his family on that night and he was reluctant to say much about it. His father was

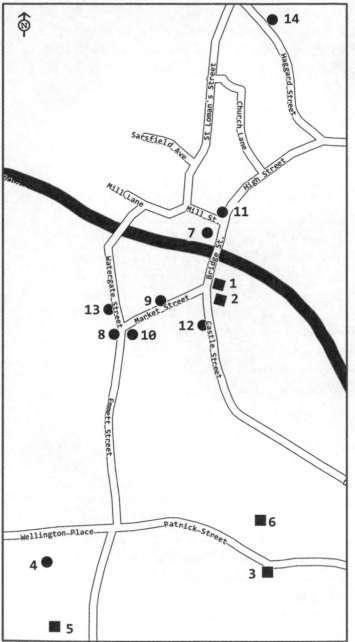

TRIM

Places Mention
in the Text

General:

1. Town Hall
2. Court House
3. Workhouse
4. Fair Green

British Forces:

5. RIC Barracks
6. Industrial Sch
   base of Auxili
7. Temporary Barr
   of RIC and Tan

Sinn Féin - IRA

8. Hagan's -
   centre of repu
   activities

**Houses Burned
26 - 27th
September 1920:**

9. Smyth's
10. O'Higgin's
11. Allen's

**Houses Ransack
on Same Night**

12. Lalor's
13. Mooney's

14. Location of
    Ambush on
    Crown Forces
    25th January

dragged barefoot and in his night clothing into the garden where he was beaten continually until a neighbour intervened and persuaded his attackers to relent. Later, however, they returned and began to beat him again all the time demanding to be told the whereabouts of his sons. Paddy's mother and sister were also ill-treated and insulted and an attempt was even made to make his sister disguise herself as a British soldier by putting on a great coat and then go around the town pointing out republicans. When she refused the house was torn asunder: "they smashed everything", said Paddy, "pictures, windows, furniture and religious statues."

The Lalors lived in Castle Street but it was in Market Street that most of the destruction was done. The *Meath Chronicle* of 2 October 1920 reported that "the reprisals started with the indiscriminate firing of a machine gun into houses in Market Street. The shops owned by McCormacks and Gaughrans were broken into and barrels of petrol taken out." The parents of the Mooneys, O'Hagans and O'Higgins were visited and treated the same as the Lalors, and the home and business of the latter were burned out. Also in this street was Smyth's bakery and mineral water works. The owners had no sympathies whatever with Sinn Féin, let alone the Volunteers, but their property also was sent up in flames. The explanation of this was probably, as Séamus Finn pointed out, that "Smyth's employed about a hundred persons and the object of the burning was to create unemployment." Another target was the residence and drapery shop of the Allen brothers in High Street; Bob was chairman of the Sinn Féin Comhairle Ceantair in South Meath but Harry took no part in politics. Their business was looted and burned with a loss of about eight thousand pounds worth of stock. Finally, the offices of Trim UDC were ransacked and also set alight resulting in the loss of many town records, some of them dating back about six hundred years.

After about two hours the violence and destruction came to an end. The identity of the men who burned and looted Trim is not known for certain. Seán Boylan referred to "several lorry loads of military and Auxiliaries from Beggar's Bush Barracks in Dublin", while Séamus Finn thought that they were "about two hundred Auxiliaries and Black and Tans from Drogheda" (he may have meant here the camp at Gormanston close to Drogheda which was the centre for the Black and

Tans). Paddy Lalor, however, is adamant that the reprisals were carried out solely and exclusively by the RIC. "There was not one Englishman amongst them", his father later told him, "they all had Irish accents as flat as our own." A few years later, after he had joined the Garda Síochana, Paddy met a man at the Phoenix Park depot where he was based, and this man told him that it was he who had opened the gates that night to let out the lorries going to Trim. "The Phoenix Park depot in 1920 was used by the RIC and not by Auxiliaries, Black and Tans or military", concluded Paddy.

Knowledge of the exact identity of their tormentors was probably of little interest to the people of Trim at the time. The *Drogheda Independent* of 2 October 1920 painted the following picture of a near ghost town and its dazed population:

> Terrified women and shivering half-clad children spent the weary
> hours of Sunday night along the banks of the river Boyne ... there
> was a belief that another attack would be made on Monday night
> .... the town was deserted, shops and schools closed, people were
> departing to their relations in the countryside ... about seventy
> people have been taken in, almost like refugees, to the workhouse.

It was a week before life returned to normal in the town and Trim UDC felt obliged to set up a civil guard to ensure that the pubs stayed closed and that looters would be dealt with.

There was widespread condemnation of the reprisals, most of it echoing the sentiments expressed by the *Drogheda Independent* which placed the blame firmly on the shoulders of the British administrators. In particular, the editorial writer singled out General Macready, Commander-in-Chief of the British Army in Ireland, for his advocacy of reprisals, both official and unofficial. In connection with this, the editorial went on:

> there is not a subordinate of his who will not have read from the
> pronouncement a plenary absolution for anything that may be
> done in pursuit of such a hideous policy ... and the results must
> be ... similar to those which have made such red ruin in Trim
> and Balbriggan.

From a conference of clergy being held in Navan on the Monday, Bishop Gaughran issued a statement reported in the *Meath Chronicle* on 2 October in which he:

> emphatically protested against the British Black and Tan troops in burning and sacking the town after the regular military and police had withdrawn, satisfied with the guarantee given by the priests that they would be responsible for the peace of the town. Such action is the negation of all government.

It is noteworthy, however, that the formidable bishop balanced this with a firm verbal attack on the Volunteers:

> who attacked the police barracks and endangered human life ... however upright and patriotic the motives of those responsible, we cannot think that as Irishmen and Catholics they will, in the calmness of reflection, endorse a course of action which is neither approved of by their church nor calculated to advance the cause they have so much at heart.

While this was mild compared to his vehement denunciation of the killers of Constable Agar in Ballivor a year earlier, it showed that the bishop was, if nothing else, consistent.

The destruction of Trim left a bitter taste. Amongst those Volunteers, the Lalors, O'Higgins, O'Hagans and Mooneys, whose parents had been beaten up and whose houses had been burned to a shell, the euphoria of Sunday morning must have quickly evaporated. For them, at least, if not for all the Volunteers, the stunning success of the barrack's raid must have, by Monday morning, seemed more like a pyrrhic victory.

On Tuesday, 5 October, the first group of Black and Tans to be stationed in the county was imposed on the people of Navan. The *Meath Chronicle* of 9 October 1920 reported that, almost characteristically, they visited the town's pubs, and it warned readers "to be particularly careful and to give no excuse for trouble." Although several lorry loads arrived that day it seems that only about a dozen stayed on permanently. It is difficult to know exactly where else Black and Tans were based in the county; most of those veterans spoken to tended to use the phrase 'Black and Tans' as a generic term to cover all Crown forces, both police and military. Whether the billeting of the Tans in Meath was a direct consequence of the Trim operation or whether it had been planned to send them irrespective of this is not clear, but what is certain is that over the next three months, up to the end of 1920, and continuing into the following year, raids, swoops and widespread arrests by the authorities became a feature of everyday life in the county.

It is remarkable then that those involved in the Trim raid seem to have escaped the attentions of the police. One exception was Paddy Lalor but his detention was to prove short-lived. Paddy had been on the run since the destruction of Trim and, along with his brother Joe and Pat Duigenan, had been staying in the home of a land steward at Newtown, a few miles outside the town. The land steward's name was Vaughan and he was a native of Oranmore, county Galway. "He had been only in the area a few months", remembered Paddy, "but he was sympathetic to us and let us sleep out in a barn or even sometimes in the kitchen of his house." Paddy recalled that many of the guns taken from the Trim barracks on 26 September had originally been hidden in a farm on the Scurlogstown-Laracor road, but then were moved to the barn on the farm looked after by this land steward. Later they were moved elsewhere which was fortunate for the Volunteers, because one night towards the end of October a party of police and soldiers suddenly appeared outside the house where the two Lalors and Pat Duigenan were sleeping. "The three of us were caught", said Paddy,

> and then the RIC sergeant who was in charge went to the barn and then went straight to the exact place where the weapons had been kept up to a few nights earlier. He was obviously well informed.

The three men were taken to Navan where they were kept for about a week in a filthy cell. After that they were freed. They got off leniently compared to the land steward who had sheltered them. Mr. Vaughan, apparently, was 'lifted' the following month and was taken to Dublin where, in Paddy Lalor's words, "he was beaten to pulp." Even worse was to follow when on his return to Trim he found that his job was gone and he had to leave the area for good.

In its last issue for the year 1920, that of 25 December, the *Meath Chronicle* published a list of the Meath men then being held in various prisons and camps under the Restoration of Order Act. The following is a summary of that list, given area by area:

Navan: Joe Woods and Ciarán O'Connell, both of whom held officer rank in the Volunteers; Leo McKenna, who had been released following the hunger strike earlier in the year; Michael McKeon, Flowerhill; Joe Bailey, a hardware shop assistant; Peter McNellis, draper's assistant; Michael Gaynor, railway employee; Joseph Boyle of Flower Hill, painter; Andrew Finnerty, grocer's assistant; Thomas Clarke, tailor; Patrick Keating, tailor; Joseph Gleeson, stationer and Richard Doran. All of these men were part of the Navan Company. Also detained at this time was Pat Loughran, the Battalion O/C.

From outside Navan, those under arrest at this time included: B. Gartland, Kilberry; J. Meade, Wilkinstown; two Dorans from Kilberry and Joe Ryan of Gormanlough. Again all were members of the Volunteers. Also included in the list were figures such as James Quigley, the county surveyor, and Seán MacNaMidhe by now chairman of Navan UDC and also headmaster of Navan Technical School. We have met both of these men before, but although of republican views, neither of them were Volunteers. Another political figure in jail was the chairman of Navan RDC, James Ginnity of Rushwee, and with him was another member of that council mentioned earlier, Joseph Ledwidge of Slane, brother of the dead poet Francis.

Kells: John Farrelly, Carnaross; John Keogh, Ballinlough; Nicholas Gaynor, Ballinlough; Justin McKenna, solicitor, Mullagh; Philip Farrelly, Ballinagon; Andrew Carroll, grocer's assistant, Crossakiel; Bernard McKeon; F. O'Higgins, Kilskyre; Pat Magee, Kilmainhamwood; Patrick Cusack, Kilmainhamwood; J. Brennan, chairman of Kells UDC; Christopher McCabe, a blacksmith and also a member of Kells UDC; Domhnall O'Sullivan; John Morris, solicitor's assistant; Patrick Keelan, Patrick Smith and John Gillic, all tailors, Kells; John Maguire, blacksmith; John Bray, labourer; Joseph Morris, clerk; Robert Mullen, carpenter; John English, chairman of the Kells Board of Guardians; John Fitzsimons and Patrick Flynn, both labourers; N. Farrelly, Crossakiel; Patrick Clark, van driver; Patrick Hand, farmer, Kilskyre; Patrick Hopkins, county councillor and Michael Skelly, urban councillor.

Not having been able to secure lists of members of Volunteer companies for this area, it is impossible to say who was and who was not a member. But of those named, John Keogh was Battalion O/C, having, as we have seen, taken over following the death of Cogan; the Farrellys were also prominent members, while Bob Mullan was captain of the Kells Company.

Oldcastle: H. Ward, Cloughmaio; Thomas McCabe, county councillor; Michael McEnroe, rural councillor; P.J. Bartley, clerk; Michael McGinn, clerk; Michael and William Grace; James McGinn, farmer; Matt Gibney, farmer; Leo Twomey, barber; P. Timmon, linesman; John Husband, rural councillor; Patrick Garrigan, coachman, Crossdrum; Hugh Curran, Tierworker; Harry Sheridan, Tom Gavin and Owen Clarke. The last three named had all been with Cogan in the car on the night he was killed.

Surprisingly, few names are given for the Trim area, the most notable amongst them being Michael Giles who had participated in the Trim raid. The above represents but a summary of the names given in the *Chronicle* where over a hundred names are listed.

Life in prison at that time was not as bad as it may have sounded. For Owen Clarke the worst part was getting there. After his arrest he spent two weeks in Dunshaughlin workhouse and another two in Arbour Hill. After that, along with a large number of other prisoners, he was taken on a destroyer ship to Belfast and thence to Ballykinlar Camp in county Down. "It was a very hot day", Owen said, "and we had to walk the last three miles carrying our baggage even though we were handcuffed." Owen spent about three months in Ballykinlar. There were two separate camps, holding a total of up to five hundred men. Owen remembered meeting other Meath men there, such as Andrew Finnerty and a brother of Pat Fitzsimons. The prisoners more or less ran the camp themselves organising their own meals, games, Irish classes and drama. The commandant of Owen's camp was Eoin O'Duffy, a member of the Volunteers' headquarters staff and later to be leader of the Blueshirts in the 1930s. The relaxed atmosphere can be seen in that Owen was at one stage released on parole to testify at a court case in Oldcastle. The Volunteer leader in the camp, however, determined to make use of this opportunity and he was ordered to bring back wire cutters. Owen recalled getting these back in concealed in his leggings. Shortly afterwards two men escaped from the camp. Owen thinks that they were wanted to do a job on the outside but, as it turned out, both were soon rearrested.

An indication of the increased tensions in the county can be seen in the fact that in the space of a month there were four different accidents, three of which ended in fatalities, and all of them arising directly from the Troubles. At the beginning of November, in Navan, a British soldier named Clifford was involved in an accident while reversing a Crossley Tender up Barrack Lane. It seems that there were a number of bombs in the tender and that he struck a lever against them: the unfortunate soldier was seriously injured and had to have his right leg amputated. Following closely on from this came the first civilian casualty of the war in Meath. He was a sixty-seven year old journalist named Austin Cowley who, on the evening of Sunday 21 November, while walking through the grounds of the military-occupied workhouse in Navan, was called on to halt by a sentry. Cowley, who was, it seems, slightly deaf, did not heed the warning and was shot dead.

Just over a week later, Sergeant Keighary, an RIC officer of twenty years experience, was the victim of a similar misunderstanding. While on duty at Kilcarn on a dark and very rainy night, he signalled a lorry approaching Navan to halt. Apparently the sergeant did not realise that it was a military lorry, nor did the occupants realise that it was a police officer who was attempting to stop them. It seems then that both sides began to fire on each other and, before they could correct their blunder, Sergeant Keighary lay dead on the side of the road.

Shortly afterwards a similar mix-up resulted in the death of a young Volunteer from Dunboyne named Bernard Reilly. Seán Boylan recounted the incident as follows:

> The residence of Mr. J.J. McCarthy of Courthill, Dunboyne, was
> used by Mick Collins, Gearóid O'Sullivan, Austin Stack, Harry

Boland and other GHQ officers as a safe retreat from time to time. Mr. McCarthy, who was a native of Kerry, was a Justice of the Peace. He had often offered to resign but was prevailed upon by Michael Collins not to do so. Dunboyne Castle, the residence of Leonard Morrogh, overlooked McCarthy's house. Leonard Morrogh had an English nurse employed. Her name was Lang. From her window she could observe the comings and goings of strangers to McCarthy's. It was thought that she reported all this to the RIC for, one day, McCarthy received information from a friend of his in the RIC that his house was to be raided by the RIC. His friend was Head Constable Bonham who was an RIC instructor at Dollymount, Dublin. It appears that Bonham threatened to resign if McCarthy's was raided.

As soon as the information was conveyed to me that McCarthy's was to be raided I placed an ambush party in the old cemetery nearby to await the raiding party. During an inspection by an IRA officer of an outpost occupied by a section of the IRA a young Volunteer named Bernard Reilly was called on to halt. It appears that he (the Volunteer) replied in an English accent (his mother was English). He was shot dead in error. It was on the night of 9 December 1920. When I heard that he had been shot I sent Volunteer Joseph Lalor of Trim, who happened to be in the area at the time, to Fr Kelly to tell him what had happened and to ask him to render spiritual aid to Reilly. I had realised at once that an inquest would be held and that Fr Kelly, who did not know Volunteer Joseph Lalor, could truthfully say he had never met the man before.

At the inquiry at Dublin Castle, Fr Kelly was threatened with detention if he did not disclose the name of the Volunteer who called on him but he was able to convince them that he did not know the man. After the inquest the body was handed over to his parents and was later buried in Dunboyne … the expected raid on McCarthy's never took place. Whether this was due to the threatened resignation of Head Constable Bonham, we do not know. I do know, however, that Nurse Lang sent a letter to the military officer in charge of the area informing him that I had called to McCarthy's on a subsequent occasion with a number of tools to demolish bridges in the area. The officer sent this letter to Leonard Morrogh for verification, after which she was dismissed.

The circumstances surrounding the death of Volunteer Reilly are remembered in much the same way by Séamus Finn although with some slight variations. He wrote that McCarthy's house was being watched and that, to counteract this, the Volunteers had set up their night-time vigil. The understanding was that no Volunteer would leave his position until a whistle sounded. The night in question was, however, according to Finn, a bitterly cold one, and it seems that Reilly got up from his prone position and began to walk around to try to warm himself. When he was challenged by a fellow Volunteer he failed to reply and was shot.

Thus ended a strange sequence of four accidents, three of which proved fatal, within a month. In the case of one of these four incidents it was hinted that they were not as accidental as they seemed and that they were in fact deliberate killings engineered by 'comrades' of the victims. There were indications of double-dealing and spying and informing. At a later stage it will be shown that such practices were not at all unknown in the county during the years under scrutiny, but as regards the incidents just considered there is no definite evidence to show that the dead or injured men were in any way victims of carefully contrived 'accidental' shootings.

In October 1920 Seán Boylan recalled presiding "at a joint meeting of the officers of the Fourth and Fifth Battalions which was held in the Carnaross Company area." At this meeting certain differences arose between Boylan and some of his officers; these would hardly amount to a mutiny but there was a certain reluctance on the part of these to obey orders and carry out instructions. Boylan went on:

> The Fifth Battalion officers present included Tom Manning, Commandant (I had appointed him O/C in place of John Keogh who had been arrested a couple of weeks earlier); Peter O'Higgins, Adjutant; Barney Harte, Quartermaster. The Fourth Battalion officers present were Patrick Farrelly, Commandant; Thomas O'Reilly, Vice O/C; M. Cahill, Adjutant; Michael Govern, Quartermaster.

Charlie Conaty who, as first lieutenant of the Stonefield Company, was present at this meeting and recalled that:

> Boylan, who presided, announced that an ambush of enemy forces would have to be carried out in each battalion area and he suggested that the preparation of plans for the attacks be made immediately. Tom Manning, our Battalion O/C, stood up and opposed the idea, saying that we had insufficient arms or ammunition to meet any reprisals which were likely to follow. He was supported by Peter O'Higgins and other officers ... the officers of the Fourth Battalion agreed to formulate plans for an ambush in their area.

Boylan, by his own admission, was very annoyed at the attitude of the recalcitrant officers especially when he:

> realised the effect it would have on the morale of the Volunteers of the area. I suspended each one of them on the spot and informed them that they would be courtmartialled within the next seven days.

Following this Boylan remained in the area for some weeks to reorganise his battalion and restore morale. A new team of officers was appointed, consisting of David Smith of Whitegate as Commandant; Peter O'Connell, Stonefield, Adjutant; Brian Daly, Carnaross Company, Quartermaster; Patrick McDonnell, Stonefield, Intelligence Officer and Matt Tevlin, Carnaross Company, Engineer. Boylan picked his men well and morale in the area was quickly restored. It was from the companies of the Fifth Battalion that the strongest and most consistent thrusts and attacks against the British forces in the county were to come in the following year as the war entered its final phase.

General guidelines for the direction that the war was to take in 1921 seem to have been decided upon at a meeting in Delvin workhouse sometime in December (Charlie Conaty remembered that it was on a Sunday night). Those present included the brigade staff (Boylan, Finn,

Cullen and O'Higgins); all officers at battalion level in the brigade
area and Major-General J.J. (Ginger) O'Connell who held the rank of
Assistant Chief of Staff of the Volunteers, and who had been sent from
headquarters to preside at the gathering. Charlie Conaty recalled that
it was decided:

> to organise and formulate plans for attacks on enemy patrols and
> outposts. Séamus O'Higgins, brigade quartermaster, was to be
> supplied with a complete list of all arms in the brigade area and
> after some discussion it was arranged that Eamon Cullen should
> come into the Fifth Battalion area to instruct us in the making
> of mines and bombs.

Seán Boylan, in recounting this meeting, stressed the point that such
attacks were then vital in order "to relieve pressure by enemy forces in
Cork and elsewhere."

Peter O'Connell, Adjutant of the Fifth Battalion and in attendance
in Delvin, thought that it was here also that the idea of knocking and
breaking bridges was first mooted. "I think that it was Ginger O'Connell
himself who suggested it", he said. For the early months of 1921 the two
local newspapers are punctuated with reports concerning this tactic.
Sometimes dynamite was used but this was scarce. More often, as Peter
O'Connell said, "it was very hard and slow work needing crowbars and
pick-axes." The idea, of course, was to delay, or to stifle altogether, lorry
and car movement by the police and military. Peter was dubious as to
whether it was worth all the effort:

> The police soon overcame the problem by using fifteen foot steel
> girders which they carried around in the lorries. These would
> simply be laid across the broken road or bridge and the vehicles
> could drive over them.

The policy of bridge demolition backfired in an unexpected and tragic
manner in February 1921. A man cycling home one evening did not
notice the break in a road at Carlanstown and fell in, suffering severe
head injuries from which he soon expired. This, in fact, was John

McMahon, referred to in the previous chapter as the representative of Nobber electoral area on the Meath County Council from 1914 to 1920. "I almost fell into one of the craters myself", mused Peter O'Connell,

> It was on a night that we were returning from a battalion council meeting. We had just done the job a few nights earlier and I was nearly on top of it before I remembered. Sometimes we marked the broken bridges using bushes or poles on the road a few hundred yards in advance. But these precautions were not taken very often. I heard another case of a man in Mullagh who fell into a crater and fractured his skull.

Preaching in Mullingar Cathedral on Christmas Day 1920, Bishop Gaughran reflected that:

> the outlook was gloomy; we are surrounded by dangers and trials unparalleled in the history of the country; we cannot tell what has to be faced on each morrow but if the people conform to the will of God in these very dark hours He will eventually bring good out of the evil which he has allowed.

A *Drogheda Independent* editorial of 15 January 1921 struck a similar note, as it reviewed the disturbed state of the country:

> The conditions prevailing in this country at the present time are such that no living Irishman can recall anything to compare with them within the range of his own experience. Martial law is in force in eight counties; the policy of reprisals has been brought into play in perhaps three-quarters of the country; law seems everywhere to have abrogated in favour of anarchy; women and children over a large area of the island live in a state of abject terror by night and day; the normal conditions of existence have ceased to be and the legitimate business of life has been paralysed over a large part of the kingdom.

The writer went on to blame the British Prime Minister for all the above calamities, thus continuing a long-running personalised campaign against Lloyd George, attacks on whom had been appearing intermittently in the columns of this newspaper over the previous two years. The writer claimed:

> It would be difficult to persuade the Irish leaders to enter negotiations with a minister with such a dubious record on Irish affairs like Lloyd George … the old adage 'once bitten, twice shy' finds remarkably fit application here.

The *Drogheda Independent* had been, just a few years earlier, a staunch supporter of the status quo, but by 1921 it was very much anti-British in its comments and reports, sometimes even introducing a note of ridicule, always a lethal weapon in rural Ireland. On 1 January 1921, for instance, a report which gave a list of houses raided in the Navan area ended in mock solemnity that "a haystack in Smith's was also assiduously searched", while an item headed 'A Rebel Cow' stated sneeringly that:

> some of the military stationed at Oldcastle when returning home last Friday night called on a cow to halt and having failed to answer the third challenge the beast was shot dead.

On a more serious level, however, the 'anarchy' referred to in the newspaper editorial just quoted may have been prompted by an incident in Slane just before that. It was, in fact, on Christmas Day 1920 but certain persons were not showing much goodwill to their fellow man. A young man named Nangle, according to the *Drogheda Independent* of 1 January 1921, claimed that, while walking near Slane Castle on the night in question six revolver shots were fired at him, wounding him in the ankle. Nangle was insistent that his two assailants whom he had just passed on the road were RIC men and that he could identify one of them. It is significant that when the reporter contacted the RIC in Slane they refused to deny the story.

The year 1921 opened with the Black and Tans sending their notion of a New Year's greeting to the people of Meath. Posted on telegraph poles in Navan the message read as follows:

> 'It has come to our notice that heads of the IRA have ordered an aggressive policy towards all ranks of the RIC in the immediate future. We have no desire to disturb the hitherto peaceable condition of this county but we hereby give warning that if hostile action is offered to any military or police officer in county Meath the most drastic action will be taken. It is therefore a matter for the men of responsibility in this county to ensure that our wrath is not drawn on the people' – Black and Tans.

Another indication that the county was by now being viewed as a centre of growing rebellion can be seen in a further notice issued from Dublin Castle later that month. This stated that "if outrages continued, known rebels will be carried as hostages for the safe conduct of the occupants in all vehicles." This warning applied specifically to Dublin city, county Dublin and county Meath. The threat here does not appear to have been carried out too often in Meath but over the next six months in the streets of Dublin it was quite commonplace to see military lorries with Volunteer prisoners tied to the sides as the crown forces defied any potential ambushers to open fire or bomb them.

The hitherto untroubled village of Moynalty became the first focal point of anti-British activity in 1921. There was a Volunteer company in the area of which Paddy O'Reilly was the captain. "We had twenty-three men at the time of our greatest strength", Paddy recalled, "but things were fairly quiet here up to this." The company had collected a good number of shotguns, many of which were given to them willingly, and these were kept buried under the floor of a disused farmhouse at Salford, just outside the village. Paddy thought that the authorities got word of this from an overheard or indiscreet conversation in a pub in Mullagh. Whatever the source of the information the outcome was that early on Sunday morning, 23 January, District Inspector Rowland and a number of constables from Kells arrived into the village, went straight to the farmhouse, dug up the hidden weapons and then loaded them on to a car. "A little girl was sent to tell me what was going on", said Paddy, "and I gathered up some of the men. In fact there were eight of us against eight of them."

The Volunteer faction arrived just in time as the police were about to leave with their haul. In the ensuing gun battle the police had to abandon the car and make a disorganised retreat back to the house of the sympathetic ex-British army officer, Lieutenant-Colonel Farrell. Paddy thought that one constable may have been wounded but they never knew for sure. "Once we got the guns back we didn't care about them. Later on they were rescued by police reinforcements sent from the Nobber area," he said. The police party went home empty-handed because not only did they let slip their captured consignment of guns but they also learned later that their motor car had been burned out in a nearby field. "Jimmy Cullen drove the car to Feagh where it was burned," remembered Paddy. "At the time he was the only one in the area who was able to drive."

Towards the end of this month of January the Trim Company of Volunteers began again to make life unpleasant for the police in the town. Since the burning of the barracks in September, things seemed to have quietened down a bit, although a report in the *Drogheda Independent* of 29 January 1921 remarked that:

> matters have never righted themselves in Trim and more incidents of an unpleasant nature have taken place there than in any other portion of the County Meath.

The writer may have been referring to the behaviour of the RIC in the town in the months immediately following the loss of their barracks. Paddy Lalor recalled that the regrouped police were particularly aggressive towards the townspeople and that there was one particular sergeant who used to go about slapping people across the face for no reason whatever.

About the middle of October a force of around fifteen RIC, including a Head Constable and a District Inspector, had returned to the town and set up 'barracks' in a commandeered house in High Street and later in a bigger building in Mill Street. It was while on a routine patrol on the night of Tuesday, 25 January, that six of the garrison literally walked into an ambush by the local Volunteer company.

Jimmy Sherry was among the ambushing party that night. Jimmy joined the Volunteers in February 1917 when he was aged only sixteen; his brothers Tom, Ned and Bill were already members. "My mother's people were in the Fenians in the old days", he said, "so I suppose there was a tradition there."

Jimmy remembered that word had come down to them, probably after the meeting in Delvin workhouse mentioned earlier, to organise ambushes to keep the British forces under pressure in the county and thus to prevent their transfer to areas of greater Volunteer activity such as Cork. The local newspaper reports at the time estimated that there were about twenty men in the ambush but there were in fact only six according to Jimmy. "There were 'The Gael' McArdle, the two Hynes brothers, Mick and Pat, my own brother Ned and myself and one other I can't just remember", said Jimmy. "McArdle was a former British army sniper. The six of us got in behind a wall at Haggard Street which was at the edge of the town and so gave us an escape route across the fields."

The patrolling police were hit hard that night and the attack on them ended only when reinforcements came on the scene. By then three of them lay wounded, the *Drogheda Independent* of 5 February 1921 reported their names as Constables Barney and Packman, who were English, and a Scotsman, Constable McQuat.

A week later, the first named, who had been wounded in the head, died in a Dublin hospital. Following this attack another bout of panic gripped Trim as the populace anticipated a second night of reprisals. Schools closed, business came to a standstill and a large number of people left their homes, many of them taking refuge in the town's workhouse. Although there was some intimidation, warning notices urging the occupants to leave town were placed on the doors of the businesses of Sinn Féiners such as Harry Allen and Bernard Reilly of Market Street, the local clergy secured a guarantee that there would be no repeat of the September reprisals. This time the guarantee was honoured.

The following Sunday, however, the police walked into another ambush, this time at Wellington Street. The *Drogheda Independent* of 5 February 1921 described the noise as a "tornado of firing" which went on for fifteen minutes. Paddy Lalor recalled this incident as a one-man ambush carried out by his brother Joe when he threw a hand grenade at the police party and followed up with gunfire. "Joe always wanted to be in the action", said Paddy, "he didn't have the patience to be waiting for the go ahead from higher up." There were no casualties on this occasion but it provoked an angry reaction from jittery priests and townspeople who condemned it and claimed that it had not been carried out by locals.

The more aggressive policies decided on in Delvin and being pursued in Trim were also attempted in January in both Navan and Oldcastle, although in both cases the operations were to prove abortive. Plans for an attack on Oldcastle RIC barracks were discussed at a meeting in Rahard attended by Seán Boylan, Séamus Finn, Eamon Cullen and members of the Fifth Battalion Council. "We went into the number of arms and ammunition available", recalled Peter O'Connell,

> the vantage points to be used and the possibility of preventing reinforcements reaching Oldcastle from a military post at Crossdrum situated about a mile from the town.

The night of 8 January was fixed for the attack and in the meantime Eamon Cullen instructed a number of Volunteers in the manufacture of home-made land mines. By the scheduled date the Volunteers had a couple of land mines ready for use.

Peter O'Connell's evocative retelling of the mobilisation of the Volunteers on that night brings home the very rudimentary conditions under which they were labouring at the time, conditions which made their avowed aim of ousting the forces of the British Empire seem almost risible:

> On the night of 8 January, Whitegate and Stonefield Companies met at seven o'clock at Tandera and took the mines with them by hand to Lisnagon. Here it was decided to commandeer a vehicle to take the mines to Oldcastle. Two men went to Crosswater, where they procured a horse and trap with a driver after which we proceeded in a body to Boolies, Oldcastle, where the rest of the battalion were mobilising. Some of the men arrived on bicycles, others had walked the railway line. The Carnaross men passed us on the way in two spring carts. It was a distance of six

miles for the men of Stonefield Company.

Charlie Conaty, who was present that night, remembered that the men, who numbered up to fifty, were well armed: "four or five carried rifles, a few had revolvers while the remainder had shotguns." Apart from the Stonefield, Carnaross and Whitegate companies, men were also present from the units in Ballinlough and Oldcastle itself. David Smith, Phil Tevlin and Pat Farrelly were the officers in charge of the operation, but unfortunately for them, their carefully laid plans came to an abrupt end. "When I got there", said Charlie Conaty:

> I noticed a man dressed in black walking up and down near our men. After a while he approached a group of our men and asked, "Who is in charge?" He warned them that we were going to our deaths, that the military were in the town and were aware of our intentions and waiting for us ... The man in black was a local priest. Paddy McDonnell, Battalion Intelligence Officer and Police Officer of the Fifth Battalion, had just previously commandeered a taxi which he intended to drive into the town with the object of drawing out the police. Needless to say he did not do so when he heard of the situation.

After some consultation the senior officers decided to call off the attack and send the men home. There was much anger over this fiasco. Seán Boylan saw it as "a great blow to the morale of the Volunteers when the enemy had such first-hand knowledge of their movements" and at the time he could only conclude "that the information was supplied by someone within the ranks of the IRA." Some of the men that night were more specific in their suspicions of the culprits for, as Peter O'Connell put it, "they blamed the Oldcastle and Ballinacree men for informing the clergy."

An equally ambitious scheme planned for Navan on the same night, 8 January, ended similarly. Since the large scale arrests towards the end of 1920 which had deprived them of officers at both company and battalion level such as Leo McKenna, Pat Loughran, Joe Woods and Ciarán O'Connell, the Navan men had had to reorganise themselves. It was at this time that Pat Fitzsimons became Battalion O/C (replacing

Loughran) and that the Hilliard brothers came to occupy prominent positions, James becoming Battalion Quartermaster and Mick being appointed company captain.

Born in 1903, Mick Hilliard spent a number of years attending the Diocesan College (now St. Finian's) in Mullingar which he left in 1920 to devote himself to the struggle against Britain. This was the start of a long political career as a member of Navan UDC (1934–42), as a Fianna Fáil TD for the old Meath-Westmeath constituency (1943–48) and then the Meath constituency (1948–73), and reaching a pinnacle when he served as Minister of Posts and Telegraphs (1959–65) and later as Minister of Defence (1965–69).

Returning to the events of 1921, the plan was to carry out an ambush on an enemy patrol in Navan. The local company was to be assisted by other Volunteers in the battalion area. Both Bobby Byrne and Patsy Bennett remembered the plans for this operation, although neither could put an exact date on it. Bobby could recall only that it was a "few months" after the burning of Trim while Patsy thought that it was "sometime early in 1921." Seán Boylan gave the date 8 January which is doubtless accurate since he associates it with the proposed attack in Oldcastle on the same night, and it certainly does not contradict the approximate dates given by the other two men. Another point of interest here is that all three agreed that there were two projected ambushes, neither of which materialised; but whereas Boylan stated that "the men were in position for two nights in succession", the other two thought there was a gap between the two occasions, "about a fortnight" being Bobby Byrne's estimate.

The plan, it seems, was to ambush a foot patrol of military and police who, as regular as clockwork every night, marched around the town. Their route took them from the soldiers' base in the old workhouse (now part of the town's hospital) at the top of Brews Hill, down that street, through Trimgate Street to the Market Square where they turned right and marched down Ludlow Street and Academy Street as far as the railway bridge on Dublin Road which marked the southernmost point of the town at that time. After that the party made its way back to its base via Circular Road, Railway Street and Brews Hill. As Bobby Byrne remembered it, men were to be placed at three points along this route, their purpose being not just to ambush the patrol but also to deal with the reinforcements that would be sent out subsequently. The points chosen were, firstly, on the roofs of the sheds along the top of the jumping enclosure, now the grounds of Navan O'Mahony's football club, which extended several hundred yards along one side of Brews Hill; secondly, in the chapel yard in Trimgate Street and, thirdly, on the bridge on the Dublin Road from which height military and police could easily be picked off.

Apart from the Navan men, Volunteers from Bohermeen, Martry and Commons companies were also involved. The Bohermeen and Martry men came into the town by walking the railway line which brought them out to the far end of the town at Beechmount. Here they were to be met by two scouts who would then lead them to their positions. "Tom Reilly and myself were the scouts that night", said Bobby Byrne,

> We were to meet the Bohermeen men at Lawlor's haggard in Beechmount. I remember that 'Tara' was the password they had to give us. But after waiting there a long time there was no sign of the men, so we reported back to Pat Fitzsimons, Tom Duffy and the other officers who were waiting in the Banba Hall on the Fair Green. They had no option but to call off the whole thing.

Later it was discovered that the Bohermeen-Martry men were in fact waiting for directions in the Beechmount area. "Although in the general vicinity they had gone to the wrong meeting point and we did not go out far enough to meet them", said Bobby. "Maybe it was no harm", reflected Bobby,

> since I often thought since that if the ambush had gone ahead and police or soldiers were killed the town might have been subjected to the kind of terror and burning that Trim had suffered.

It is almost certain that it was for a fortnight later that the plans were rescheduled. This time all the men took up their positions. "I was in the chapel yard that night", said Patsy Bennett, "but we waited a long time and no military appeared." Patsy thought that this may have happened a second night and this would fit in with Seán Boylan's statement, quoted earlier, that "the men were in position for two nights in succession." Whatever the exact circumstances there was no doubt in Patsy's mind about one thing: "the military were obviously warned off in advance because they never missed their night's patrol."

Seán Boylan was quite certain as to who was responsible for the debacle. In his statement he named two men; one of them was a rank-and-file member of the Volunteers while the other held a prominent position in the organisation. Regarding the latter, Boylan stated:

> some days before the date fixed I gave [---] two hundred buckshot cartridges for use in the attack. I handed them over to him in Thomas Gibney's house in Bohermeen. The local company, with a few Volunteers from other companies who were to bring off the attack, never got the ammunition from [---]. They were in position for two nights in succession, armed with shotguns.

Boylan goes on to say that it was later reported to him by another of officer rank that when the men were in position on the second night, the other 'culprit', the rank and file man just alluded to:

> sent a messenger from his home to the ambush party to say that I [Boylan] had called to his house and left word that the ambush was to be called off. I was never in his house in my life.

Later, in November 1921, Boylan recounted, he called a special meeting of the Brigade Staff to inquire into the failure of the officer to supply the cartridges on the night in question and that the man "admitted the fact and signed a statement to that effect." Boylan goes even further, alleging that the man "was in constant touch with the RIC in Navan and elsewhere", in other words that he was a spy or informer. This shadowy area will be considered at a later stage but, for the time being and probably forever, the exact position regarding the ambush plans for Navan, the number of such ambushes planned and the reasons why they never materialised must remain unclear.

Apart from the by now routine demolition of bridges and the blocking of roads by felled trees the only other incident of note in the month of January 1921 was a brief attack on Longwood police barracks. What was probably, however, the most unlikely event for the duration of the Troubles in Meath came towards the end of this same month with the arrest by crown forces of Lord Dunsany. The peer was, as the *Drogheda Independent* of 29 January 1921 verbosely put it, "unceremoniously taken from his bed, denied the privilege of indulging his appetite, and hurriedly driven in a motor lorry to Dunshaughlin."

The forty-two year old Lord and writer, the essence of loyalty to the crown, had not suddenly turned rebel but was in fact the victim of very stringent security policies being pursued by the administration: Dunsany was charged with "having arms not under effective military control." At his trial a few weeks later his counsel made great play of the Lord's impeccable background and record of service: Eton public school, the Coldstream Guards, service in the Boer War and the Great War. Counsel also stated that at Easter 1916 his client had driven to Dublin to offer his assistance in the suppression of the Rising, but had been ambushed and shot in the face near the Four Courts. In his own defence Lord Dunsany stressed that his castle "was one of the castles of the Pale and had always stood on the side of the crown ... no one had ever lived in it who was not loyal." Addressing himself to the charge proffered against him, he said that he had handed over several guns to the police but had kept a few for the simple and practical purpose of "ridding his land of rabbits." Neither Dunsany's nor his counsel's protestations of loyalty could save him from a hefty fine of £25 which brought an end to this most ironic of episodes in the Troubles.

February began with the arrival in Trim, on the first day of the month, of a company of Auxiliaries. The force occupied the Industrial School in the town. This building, which stood on the site of the present day Convent of Mercy secondary school, at the time housed orphans and delinquents, but both Paddy Lalor and Jimmy Sherry remembered it as a place where useful practical skills such as carpentry, tailoring and cookery were taught to the boys and girls. Most of these were now moved out and resettled in the local workhouse. "There was a dome at the top of the school", said Paddy Lalor, "and I remember the Auxies setting up a machine gun and searchlight there." Whether or not the placing of the Auxiliaries in Trim was a direct response to Volunteer activities in the area is now impossible to say, but just a few days later, on 5 February, the south Meath area experienced even more excitement with the burning of the Langford's house at Summerhill.

The burning down of the 'big houses' had already become a feature of the war elsewhere in the country. These houses were usually the property of the Protestant Unionist Ascendancy class whose pro-British outlook made their homes fair game in the unceasing war of reprisals now being waged by both sides. Summerhill House, described in the *Meath Chronicle* of 12 February, 1921 as "the most beautiful in the county", had been the ancestral home of the Langford family for almost two hundred years. Lord Langford himself had died the previous summer and the tenant at this time was a Colonel Rowley.

It is fairly certain however that the burning of the house was neither a reprisal nor an act of mindless destruction but rather a result of the strategic-military situation at that time. Seán Boylan recalled that:

> in the spring of 1921 I received a message from GHQ to the effect that the Auxiliaries were about to occupy Summerhill Castle, the property of Lord Langford ... it appears that the information was received by Mick Collins from one of his men in Dublin Castle who had seen a decoded message to that effect. I called on Battalion Adjutant Bernard Dunne and instructed him to have Summerhill Castle burned down immediately. He conveyed the message to Michael Graham, captain of the Summerhill Company, who carried out the order within twenty four hours. It appears to have taken some time to set it alight as they had to use fifty six gallons of paraffin oil before it went up in flames.

Boylan then explained the necessity for this drastic measure as being the fact that the house:

> was situated at a very strategic point on high ground which commanded one of the routes to the west. The Auxiliaries with

field glasses could have swept the country. Following the burning of Trim RIC barracks they had established a strong post in Trim and the intention was to establish another at Summerhill.

That the burning of Summerhill House may have been grounded in sound military strategy was of little consolation to its proprietors. In the blaze many valuable pieces of furniture and paintings were lost. A feature of the residence had been a magnificent garden and a miniature lake which stood on the top of the house. In fact, when the police and firefighters came on the scene they used bullets to puncture the receptacle that held the lake in the hope that the water cascading downwards would extinguish the flames. This proved a vain hope, and total damage was later estimated at far in excess of a million pounds.

If it is in fact true, and there is no reason to suggest other than what Boylan has stated, that it was intended to have two bases for the Auxiliaries in the south of the county, then this is a strong indication that the area was being viewed as increasingly troublesome. From 9 February the town of Trim was subjected to a curfew lasting from ten o'clock until five in the morning, the only exemptions being doctors, nurses and clergy. A report in the *Chronicle* later in the year – just after the Truce in July – stated that Trim was the only area in the county where such restrictions had been imposed during the Troubles. Although the same newspaper in February gave the number of Auxiliaries stationed in the Industrial School as about four hundred, this was undoubtedly an exaggeration. Robert Kee estimated that the total number of Auxiliaries in the country at this time was 1,500 and it is extremely unlikely that over a quarter of these were based in Trim. Paddy Lalor's estimate of one hundred would certainly be much nearer the mark. It is also most interesting to note another statement by Kee that by the spring of 1921 there were fifteen companies of Auxiliaries in the country. Most of these were based in Dublin, Cork and the other Munster counties which were the areas of most intense fighting while Meath was one of only four other counties which 'hosted' a company, the others were Longford, Sligo and Roscommon.

"'Gentlemen officers', they called them, to distinguish them from the Tans … They were more like 'gentlemen thugs'", was how Paddy

Lalor caustically recalled the company of the Auxiliaries. It was perhaps inevitable that their presence combined with the curfew soon resulted in a sharp fall-off in the level of Volunteer activity in the Trim area. The newcomers made their mark in other ways. "They gave real hell to the townsfolk", was how Séamus Finn put it, and within a very short time they were involved in a most unsavoury incident that was to gain nationwide notoriety and result in the resignation of their commander-in-chief.

This began at about two o'clock in the afternoon of 9 February when a party of about forty Auxiliaries arrived in the village of Robinstown, a few miles outside the town (there were also some military and RIC with them). They went straight to the grocery and licensed premises of Chandlers, forced their way in, alleging that they were searching for arms and ammunition, and then proceeded to tear the place asunder. What was astonishing in all this was the fact that the Chandler family was Protestant and Unionist. "Their place", wrote Séamus Finn, "was a rendezvous of the Meath hunt in its palmiest days and consequently its owner was not without influence in official circles."

The owner was, in fact, Mrs Chandler, an old and partially invalided widow, and the business was managed by her son Richard. It was he who informed the intruders that there were no arms or ammunition on the premises following which, according to Finn, "they beat him and kicked him down the stairs. Then", Finn continued, "they set about looting his hostelry, a task that was after their own hearts and for which they were well equipped." In the local newspaper reports of the following weekend and in the testimony given by witnesses in the subsequent farcical trial in May and June, a clear idea may be got of the havoc wrecked on the premises. It is worth pointing out that in her evidence, Mrs Chandler exonerated the 'tin hats' – slang for military – of any part in this vandalism and placed the blame entirely on the Auxiliaries. The trespassers took bottles of alcohol, spirits and wine which they broke or took away or consumed there and then to a total value of about a hundred pounds. Some of them went upstairs and began throwing blankets and sheets out of the bedroom windows down into the yard where others put them into the lorries. From the grocery they took boxes of chocolates, cakes, a case of condensed milk, several bags of sugar and sixty pounds of bacon, candles, soap and boot polish. From the house a list of valuable items was stolen, including salt cellars, silver forks, watches, rings, brooches and an amount of money in gold and silver coin.

As though this were not enough, they also made off with some hens and other fowl. Some of the hens were mutilated and Paddy Lalor remembered hearing the story of the Auxiliaries coming into the town that evening with bits of hens impaled on their bayonets. The terrifying spectacle lasted over two hours during which, Mrs Chandler later told the court, "They shot their guns at random in the air, took the contents of the till and acted like pigs". When they left they took Richard Chandler with them and he was kept for some time in their Trim base. Not content with this, it emerged at the trial that, on the way back they stopped off at the house of a local schoolmistress and stole a quantity of clothing.

But for Mrs Chandler the miseries and persecutions of this day were only half over. At about ten o'clock five or six of the Auxiliaries returned to the premises, intimidated both Mrs Chandler and her daughter, threatened to blow up the place, went from room to room ransacking them of whatever was left and took off with even more drink, including twenty three bottles of champagne.

The commander-in-chief of all the Auxiliaries in Ireland at this time was Brigadier-General Frank Crozier, a veteran of both the Boer and the Great War. Crozier has left behind him a number of books of his memoirs including *Impressions and Recollections* (T.W. Laurie, 1930) and *Ireland Forever* (Jonathan Cape, 1932), both of which touch on the events under consideration. Crozier describes how, following the looting in Robinstown, two Auxiliaries came to him in Dublin and reported what had taken place. They did so "at the peril of their lives", wrote Crozier, "as their comrades would undoubtedly have killed them had they known". Crozier then came to Trim where he carried out an investigation as a result of which he placed five Auxiliaries under arrest and suspended twenty one others. On the following day, 14 February, all of these were taken to Beggar's Bush Barracks in Dublin. As they passed their former barracks in Trim, the *Meath Chronicle* of 26 February 1921 reported, they jeered, hissed and shook their fists in its direction, a clear

Charlie Conaty (extreme right) in a family photograph taken about 1925. Also present are is younger brother, Pat, his father, Patrick and his sister, Kathleen, a member of Cumann na ιBan during the Troubles.

Peter O'Connell, centre, front row, during his time with the Free State army. As can be seen n the writing on the wall, the photograph was taken at the Curragh in September 1923. On ∍r's left is Joseph Boylan, a brother of Seán.

3. Mick Hilliard (centre) addressing a republican meeting in Drogheda, probably in the earl[y] 1930s. On the left is Eamon de Valera with Frank Aiken on the right.

4. Matt Wallace (extreme left) in his days working for Meath County Council. The photogr[aph] was taken at Soldier's Hill, Lismullin in 1927.

J. BOYLAN (Sec.), J. MULLALLY, E. KANE, J. MAGUIRE, C. LYNAM H. H. MULLALLY, R. REILLY, J. REILLY, O. BUTLER.
P. REILLY, P. CLUSKER, J. McGOVERN, P. BYRNE, J. BOYLAN (Capt.), N. MORAN, J. MURPHY, M. KELLY, P. MULLALLY (Treas.),
P. LEE, N. F. DUNICAN, W. McGOVERN, M. BRADY.

[38 St. Thomas's Terrace, S.C.R.

5. Dunboyne hurling team with Sean Boylan as captain (centre of middle row). Several others mentioned in this book are also included.

6. Dunshaughlin Board of Guardians, 1922

(L to R): Fred Morris, Margaret Murray, Bart Fitzsimons, Michael Reid, David Hall, William Doran

7. British troops in Athboy, 1920

8. Séamus Cogan

9. Bobby Byrne

10. Pat Fitzsimons

11. Willie Coogan at the time of his service with the Free State army in Cork during the Civil War.

12. Sean MacNaMidhe

13. Francis Ledwidge

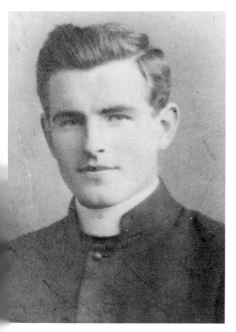

4. Patrick McDonnell

15. Michael Duffy

Trim, September 1920

17–19. Trim, September 1920

display of contempt for those inside whom they regarded as informers.

After a court martial in Beggar's Bush, presided over by Crozier himself, all twenty-six were dismissed from the force. Later that day, General Tudor, the head of the RIC, gave his approval for this action. The exact events of the next couple of weeks are not very clear but it is certain that the dismissed men began to exert pressure first on Dublin Castle and then in London by, it seems, threatening the authorities that unless they were reinstated they would publicly reveal the truth about the reprisals with which they were synonymous.

By 17 February both General Tudor and Dublin Castle were asking Crozier to reinstate the men but he refused stating that they "were unsuitable for our requirements because the police oath bound them to prevent and detect crime which they were not doing". As for political interference he "did not care tuppence about cabinets, political parties and Prime Ministers if they interfered with my command." Others were not of such high principles and, while Crozier was on a few days' leave in Wales, most of the dismissed men were taken back into the Auxiliaries and returned to Ireland. Crozier resigned at once and in his letter to General Tudor gave as his reason that he was:

> all out to have discipline unquestionable ... I consider that theft on the part of policemen in the course of their duty is unpardonable and I cannot honestly associate myself with a force in which such acts are condoned.

The whole episode must have had a sobering effect on the Brigadier-General for, in the course of his somewhat garbled memoirs, certain sympathy towards Irish nationalism is occasionally interspersed amongst his fanatical imperialism.

But the 'Trim incident', as it soon became known, did not end with the reinstatement of the men. The matter was raised on several occasions in the House of Commons, and it was probably to appease public and international opinion that a police inquiry and arising out of this, a public trial, was held. Regarding the former, Crozier wrote that:

> I returned to Dublin, after I had resigned, at the request of the

Chief Secretary, in order to help to solve the Trim question. The
inquiry which was held by the police was a pure farce. The Court
Martial Department of GHQ told them so and told me so also.

The trial, referred to earlier, was equally farcical. This began on 28 May
in the City Hall, Dublin and for its duration it received front page
coverage every day in the *Evening Herald*.

There were actually two trials, the first dealing with the events of
the afternoon of 9 February, and the other with the occurrences of that
night. In the first trial the court heard evidence from Mrs Chandler, the
schoolmistress whose house had been broken into and clothing taken,
and a number of Auxiliaries who described how the booty, including
hens and ducks, was divided up that evening in Trim. This was countered
by the defence, both counsel and accused, in an amazing series of bland
denials. They had never been near Chandler's house at all, just searching
some buildings at the back; this search had lasted only ten minutes;
they had not got to Trim until after four o'clock because they had gone
astray. When, in answer to this, prosecution pointed out that local RIC
men were with them, no explanation was forthcoming. There had been
no drinking or looting whatever. A bag, said by one of the witnesses
to contain stolen clothing, was actually used to carry ammunition for
machine guns; and the hens and ducks had been bought at a private
house on the way back to the town.

Whether the judge was impressed by this stonewalling or whether
the whole thing really had been 'fixed' beforehand will never be known,
but of the eighteen originally indicted on charges of conspiracy and
stealing money, goods and chattels, not one was found guilty. In fact,
even before the trial began charges against five of them were dropped. In
the case of another one it was ruled that there was no evidence against
him; and the other twelve were found not guilty of all the charges
against them.

The second trial followed a similar pattern. Nine men, these included
four just acquitted in the first trial, were charged with four counts of
robbery, larceny and receiving. Prosecution counsel, Mrs Chandler and
a couple of sympathetic Auxiliaries recounted the happenings of the
night in question. A defence witness stated that after ammunition had

been found in the house that afternoon it had been decided to send back a few men to make a more thorough search. This time the accused even surpassed their colleagues of the earlier trial in the extent of their outrageous statements: the sugar had been bought that day from one of the biggest firms in Dublin; any drink, referred to euphemistically as "refreshments", given to them that night had been offered free by the man of the house (presumably Richard Chandler) even though they had tried to pay him two pounds at the bar; two of the accused insisted that there had been no looting or stealing, one of them maintaining that he was "dead against that sort of thing" and adding that he would be the "first to put the man who would do it under immediate arrest."

It was at this point, on 7 June, that newspaper coverage of the trial ceased. The case was clearly drawing to a close but the final sessions were not reported nor was a verdict recorded in the press. There is little doubt but that the authorities censored reporting of the case which was a very sensitive one. The first trial had been clearly a whitewash and already two of the defendants in this second trial had been acquitted. A similar verdict passed on the other seven would have stretched public credibility. Although Crozier at one point states that five of the accused served prison sentences, it can be taken for granted that the sentences were fairly light and that their colleagues got away scot free.

Shortly after midnight on the morning of 18 February two men forced their way into the home of Bernard O'Brien, a publican, of Academy Street in Navan. They entered his bedroom and, as O'Brien later told a newspaper reporter, he was in fear of his life. But he was lucky because all they wanted from him was a small piece of information: where exactly on the street did the Navan postmaster, Thomas Hodgett, live? Having obtained this information the intruders left. This was the prelude to one of the most disturbing and tragic episodes in Meath in these years and it reflected a nationwide trend as civilians were becoming inexorably drawn into the violence.

The two men, having left O'Brien's, made their way to Hodgetts just a few doors away. Mrs Hodgett later recalled being woken by a loud knocking on the door and voices shouting that they were the police and demanding entry. When she opened up two men burst past her into the house and ordered her to fetch her husband. The men spoke in a language which she could only describe as "gibberish" and which certainly was not Irish, although she suspected that they may have been trying to give the impression that it was. Furthermore they spoke in what she considered to be assumed Irish accents. Amidst all this confusion one thing she could make out was that by now they were claiming to be Sinn Féiners and that they "would show what Sinn Féin could do." When Mr Hodgett came down to the hallway the two men ordered him to get dressed. What followed must have been a pathetic scene: Hodgett had suffered a stroke of paralysis just a short time before and one side of him was helpless. His wife had to help him dress but before this was completed the two thugs dragged him away, minus one sock and with one boot unlaced.

Thomas Hodgett was never seen alive again; a short time later that night a number of residents in Watergate Street heard a single shot, and on the following morning large pools of blood were to be seen on the Blackwater Bridge at the bottom of Flowerhill. For a few days afterwards, the rivers Boyne and Blackwater were dragged but to no avail. It was not until 25 March, it was, ironically, Good Friday, that the body was recovered from the Boyne having been spotted by anglers. That it was the postmaster was in no doubt: the body was dressed exactly as when his wife had last seen him with one boot unlaced and without one stocking. There was evidence of just one bullet wound. The town witnessed a huge funeral on Easter Sunday and, said a *Meath Chronicle* report of 2 April, 1921, "there was scarcely a home in the town but had one or more members present."

Who murdered Thomas Hodgett? No one was ever convicted of the murder or even charged with the crime but certain conclusions may be drawn. Two things should first be pointed out about the postmaster. Firstly, as emphasised at the time, he took no part whatever in politics; and secondly, his background, which may be of some significance, was that of a Protestant and almost certainly Unionist from Dungannon, county Tyrone. Given this background then and even given the fact that sectarian attacks on Protestant Unionists or their property, as in the case of Summerhill House, were not unknown in southern Ireland at this time, then the theory may be considered that Hodgett was the victim of a blackguardly murder plot by local Volunteers. But this notion may be discounted and for a number of reasons.

Local men would hardly have found it necessary to break into another man's house to find out the residence of the postmaster, who had been living there for four years. Then there is the testimony of Mrs Hodgett that the trespassers spoke with assumed Irish accents and that they continually stressed that they were Sinn Féiners. Such actions and vehement protestations leave one with the impression of men trying to make Sinn Féin the scapegoat for their deed. Finally, and arising out of the last point, is Mrs Hodgett's statement to a local reporter that she was certain that the Volunteers had nothing to do with the matter. Of course, none of this represents conclusive evidence against Volunteer complicity but over sixty years later the best that can be obtained are strong indications and hints.

Let us examine the evidence that implicates the crown forces in the town, and specifically the Black and Tans. Remember that crimes such as this one, the midnight dragging of men from their beds followed by beatings and murders, were by now the hallmarks of the Black and Tans. Those familiar with the town, such as the local RIC, would hardly have needed to break into O'Brien's house to inquire as to the whereabouts of his neighbour. Also, if, as is almost certain, the blood on the Blackwater Bridge was that of the postmaster, then another point may be made. To reach the bridge from Academy Street the two men would have had to take their captive up Ludlow Street, through the Market Square and down Watergate Street. This they almost certainly did as Bobby Byrne recalled that on the night in question his mother was awakened by some shouting and, looking out the window in the darkness, she could just make out a man being dragged by two others at the top of Ludlow Street. This route brought the abductors right through the centre of the town and, remarkably, past the RIC barracks, (later the Garda station), in Watergate Street, just about a hundred yards from the bridge: hardly a route that would be chosen by a Volunteer murder gang, however reckless. Again there is no definitive proof here but some clear pointers.

What about a motive for the murder? On the Volunteer side we have seen that Hodgett's background could just possibly have made him the victim of a mindless sectarian murder. But, as we have also seen,

Mrs Hodgett certainly did not think so, and in April she elaborated on the matter. The *Meath Chronicle* reported on 9 April, 1921, that an article in the *Irish Independent* had commented that the murder of the postmaster in Navan had been due "to his friendly relations with police or military authorities". Mrs Grace Hodgett wrote to the newspaper bluntly refuting this and stating that her late husband, on more than one occasion, had reported police for robbery at a sub-post office and, although he had given evidence to the authorities in this matter, nothing had been done about it. Similarly, most of those veterans spoken to in researching this account had vague memories of this episode having sprung from friction between the postmaster and the police. These vague remembrances were crystallised on seeing a statement to the Bureau of Military History, the author of which indicated that he would prefer to remain anonymous.

This man, who was certainly in a position to know what was going on, stated that by early 1921 the Navan Company of Volunteers had made a contact inside the post office and that much valuable information concerning police and military intentions was being passed on to them by him. It seems that, to find and counteract this source, the Head Constable in Navan whose name was Queenan, tried to get his daughter a position in the post office but that Mr Hodgett refused on the grounds that it was not being done through the proper channels. This, the source thought, may have been the immediate cause for the murder, although there is absolutely no suggestion or implication here that it was carried out by the Head Constable or even on his orders. Séamus Finn stated that intelligence work soon ascertained the identity of the two killers, who were earmarked for execution and were saved only by the calling of the truce in July.

Meanwhile, back in north Meath the Fifth Battalion men were running into more difficulties in trying to carry out their plans. Towards the end of January, remembered Charlie Conaty:

> a few of us met in a house near Virginia Road railway station. Those present included Pat Farrelly, David Smith, Peter O'Connell, Tom and Patrick McDonnell, Mick Wynne, myself and three others. Here we arranged to try once again to attack

the RIC patrol in Oldcastle and decided to do so on the fair day early in February. Selected men from each company were to be asked to take part.

Peter O'Connell took the story from here:

> We had decided to carry out the attack from behind a stone wall on the road. We tried to get in touch with Tom Callan of Oldcastle Company but failed to contact him so we postponed our attack until the following night.

It was lucky for them that it was called off because the next day they were informed by Patrick McDonnell, the battalion's intelligence officer, according to Peter O'Connell, that:

> the RIC had actually taken up positions and lined the very walls from which we were to open the attack the night before. He told us that the RIC were waiting for us and knew of our intentions.

Once again the attack was postponed and Peter even recalled that:

> other ambushes were laid at Whitegate, Rathbrack, Maghera and other places, but they never materialised because the RIC always seemed to have foreknowledge of our plans.

Concerning this Seán Boylan was once again convinced "that the information was supplied from within the Volunteer organisation."

All these frustrations were put firmly aside on the night of Tuesday, 22 February, when the RIC were dealt the hardest blow struck at them in Meath in these years. Given the leakage of information which had foiled several planned ambushes, it was perhaps inevitable that it took an almost spontaneous action on the part of the Carnaross Company to achieve a successful strike at the police. This happened at Dervor Hill, just south of the village of Carnaross, on the Kells to Virginia road. Jack Lynch recalled:

That evening Matty Smith, our company captain, heard that a lorry load of police and Tans had passed through the area on the way to Virginia. There they raided a number of houses and a hall from which they took some musical instruments. Matty decided to try to ambush them on the way back but there was little time to get organised and only about twelve of us were present.

The men took up positions on both sides of the road and most of them were armed with shotguns. "There were nine or ten of them in the open lorry when they passed", recalled Jack,

> Five of them were wounded and one of these fell out of the lorry altogether. So did the band instruments which were scattered around the road. Later I met the driver of the lorry and he told me that his finger was shot off that night.

The police, apparently, made a feeble attempt at returning fire but made no attempt to stop and fight. This was probably on the orders of District Inspector Rowland whom the *Meath Chronicle* of 5 March later reported as having been "badly wounded in the back and in a critical condition in a Dublin hospital." The wounded policeman who fell out of the lorry made his way back to Kells without his cap, which for years afterwards was kept as a souvenir in the district. Jack Lynch continued:

> The following morning a few lorry loads of police and Tans came out from Kells and went straight to the homes of the Farrellys and Tevlins. They threatened to burn down these and other houses but our parish priest, Fr Kelly, appealed to the police officers whom he was friendly with and this stopped it. After Dervor nearly the whole company was on the run. Mostly we stayed in disused farmhouses where we piled up hay on the floor. Some of the women in the Cumann na mBan would bring us food. It was just as well they did because I remember once that a few of us killed and cooked a chicken but forgot to clean it out so it wasn't very nice to eat!

Jack and the others had some narrow escapes over the next couple of months but mostly they felt safe. He remembered that a farmhouse in Maperath, where they stayed a lot of the time, was beside a small rise in the ground called Leddy's Hill and from this at night time they could look across towards Kells and the lights of military or police lorries could be spotted from the very moment that they left the barracks and the whole way out towards Carnaross, thus giving them plenty of advance warning of raids by the authorities.

Elsewhere there is little to report for the month of February apart from the continuance of police raids, arrests and trials. In one of these trials three Stapleton brothers from the Commons, Navan were charged with possession of firearms, explosives and ammunition alleged to have been discovered hidden in a haystack beside their house. Daniel and Thomas were sentenced to eighteen months and Val to a year, all with hard labour. Val was certainly a Volunteer in the Commons Company which was led by another brother Paddy, who was soon to become a Battalion Vice-Commandant. Also that month a second trial deprived the already much depleted Navan company of yet another of its officers, when Eugene O'Gorman, its intelligence officer, was given eighteen months hard labour on a charge similar to that on which the Stapletons had been indicted. Richard O'Gorman, his brother, suffered a similar fate. Both men worked as bootmakers on Brews Hill and the court was told that a search of their house had unearthed two revolvers, two hundred rounds of ammunition and three sticks of explosives. The brothers refused to recognise the court and Eugene alleged that the police had planted the evidence during the search. Also imprisoned in this month was Paddy Giles, the leading figure in the Longwood Company, who had been arrested in the aftermath of the attack on the police barracks there in January and was now given one year with hard labour.

On the first day of March, the body of a man was found on a lane in the Beechmount area on the outskirts of Navan. The body was never identified and the remains of the stranger were interred in the graveyard adjoining Navan workhouse. This was a bleak ending to a young life for, to paraphrase the *Meath Chronicle* report of 5 March 1921 on the incident, the man had been brutally murdered, shot in the face and chest, and his body was found lying in a pool of blood. At the time, the *Drogheda Independent* of 5 March assured its readers that "many who have examined all the circumstances are of the opinion that the occurrence is not one of a political nature." If, presumably, the writer meant that the killing was not in any way connected with the Troubles in the county, then he was mistaken, for the body discovered at Beechmount represents the first known execution of a spy in Meath in these years.

As stated earlier this whole area of spies, informers and such like is a very shadowy domain, peopled with seedy characters and full of distasteful incidents. It is also a very sensitive area since many of those warned off or punished or even executed, whether with any justification or not, as spies or informers probably still have relations living in the county. For this reason it is not intended to print any names to avoid embarrassment and pain. However, to ignore completely this aspect of the Troubles would be most unrealistic since, in the last few months leading up to the July Truce, it formed an integral, if exaggerated, part of the unrest in Meath.

Broadly speaking three distinct groups may be made of the people involved in the traffic of illicit information. The first is made up of those Volunteers who passed on information to the police regarding forthcoming operations by their companies or battalions. That such existed there can be no doubt. We have seen how Seán Boylan has stated on at least three occasions that information given to the authorities from "within the ranks" reduced well planned ambushes to non-events. This happened twice (at least) in Navan and twice (at least) in the Fifth Battalion area between Kells and Oldcastle. Several of the veterans spoken to were of the same conviction as Boylan. We have also seen that Seán Boylan was so certain of his ground that, in his statement to the Military History Bureau, he actually named the man, a prominent figure in the Volunteer structure, who jettisoned the Navan plans by allegedly refusing to pass on ammunition on the chosen night. Boylan went further and stated that he had a suspicion that this man, as well as his father, who had worked in the service of the British administration, "were in constant touch with the RIC." Furthermore, he continued:

these suspicions were later proved correct by a letter I received from an RIC constable named McGarrity who was stationed in Navan for some years prior to the Truce. It shows, if true, that [---] was being paid by the RIC for information supplied during the pre-Truce period.

The letter which followed gave a list of those purportedly selling information to the police at the time and the man in question is mentioned three times in the course of this. While this may sound conclusive evidence it is only fair to point out that the 'suspect', if he was a police informer, must have been an excellent actor who sustained the performance of his role over a protracted period, for in the years both before and after the Troubles, he made a large contribution not only to the political but also to the cultural life of the county. One other point suggested by a few of those spoken to is worthy of consideration, namely, that the giving away of information in Navan, Oldcastle and elsewhere may have been inspired by a desire on the part of some Volunteers to avoid in their localities the terrible reprisals, such as those inflicted on Trim, which could well have resulted from heavy attacks on police and military. Naturally, such a course of action, from the point of view of military discipline, could not possibly be condoned but it may explain why men of apparently impeccable republican credentials may have found themselves double-dealing with the police to ensure the safety of their community.

The second category may now be considered, although, in the case of the people involved here, the term 'spy' is much too grandiose a word to describe the prying of those who were nothing more than village gossips seeking to use the exigencies of the times as a means of converting their snooping activities into petty financial gain. In the letter, mentioned above, which Seán Boylan received from the ex-police constable, some of those allegedly in the pay of the police are named. Most were from the Navan area, but this was only natural since Boylan's contact had been based there, but there were also names from Slane, Oldcastle and Trim. The names were followed by brief comments ranging from "fairly well paid", "gave useful information" and "a good fellow" to "not much money, information not much use" and "badly paid – just a few shillings." Those identified as informers ranged from post office and bank clerks to publicans and housewives. It can be taken for granted that practically every part of the county, and not just the areas mentioned, had its police informants. It is also certain, in the case of the majority, that what they were selling was of little or no value. Peter O'Connell recalled that there were some of these people in his own area of Carnaross and Stonefield:

> We strongly suspected or knew for definite who they were but most of them had useless or wrong information. Few of our company were ever arrested on their word although a few of the Sinn Féin people were. Occasionally we might warn them but most of the time we just ignored them because they were harmless.

Not so harmless were those men comprising the third category. These were perceived by the Volunteer movement as the real spies and, as a consequence of this, most of them paid with their lives. The fact that some others did not was not in any way due to a lack of intent or effort on the part of those sent out to execute them. From the reading of contemporary local newspaper reports and from conversations with veterans of the war, it has been possible to identify nine cases, eight of them civilians and the other a British army officer. Of these, six were killed and the other three were lucky to escape with their lives. As regards these nine cases seven of them were reported in the local newspapers and the other two were related by those spoken to. At the time, of course, the local press never once stated that the murderous assaults were in any way connected with a campaign against spies and informers. But doubtless most readers were alerted to this fact when they saw a victim of such an attack described as an "ex-soldier"; at least six of the men fitted this description. Being a former member of the British Army was, as the Troubles reached a sordid climax, a dangerous thing, although it must be pointed out that within the ranks of the Meath Volunteers were men who had seen service on the British side during World War I.

The first case, and certainly the strangest, has already been touched on at the outset of this section. If the unknown man, whose body was discovered at Beechmount on 1 March was indeed a spy, then he was certainly notoriously inefficient at his work and his eccentric behaviour in the course of the previous day was designed to attract, rather than to deflect, attention to him. Both local newspapers are agreed on this point, as reported to them by residents of the town. The *Drogheda Independent* of 5 March 1921 noted that the stranger, "a young well-built man rather shabbily dressed", had arrived in the town that morning and "by his demeanour and irrational statements had attracted considerable attention." At one stage during the day he wandered out the Trim Road where he called on several houses asking for food and at various times he passed himself off as a dismissed Black and Tan, a Sinn Féiner and as a man just out of prison. One person claimed that he carried a small automatic pistol while others testified that there were two tattoos on his chest, one inscribed 'HMS Victory' and the other 'Ireland Forever'.

One source, who preferred to remain anonymous, recalled that the man entered a pub in the town and let it be known that he wished to meet the local Volunteer leaders. It seems that in the course of the afternoon he was sent from one Volunteer to another, all of them keeping him engaged in conversation. That evening he was brought to the Banba Hall, the meeting place of the town's Sinn Féin club, on the Fair Green where he was questioned. Under pressure, apparently, he gave his name as Michael O'Brien from Tipperary, but later lapsed into a Scottish accent. He also stated that in prison he had met Dick Chandler and that Chandler had told him to get in touch with Seán Boylan on his release. After further questioning the stranger was taken out to Beechmount where he was executed, his body being found early the next morning. This whole episode will forever remain as much a mystery as the identity of the central figure in it.

The next two cases followed closely on each other. Early in the morning of Sunday, 27 March, a labourer who lived alone in a cottage in Kilberry heard shouting outside his home. When he went out, he later recounted, he was shot several times in the stomach and was battered on the head with the butt end of a revolver. Miraculously, he managed to crawl back to his cottage and into bed where later that morning his sister found him in a critical condition. Nearby was found a piece of paper with the words, 'convicted spy; let informers beware'. Amazingly, the man survived but within a month his cottage was burned to the ground. On Sunday, 10 April, a middle-aged man was the target of a vicious attack by two men near the railway bridge on the Trim Road, Navan. The man alleged that he had been assaulted with a razor which inflicted three severe wounds on his throat; fortunately for him he also survived. In both these cases the men on the receiving end were ex-British soldiers.

On 26 May, a man fishing in the Blackwater River at Newgate, about a mile outside Navan on the Kells Road, noticed a body in the water. On investigation he found that the hands were bound around the neck, wire was fastened around the waist and a handkerchief was tied over the mouth and chin. An inquest later concluded that death was due to strangulation. It was soon obvious that the dead man was Sergeant Harrod, a thirty-three year old officer of the South Wales Borderers, who had been missing for ten days. The *Meath Chronicle* of 4 June, 1921 reported that "he had left the military quarters in Navan on the previous Monday week and had last been seen walking towards Ardbraccan." It seems that his reason for going out here was that he was courting a servant girl employed in the big house of John Law, the strongly pro-British councillor mentioned in the previous chapter. "But he was collecting information as well", a source stated:

> There were a couple of Volunteers on the run and they were hiding out in some old sheds around there. The soldier was always snooping around and we warned him not to come back but he still did.

Whether or not it is correct to classify Sergeant Harrod as a spy is open to question but it is interesting to note that he was the one and only British soldier to be killed in Meath during these years. It is also worth pointing out here that most of those old IRA men spoken to bore no malice whatever to the military, which was in marked contrast to their attitude to the RIC and their cohorts in the Black and Tans and Auxiliaries. Indeed at the time of his arrest in October 1920, Paddy Lalor requested that he be brought to Navan by the military rather than the police since he was in fear of being beaten up but this request was refused, while Peter O'Connell recalled being searched on many occasions by the military who were always pleasant and well-mannered towards him and his fellow Volunteers.

The next two instances followed on successive nights in June and again both men involved were former British soldiers. On the night of 12 June a gardener from Warrenstown, Dunsany, was taken forcibly from his home. His two abductors obviously had murder in their hearts since they told him they were giving him a couple of minutes to say his prayers; but the gardener, according to the *Chronicle* report of 18 June, 1921, managed to evade his captors and after a short struggle hid himself safely in a ditch. Not so lucky on the following night, and just a few miles away in Ratoath, was a twenty-one year old man who had been demobilised from the British Army just six months before. The man had served in France with the Dublin Fusiliers and had twice been wounded during the Great War. On the fatal night he was taken from his home, his distraught father was assured that he would be soon brought back; he was, but not alive. Tom Manning had good reason to recall that night because, earlier on, the intended victim had been in his house in Kilbride. Glad of the chance to put the matter on the record Tom concluded:

> He was a nice young lad but he was definitely giving information to the police. He had been seen sneaking in and out of the barracks in Dunshaughlin on many occasions and several times he had been warned. He used to come down to our house on the pretence of being sociable and he would stay late playing the fiddle. But we always suspected that he was trying to pick up information since our house was the centre for the Kilbride Volunteers. He was even in the house earlier on the night he was killed and because of that I was suspected and blamed for it. A couple of nights later I was stopped by some Black and Tans who wanted to question me about the matter. But it was dark and since I was near home and knew the country inside out I decided to make a break for it and lucky enough I got away. I had no part at all in the killing in Ratoath.

On 5 July another body was fished out of a river, this time the Boyne, at Trubley, Kilmessan. It was a surprise that it ever surfaced as it was weighed down by two axles. One wound in the back of the head told the story of the killing. There was little problem with identification since a local man, again an ex-army man who had fought at Gallipoli in 1915, had been missing for the previous week and doubtless his family had resigned themselves to the worst.

This leaves the two cases which went unreported in the newspapers at the time, probably for the simple reason that the bodies were never recovered. First there was the case of 'The Thatcher', an anonymous figure who has passed into the folk memory in the Bohermeen and Rathmore areas. Patsy Bennett had some memories of the case:

> He was a roof thatcher working in the Rathmore area. I don't think he was a local man. But I heard that during his work he used to be picking up bits and pieces of information and going to the police in Athboy at night. Some of the companies in the Athboy area dealt with him and he was buried in Bohermeen bog.

Finally, there was the spy who, in the last few months of the Troubles, was giving information which was making life positively uneasy for the Volunteers in the north of the county. Peter O'Connell remembered it this way:

> There was great military activity in the month of May. All prominent Volunteers' homes were being raided. It was evident that the enemy had several agents in the district at the time. We got two very important letters from a young man named Jack Tuite, a post office clerk at Kells. They were directed to the authorities and had been sent from the Virginia Road or Stonefield district. The letters contained the names of all Volunteers in the Stonefield and Whitegate areas.

Peter recalled that a man was arrested, tried and executed in the Carnaross area and then buried somewhere in Moynalty. He was yet another ex-soldier.

All of this may make unpleasant reading or even upset some people's romantic notions that nothing so underhand or unsavoury was indulged in by the Volunteers in the old days. But in every war, the democratic niceties of legal procedure are hastily put aside so that one must stop to ask: did these men get a fair trial? Were they really guilty? Were their executions justified? Those veterans with whom this matter was discussed all gave positive answers to these questions and the comments of Séamus Finn on the matter are worth noting. Finn says that:

> these were the hardest operations that our men were asked to carry out ... the men who did so can feel sure that their efforts saved the lives and liberty of many of their comrades.

In this respect it is important to state that, for obvious reasons, those who carried out the executions were usually drawn from a different company area than where their intended victim resided. As regards the crucial matter of evidence, Finn has this to say:

> A careful watch was kept on the movements of these people and in some cases they were actually seen to contact the enemy; raids were made on the mails; certain sources of information were tapped in an effort to get complete evidence in each case ... our agents in the post office were very helpful in this respect ... not until the evidence was very clear did the men act ... in all cases confirmation was received from GHQ before each sentence.

To emphasise this point, Finn concludes that:

> twelve others who were under strong suspicion continued to live principally because of the lack of conclusive evidence against them ... those who escaped can owe their luck to the fact that we were very scrupulous and conscientious in this matter.

Despite all this one is still left with the disturbing thought of the disproportionate nature of the statistics. Between 1919 and 1921 in the county six men, and there may have been more, were executed as spies as against three Volunteers dead, one an accident; three police dead, again one an accident; and no military fatalities, if it is accepted that Sergeant Harrod was killed for spying activities. Taking into account everything that has been revealed in this chapter one is left with the impression that if some Volunteer companies had devoted as much energy and time to harassing enemy forces as they did towards rooting out and executing spies, real or imagined, then they might have taken a lot of the pressure off some of their overworked colleagues elsewhere in the county.

Returning to the events of March, on the twenty-third of that month Patrick McDonnell became the second and final Volunteer to be killed in action in Meath. McDonnell has been seen as intelligence officer of the Fifth Battalion. Peter O'Connell remembered that on the day before his death McDonnell had warned that the police were about to launch a round-up in the Stonefield and Ballinlough areas. Ironically, it was his own house that was raided. McDonnell tried to escape by running out the back door and down through the fields but a police constable shot him in the back. "He nearly made it to the bottom of the field", said Peter O'Connell, "maybe if he had fallen on the ground and rolled along the grass until he reached the hedge then he might have been saved." Aged twenty-six, McDonnell was a former clerical student who had returned home when Maynooth College, in common with most other colleges, had closed down during the conscription crisis in 1918. He was buried with military honours in the republican plot in Ballinlough graveyard beside Séamus Cogan. The two men had belonged to the same company, Stonefield, and today they are commemorated by a stone monument standing in the centre of Oldcastle, close to the spot where Cogan was killed.

In its issue of 24 March the *Meath Chronicle* reported that a concerted action saw twenty-four bridges in various parts of the county either totally demolished or considerably damaged. Not surprisingly then April began with a proclamation issued from Dublin Castle banning fairs, markets and all public assemblies in Meath. The reason given for this was the refusal of Meath County Council to carry out repairs on the roads and bridges. Only the police districts of Oldcastle and Duleek were exempt from this order, which also covered dances and football matches. The first casualty of the restrictions was a Feis Cup tournament game between Martry and Navan Gaels scheduled for the Navan Showgrounds. This ban on assembly was to stay in force until the Truce.

Race meetings must not have been affected by the proclamation because, on Thursday, 7 April, the Meath Hunt Steeplechase went ahead as arranged at the old race course at Boyerstown, a few miles outside Navan. The fine evening and the relaxed atmosphere was broken just before the fourth race when a single shot rang out and struck a police sergeant standing on duty in front of the grandstand. A mild panic ensued as the *Drogheda Independent* of 16 April 1921 reported that:

> people ran blindly, hucksters' baskets were overturned and fruit scattered around ... bookies forgot to lay their odds but took shelter instead behind their seats ... several ladies fainted.

The officer who was wounded, although not seriously, was Sergeant Johns who, as a constable, had also been wounded at Ashbourne during Easter Week, 1916. In fairness to him it must be stated that he ordered the RIC men under his control in Boyerstown not to shoot back for fear of injuring anyone. Patsy Bennett was not directly involved in this attack, although it was men from his own Commons Company who carried it out. He said:

> Johns wasn't the man they were after but a policeman by the name of Martin, who was bad news in the town but wasn't on duty that day after all. When the men got out of the race course they threw the rifle into a ditch and a gun was thrown into a field that was being ploughed and was quickly covered with soil.

No-one was arrested that day but soon afterwards the man who fired the shot was picked up by the police. This man was an ex-soldier, decorated for his bravery in the First World War, but this fact was of no benefit to him in June when, on a charge of firing at a police constable, he was given fifteen years penal servitude, by far the toughest sentence meted out to a Meath man in these years. Before this, that unenviable distinction belonged to two brothers, Frank and John Carolan of Brownstown, Dunboyne, on a charge of having arms and ammunition not under effective military control. Both men were sentenced on 13 April to three years penal servitude. Remember that on a similar charge in January, Lord Dunsany had got away with a fine of £25. The two brothers were Volunteers with Frank holding the position of Vice-Commandant of the First (Dunboyne) Battalion.

The short supply of arms and ammunition remained a problem, although by this stage the companies of the Fifth Battalion were reasonably well off in this respect. Peter O'Connell recalled that by March they had about forty shotguns, five rifles, five revolvers, a quantity of cartridges and two home-made cement mines. But a cause of concern was that some of this material was becoming ineffective due to damp. Peter said:

> As well as that the shotguns were often neglected and were not kept in working order. This could not be attributed to any fault of the men, as guns and cartridges could not be stored in any man's house at the time. Our own company entrusted them to an aged man named Pat Wynne, who stored them in quantities of corn kiln-dried mill seed which proved very satisfactory. Wynne had been a Fenian and was a most careful man ... but it was decided to launch an attack on enemy forces while we still had some serviceable ammunition and explosives left.

This decision was taken at a battalion council meeting held at Farrelly's of Cloonagrouna, Carnaross, on 27 March. The ambush was fixed for Sylvan Park near Crossakiel on the Kells to Oldcastle road.

"Our intention", said Charlie Conaty, "was to attack a patrol lorry of military who travelled the road fairly regularly." The place picked had a wall running along the road and the ground behind this wall was six feet higher than the road. April the first, a Friday, was the date fixed for the attack and on the night before the men began to gather, coming in twos and threes to a disused house close to the ambush site. There were over forty Volunteers in all involved in this drawn from the companies in Carnaross, Ballinlough, Stonefield and Whitegate. Although Séamus

Finn, the Brigade Adjutant, was present, it was David Smith, the Battalion Commandant, who was in charge of the operation. Other officers also there included Matt and Phil Tevlin, John Keogh (the former Battalion O/C who had been arrested in October but had since been released), Mick Wynne as well as both Charlie Conaty and Peter O'Connell.

The first part of the plan involved planting two land mines in the centre of the road at the ambush position. "On the evening previous to the attack," recalled Peter,

> David Smith and I instructed Ben Daly to fill a donkey cart with turf, place the mines in the centre and take them to an arranged spot convenient to the ambush site. We also instructed a number of Volunteers, including my younger brother, Thomas, to proceed to Sylvan Park early that evening to sink the mines.

By seven o'clock the next morning this work, under the direction of Matt Tevlin, was successfully completed. Now the second stage of the plan came into operation as the ambush party took up their positions. According to Charlie Conaty:

> Tom Mulvany, Pat Dunne, Ned Connors and myself, armed with rifles, were allocated a position at the entrance gate to Sylvan Park House, which was on the left-hand side of the road from Kells to Oldcastle. The shotgun men – thirty to thirty-five – were placed in extended formation above and below the land-mines on the left-hand side also. John Keogh, Pat Tobin and Harry Lee, armed with rifles, were placed away on the right-hand side at least a hundred and fifty yards nearer Oldcastle.

Also on this side were Matt Tevlin and Pat Conway who were in charge of the two exploders for the land mines, the leads of which extended to behind the ditch where the three riflemen were positioned.

Peter O'Connell continued:

> We were now all ready when an old man who lived locally came

out to have a look around. We took him to the yard of Sylvan Park House leaving two Volunteers to guard over him. Later two other persons were taken to the yard also. A postman, with his horse and van, was next to arrive. He also was taken to the yard with his horse, van and mails. We let others pass through who did not appear to have observed anything unusual. Some men passed through driving cattle. Other men on their way to work were also taken to the yard. As the crowd in the yard increased we had to increase the guard over them.

As the day passed, however, there was no sign of the military lorry which had been expected to pass at about ten o'clock that morning. At about three in the afternoon, and after a consultation amongst the officers, the despondent Volunteers decided to lift the mines, withdraw and wait for another day. It was typical of their luck then that, just as soon as the mines had been lifted, as Charlie Conaty remembered, "a signal was transmitted from Drumbaragh Hill via the Ballalley Crossroads that the lorry was coming." For obvious reasons the carefully laid plans were now thrown into disarray. Said Peter O'Connell:

> The shotgun and riflemen in position, seeing that we were about to withdraw were not sufficiently on the alert. Most of them lay into their positions. A Crossley Tender containing about ten RIC and Tans drove into the ambuscade. Three of the ambush party on the alert opened fire. They included a couple of the riflemen. The police and Tans dropped to the floor of the tender and returned the fire. The tender continued on its way going strong. One Tan got a bullet through the body. None of our men was wounded.

This was not the military lorry which had been expected. "It so happened", said Charlie Conaty,

> that the wife of the postmaster at Crossakiel had gone into the Kells Post Office and then to the barracks to report that the postman with the pony, sidecar and mails had not arrived at Crossakiel

Post Office that morning and was missing. The Tans and RIC had come out in the lorry which we attacked, to trace him.

In the weeks after this there were widespread police and military raids and swoops in the battalion area. About ten Volunteers were arrested and many others had to go on the run. Charlie Conaty and Mick Wynne had a lucky escape one day when a large consignment of crown forces appeared at Virginia Road railway station but the two men managed to bluff their way out of questioning. Most of the arrested men were taken to Kells where they were placed in cells. While in these, Peter O'Connell recalled, someone had a look through the spy holes to see if he could identify any of the prisoners. This man, yet another of the seemingly ever-present informers, was probably, according to Peter, one of the men detained on the morning of the ambush.

The Sylvan Park ambush happened on 1 April but the officers and men of the Fifth Battalion could be forgiven for thinking that it was they who had been fooled as sheer bad luck played yet another trick on them.

In late March or early April, Seán Boylan was asked to report to Barry's Hotel in Dublin where he met with some of the Volunteers headquarters staff including Michael Collins and Richard Mulcahy. Here he was shown a map of Ireland marked in sections, and he was told that:

> all brigades in the country were being divided into divisions and that I had been appointed O/C of the First Eastern Divison, which comprised counties Meath and Kildare, north Offaly, south Louth, east Cavan and part of Westmeath.

Meath was to be the nucleus of the new division which was to replace the old structures that had existed for the previous three to four years. It is worth recalling this older set-up had been hastily established at the furtive meeting in Dunderry which had used an aeríocht as cover. It had been decided then that Meath, plus a small part of Westmeath around Delvin, should make up the area of the Brigade, which was divided into six battalions centred on Dunboyne, Trim, Athboy, Kells, Oldcastle and Navan. This had remained unchanged until now although many more companies had been formed in the intervening years. It is difficult to pinpoint exactly where such companies were set up. "Few records were kept at that time", Mick Hilliard stated, "so that the location of companies exist only in the minds of those who were alive at that time and can remember." However, from picking the brains of Mick Hilliard and other veterans of the war, a fairly comprehensive picture can be obtained.

The companies that were already in existence at the time of the Dunderry gathering have been listed earlier. By 1921 the following could be added: to the First Dunboyne Battalion: Ratoath, Dunshaughlin, Curraha, Skryne, Rathfeigh, Kilmoon and Ashbourne; to the Second Trim Battalion: Kilmessan, Kiltale, and Rathmolyon; to the Fourth Kells Battalion: Carlanstown and Nobber; to the Fifth Oldcastle Battalion: Whitegate; to the Sixth Navan Battalion: Kentstown, Dunmoe, Rath-kenny, Castletown and Martry. In regard to the Third Athboy Battalion, it has not been possible to discover the existence of extra companies although it is almost certain that there were some. Adding the new to the old this gives a total of fifty two known companies within the Brigade area by April 1921. Excluding Delvin and Archerstown, this would leave fifty in the actual county of Meath. But as stated already there were probably a few more.

The term 'Irish Republican Army', or 'IRA', had by this time long been in use, although the word 'Volunteers', which has been employed throughout this account, continued in usage, as did its Irish version, 'Óglaigh na hÉireann' (and occasionally, 'Arm Phoblacht na hÉireann', Irish for 'IRA'). It was now Seán Boylan's task to rearrange all the Meath companies, as well as numerous others in the other counties under his jurisdiction, into a structure of battalions and brigades that would comprise the First Eastern Division of the Irish Republican Army. He also had to appoint staff officers at every level.

Initially, Boylan organised the divisional area into nine brigades as follows:

(a) First Brigade: took in all of the First Battalion, old Meath Brigade area, and north Kildare – headquarters in Dunboyne.
(b) Second Brigade: comprised the old Second and Sixth Battalions – headquarters in Navan.

IRA Companies, 1919-21.

(c) Third Brigade: made up of the old Fourth and Fifth Battalions, as well as East Cavan – headquarters in Kells.

(d) Fourth Brigade: the old Third Battalion and the adjoining area in Westmeath – headquarters in Delvin.

(e) Fifth Brigade: most of the rest of Westmeath – headquarters in Mullingar.

(f) Sixth Brigade: North Offaly – headquarters at Edenderry.

(g) Seventh Brigade: most of the rest of Kildare with Naas as headquarters.

(h) Eighth Brigade: north County Dublin, also known as the Fingal Brigade.

(i) Ninth Brigade: south Louth, centred on Drogheda.

While the last five need not concern us, it is clear that Meath became the kernel of the division both geographically speaking, and in the fact that four of the nine battalions were given over almost totally to the county. This domination is also reflected in the newly appointed divisional staff which differed little from the old brigade officers. Boylan himself, of course, remained on as O/C with Séamus O'Higgins still as Quartermaster and Eamonn Cullen as Director of Engineering; the Intelligence Officer was Pat Clinton of Moynalty, and he also acted as Adjutant. Séamus Finn became Vice O/C and Director of Training, and Paddy Mooney was appointed Assistant Director of Training.

The various brigade officers were as follows, the order in each case being O/C, Vice O/C, Adjutant, Quartermaster, Intelligence Officer and Engineer:

(a) First Brigade: David Hall, Mick McCormack, Bernard Dunne, James Maguire, John Costigan and William O'Neill.

(b) Second Brigade: Patrick Kelly, William Booth, Thomas Coyle, Mick Hynes, Mick Hilliard and Joseph Hughes.

(c) Third Brigade: Pat Farrelly, Seán Farrelly, T.P. McKenna, David Smith, Ralph McKenna and Dick McKenna.

(d) Fourth Brigade: Michael Hiney, Patrick Corrigan, Joe Monaghan, John Tyrell, Edward Thornton and Joseph Martin.

Each brigade was divided into battalions. Once again it is difficult to find the exact number of battalions, and their officers, for each, although from various sources the following has been obtained: as regards the Second Brigade there were four battalions, the companies and officers of each being:

No. 1 Battalion: Trim, Kilmessan, Dunderry, Kiltale

O/C	Patrick Quinn
Vice O/C	Christopher Caffrey
Adjutant	James Quinn
QM	John O'Brien

No. 2 Battalion: Johnstown, Kentstown, Yellow Furze, Dunmoe

O/C	Thomas Bowens
	Rest of staff unknown

No. 3 Battalion: Castletown, Kilberry, Rathkenny, Clongill

O/C	James Swan
Vice O/C	Patrick White
Adjutant	Jack McCaffrey
QM	Thomas Crahan

No. 4 Battalion: Navan, Bohermeen, Martry, Commons (also called Ardbraccan)

O/C	Thomas Gibney
Vice O/C	Paddy Stapleton
Adjutant	Thomas Foley
QM	James Hilliard
IO	Thomas Killoran
Engineer	Patrick O'Brien

Regarding the Third Brigade, Charlie Conaty remembered that:

there were four battalions at first – the First Newcastle, the Second

Stonefield, the Third Virginia and the Fourth Bailieboro. Subsequently, two further battalions, formed from one or other of the first four, were established and became known as the Fifth Oldcastle and Sixth Lurgan.

The companies which comprised the Stonefield Battalion were: Carnaross, Ballinlough, Stonefield, Whitegate, Oldcastle, Ballinacree, Moylough and Fennor. Except for the last named these were the same units as made up the old Fifth Battalion, although later on Oldcastle went into the newly-formed Oldcastle Battalion.

The officers of the Stonefield Battalion were: O/C: Charlie Conaty; Vice O/C: Mick Wynne; Adjutant: Peter O'Connell; QM: Brian Daly; IO: Matt Smith; Engineer: Matt Tevlin.

It has not been possible to trace the officers of the Newcastle Battalion nor the companies in it, but it is almost certain that these would be the same as in the old Fourth Kells Battalion, namely, Newcastle, Kells, Moynalty, Loughan, Kilbeg, Carlanstown and Nobber.

Returning now to the First Brigade, once again it has not been possible to ascertain the battalion officers. It can be taken for granted though that there were either four or five battalions and that the following Meath companies were distributed over three of these: Dunboyne, Kilcloon, Kilmore, Ashbourne, Longwood, Enfield and Rathmolyon. This is based on what is hopefully an intelligent guess. This would then leave five units – Athboy, Kildalkey, Ballivor, Fordstown and Boardsmill – as part of the battalions of the Fourth Brigade centred on Delvin.

Apart from these formal structures there seems to have been some steps taken towards setting up Active Service Units or Flying Columns. In June, Charlie Conaty recalled, about thirty men, most of them brigade or battalion officers, underwent a week long course of training. All of these men were by then on the run. The camp was held at Mullagh Hill and the training officer was an ex-British soldier named Joseph Carolan of Killeter, Mullagh. The intervention of the Truce ended the necessity for this scheme.

A Volunteer company had been formed in Kells early in 1917. Pádraig de Búrca had been the leading figure in it until he left the town to go to work in Dublin. Bob Mullan then became captain and after his arrest it passed to Benny Carolan. Benny remembered that in the early stages there had been much drilling and some arms practice, but most of this died out following the departure of de Búrca. "We had up to sixty men in all but this was only on paper. Most of them were gun shy except about a dozen," Benny frankly admitted. Apart from the one hundred and fifty military billeted in the fever hospital and later in the workhouse, there were also twenty-five to thirty RIC and about a dozen Black and Tans stationed in what is now the town's Garda station. These were unofficially augmented by a tiny corps of Ulster Volunteers. Benny recalls:

> There were about six of these, all Protestants from the area and all well-armed, I even remember that the local minister at the time by the name of Carson used to take part in the police searches and raids. A few years ago indeed when the house of one of them named Hamilton was being pulled down a number of rifles was found under the floorboards.

There had been little or no disturbance in Kells since the outbreak of the Troubles but in May, Benny decided, as he put it himself, "to give the lads a bit of experience." The operation was a raid on Kells post office on the night of 27 May; the aim was to disrupt enemy communications by smashing telephonic and telegraphic equipment. Benny thought that similar raids had been planned for many towns in Ireland on that night but that it was only in Kells and Waterford that they materialised.

> I took about twenty five men that night whereas about six or seven would have been enough. We had just shotguns. We forced in the back door of the post office and took the two guards prisoner. But before we had got in they must have managed to phone the police. We did the job all right before the police arrived.

Only one of the company was caught that night, as the rest managed to get away, but over the next few days another seven were arrested including Benny himself. "We spent twelve weeks in Mountjoy and then were moved to Kilmainham until the Treaty when we were released. We were never charged or tried at all", he recalled.

Benny remembered that in the cell next to him in Mountjoy was an ex-Auxiliary who claimed that he was a son-in-law of former Prime Minister Asquith. He also boasted that he was one of those dismissed as a result of the looting in Robinstown in February. "What the hell brought you over to Ireland?" Benny asked him one day. "For the shooting", came the answer. "I was bored at home."

Also imprisoned around this time was Matt Wallace. Early in June he was tried on a charge of unlawfully detaining a young man and trying to prevent him from joining the RIC. "That was in November", said Matt,

> we were carrying out police duties one night when we got a complaint about a robbery. We arrested a man by the name of Gavigan at Kiltale crossroads. When we searched him we found in his pocket a reference to join the RIC from a Colonel Hamilton of Dunsany. That night we took him to a house in Derrypatrick but the guards weren't alert enough and he managed to escape and make his way to Trim. Myself and my brother Tom spent all the next day and night lying outside Gavigan's house expecting him to return. I remember that it was very damp and cold and the time went very slowly. But he never turned up. He must have taken refuge in Trim barracks before being sent on to do his training.

Four months later, in March, Matt was arrested. "I was on the run but I went home occasionally, and this day I was chopping wood at the back of the house when a group of police arrived with Gavigan amongst them." On the evening that he was brought into Dublin the police car he was travelling in was ambushed on the quays and Matt was hammered and beaten with the rifle butts of the RIC who were guarding him. At the trial which was delayed until June three men were charged with the aforementioned offence, but the other two were acquitted. Gavigan testified that on the night of his detention fifty men had been present, a huge exaggeration according to Matt, and though he was blindfolded he could clearly see the accused as they lit matches and cigarettes. Matt refused to recognise the court and his sentence was duly promulgated.

He was sent to England where he spent six months in Wormwood Scrubs and another couple in Dorchester Prison before he was freed in January following the Treaty. "But prison wasn't too bad", he recalled,

the warders were friendly and they looked after our welfare. The only trouble we had was on 'Poppy Day', 11 November, when they commemorate the armistice. All the prisoners were told that when a bell would ring they were to stop work. There were eleven of us Irish prisoners and we all refused the order. They gave us three days in solitary for that. The time in jail went very slowly. Sewing mail bags was what I had to spend the time at. The food wasn't great either and we weren't allowed to read. But for me the worst part was not being able to smoke. I used to stand in the cells and corridors sniffing the smoke from the warders' cigarettes. On the day I was released the first thing I did was to buy not just a packet of cigarettes but a clay-pipe and tobacco as well!

On 7 June, the day after Matt Wallace had his sentence handed down, the Carnaross Company, acting on their own, carried out an ambush very similar to that attempted at Sylvan Park on 1 April. The location picked was in fact just a couple of miles away at Drumbaragh. Jack Lynch had just been freed after a week's detention in Kells barracks:

One night, after coming out from a mission in Carnaross, Pat Reilly, Kit Dunne and myself were arrested and taken to Kells. The other two were soon set free and then so was I when the parish priest used his influence, saying that he needed me to sing in the choir during the mission!

Most of the Carnaross Company were present at Drumbaragh. They first placed a mine under the road and then took up positions at the back of a high wall overlooking the road. Two lorry loads of military travelling between Oldcastle and Kells were expected that morning. The mine exploded and, as the *Meath Chronicle* reported on 11 June 1921, "completely destroyed and ripped away the engine and front of the first Crossley Tender." There was a sharp exchange of fire as the second lorry followed closely on the first. "A Colonel Gross and three or four soldiers were wounded", recalled Jack Lynch. After a while, the ambush party retreated but some of them were caught in a nearby wood and in a shoot-out Jack was scraped by a bullet in the head:

> I managed to make my way to Kieran's Well where the Cumann na mBan women dressed the wound. It healed quickly but in later years I often got headaches. By 1960 there was a sort of a growth out of my head and I had to get the shrapnel removed.

The rest of the company made their way home safely that day. Shortly afterwards Peter O'Connell remembered Matt Tevlin telling him how when still close to the scene of the ambush, he saw a number of military coming towards him: "Matt was in a field and took off his coat and pretended to be counting cattle." Then he got into friendly conversation with the soldiers who soon passed on their way.

Shortly before the Truce, it was either late June or early July, there was a huge swoop by crown forces in the Carnaross-Stonefield area. "Fourteen lorry loads of military and Tans made a sweep of the area", said Charlie Conaty. Directing this was none other than General Tudor, supreme commander of all the RIC in the country. Charlie thought that this raid was prompted by the fact that Eamon Cullen, the Divisional Engineer, was in the area. He had got off the train at Virginia Road Station the previous evening and had spent some of the night at Conaty's house. "Someone must have noticed him and passed on the information", said Charlie. Fortunately, Cullen had left during the night and made his way to Sheridan's of Drumlerry where he was due to meet Séamus Maguire, O/C of the Fifth Westmeath Brigade:

> That morning Mick Wynne and myself were tending a sick mare when we suddenly noticed a party of Black and Tans coming up the road. At that point they were no more than a hundred and fifty yards away. We made a dash to the back of the house and into a fox covert where we often hid out. From there we could see everything. The house was searched but no damage was done. I remember two soldiers sitting on the wall in which we had two rifles concealed.

Later that day the two men made their way out of the area and walked to the relative safety of Oldcastle.

The last major operation in which Meath men participated took place on 2 July. Seán Boylan gave the background as follows:

> A few days earlier two troop trains had been sent from the Curragh to Belfast for the opening of the Northern Ireland parliament by the King of England. One of those trains carried seven hundred men and the other two hundred and fifty. GHQ had decided that those trains be ambushed on the return journey. Mick Collins produced a map and suggested that one of the trains be attacked at a particular point. The name of the place was Stacumny. The times of the trains' departures were known to GHQ and the one selected for attack was the one carrying the seven hundred troops.

Stacumny is near Celbridge in north Kildare. Peter Moran of Dunboyne recalled that originally it was intended just to lay mines and blow up the train, but then a meeting of divisional officers decided on a full scale ambush in the hope of capturing a large quantity of weapons and ammunition.

The men involved were drawn from the Navan, Dunboyne and Fingal Brigades. The Fingal Brigade was by this time under the leadership of Paddy Mooney and in May they had burned out about ten coastguard stations between Dublin and Drogheda. The idea of this was to facilitate the smuggling of a cargo of Thompson machine-guns from the USA, a project which never materialised. Séamus Finn recalls that the Navan men were drawn from the Commons, Yellow Furze and Johnstown companies and were led by William Booth, while the Dunboyne men were under Barney Dunne. In all, about a hundred men mobilised in Dunboyne on the night of 1 July, after which they proceeded cross-country to Stacumny.

James O'Connell of Skryne was present that night. Just a couple of months earlier he had narrowly escaped arrest by a group of police and military. He was out when they called but they were still in the house as he was returning; only a signal to him from a window by his little sister alerted him.

"The Tans took my father instead and tied him to the side of a lorry. He was detained for three months in Arbour Hill", said James. Also present at Stacumny were Patsy Bennett, who cycled from Navan to Dunboyne, and Tom Manning who met up with the Fingal men in Ashbourne and marched across to Dunboyne. Patsy remembered Paddy Mooney telling them that if they got enough guns he would start up a flying column in Meath. Dunboyne Volunteer Christy Ennis, who had been sworn into the movement by Barney Dunne in 1919, was another of the ambush party that night.

While Eamon Cullen and the engineers were laying the mines Christy was amongst those whose job it was to block the roads round about. "Not all the roads were blocked at the right time", said Christy,

> all were supposed to be closed at about three o'clock, but one leading to Lucan was blocked as early as two. At this time there was still a military lorry in the area and it came across the roadblock.

Christy believed that it was here that the plans began to go wrong. The main thrust of the ambush was to come from a bridge overlooking the railway line. It seems that the military lorry strayed up the lane leading to this bridge and came upon the waiting attackers. "The lorry was fired on", said Christy, "but although some of the soldiers may have been wounded or even killed it managed to get through and then out of the area." He also thought that a drill session carried out by one of the officers later that morning may have attracted attention as well.

Things began to really go wrong later that morning. A small military spotter plane appeared first. "This was apparently reconnoitring the railway line in front of the troop train", stated Seán Boylan. Shortly afterwards several lorry loads of soldiers came up behind the men and opened fire. The plane then reappeared as the train came into view. "It manoeuvred down between the wires and the train signalled it to stop", said Christy Ennis, "the train came to a halt, the soldiers got out and marched to the signal box where the signalman was waving them on. This man was part of our plans."

These plans now lay in tatters as the Volunteers came under attack from all sides. "We better get out, lads, we're done for", is how James O'Connell remembered an officer putting it, though in much blunter and more colourful language, to his men. Patsy Bennett recalled being pinned down under sleepers as the bullets bounced off them:

> Eventually we escaped crouching through a field of wheat. Only for a man with a Thompson machine gun who covered our retreat it is doubtful if we would have made it.

Amazingly, not one man was lost in the retreat and all made it back safely to Dunboyne. "The only casualty I remember", said Tom Manning, "was a man who broke his leg and had to be brought back in relays to Dunboyne."

Just over a week later came the Truce which came into force at midday on 11 July. In Meath, on this day, a few final salvoes were fired in defiance. The mails between Kells and Oldcastle were seized; there were brief attacks on the barracks in Nobber and Longwood; and at Maudlin, Kells, a small party of British soldiers were fired upon. They ended their subsequent search for the attackers promptly at noon. All of this was harmless enough but it seems that there were others intent on using the Troubles, however belatedly, as a cover or a justification for a final bout of mindless vandalism. At Balbradagh, Robinstown the residence of George Tisdall, a Justice of the Peace, was the target of arsonists and was burned to the ground early that morning.

Three other organisations, all of them already fleetingly referred to in this chapter, had a part in the military struggle. Firstly, there was the Fianna Éireann, a sort of youth branch of the Volunteers. The boys involved in this carried out duties such as scouting, carrying messages, delivering despatches and so on. The only place where it can with certainty be said that the Fianna were organised was in Navan where there was a group of fifteen. The names of these as given in the copybook mentioned earlier were: John Clarke, John O'Mahony, Joe Smith, John Fry, Michael Cregan, Joe Clarke, Matt Russell, Michael Reilly, Val Reilly, James Perry, Laurence McKeon, James Cuffe, Joseph Lumsden, Thomas Kennedy and J. Loughran.

Secondly, the Cumann na mBan was the womens' organisation,

often made up of the sisters of Volunteers. Their role included visiting the men in prison, preparing food and bringing it to Volunteers on the run, providing first aid, carrying despatches and so on. Occasionally they became more directly involved. Jimmy Sherry related to Garrett Fox the following incident which happened shortly before the Truce:

> An RIC Head Constable who was to give strong evidence against Seán MacEoin at his court martial was sent to Trim for safer keeping. The Trim Company became aware of the fact and Bridget Duigenan, a leader of Cumann na mBan, was asked to keep an eye on him, so that he could be 'knocked off'. One Sunday evening he went out for a walk towards Peterstown Cross. The company got the tip-off and myself and 'Gael' McArdle were posted to the Peterstown end and two other members to Marcy Regan's premises end. The Head Constable came towards the Peterstown side and we got ready. But then a group of children appeared and it was decided not to fire although 'Gael' had been a British army sniper. It was decided to follow the enemy but as he came to the main road a load of Tans came along and picked him up.

Apart from the branch in Trim, the Cumann na mBan were also organised in Dunboyne, Carnaross, Ballinlough and Newcastle. There were undoubtedly several more branches. From Mrs Jack Lynch of Carnaross was obtained the list of women involved in that locality's unit: Alice Tevlin (née Dunne), captain; Julia Daly, Peg Daly, Julia McNamee, Kate Dougharty (née Dunne), Rose Mullally (née Mulvaney), Mary Lynch (née Mullally), Brigid Farrelly (née Dunne), Mary Daly (née Gilsenan), Ciss Gartland (née Mulvaney), Margaret Connolly (née Farrelly) and Mary Caffrey (née Dunne).

Finally, there was the Irish Republican Brotherhood (IRB). This was an ultra-secret organisation, and because of this characteristic it is difficult to assess its role. In his statement to the Military History Bureau, Seán Boylan gave some idea of the evolution and purpose of the IRB in Meath:

> I joined the IRB in 1915 when an organiser named Benson ...

visited the Dunboyne area. I was the first to join in the area. Others who joined at about the same time were Michael Kelly, John Kelly, Peter Byrne, Aidan Crean, my brother Ned, Christopher Lynam, Peter Keating, Frank Carolan and James Maguire. My brother Ned was appointed head of the circle here in Dunboyne. After 1916 I was appointed head and continued in that position until the Truce in July 1921.

After my appointment I attended meetings at 35 Lower Gardiner Street, Dublin. Mick Collins occasionally attended. At the time we were attached to the Dublin Board. A short time later county boards were set up. I became head of the Meath County Board. We held regular meetings. Each meeting was attended by a visitor from another county board and we in turn sent a visitor to an adjoining county board meeting.

Our main purpose at first was to spread the organisation in the county. The name of a potential member was first proposed and seconded and placed before the board for acceptance ... In a short time circles were established in every parish. Discussions at the meetings included matters relating to the acquisition of arms and the formulation of schemes and decisions relative to national policy and the appointment of suitable men to direct and guide that policy.

Later on Boylan recounts organising county boards in Kildare, Westmeath, Louth, South Cavan and North Dublin.

Not everyone who was a member of the Volunteers was in the IRB: in fact only a small percentage was. As Boylan said potential recruits had to be proposed and seconded and Paddy Lalor, himself a member, recalled that an objection by even one man could veto membership. Both Paddy and Jimmy Sherry remembered that of the almost forty Volunteers in the Trim company, only about ten were in the local IRB circle. Jimmy became a member in 1920 but whereas he had three brothers in the Volunteers, only one, Tom, was in the more secretive organisation. "When first approached", said Paddy, "you would be asked if you had any religious qualms about joining." On this point Jimmy remembered that at the time some of the clergy in Trim would not give absolution to IRB men and that they used to go to a priest in Church Street, Dublin where, as he put it, "no questions were asked."

Charlie Conaty joined late in 1920 on the proposal of Sean Boylan. "Less than half the Stonefield company were in the IRB", he recalled, "A few months later I was elected as centre for the area of north Meath even though I was the youngest present." While IRB meetings may have often discussed military plans these were still largely the domain of Volunteer Battalion and Brigade Council meetings. Jimmy Sherry was not totally convinced of the need for the IRB, the oath for which he said, "was practically the same as for the Volunteers." Both Paddy Lalor and Peter O'Connell, another IRB man, used the word 'solidarity' when reflecting on the role of the organisation. By this they probably meant the need for the more dedicated men to stick together if ever the less committed began to waver in their republican convictions. It was ironic then the way things turned out. Charlie Conaty put it this way:

> There was probably a need for the IRB so as to avoid a sell-out. Yet later on I would almost certainly have taken the anti-Treaty side only that word came down from the Supreme Council of the IRB to accept the settlement.

As the Fianna Éireann and Cumann na mBan were largely peripheral, and as the role of the IRB remains somewhat inscrutable, the most central organisation in the military struggle was, of course, the Volunteers or IRA. What was the strength of the IRA in Meath? Again records were not kept at the time but in the mid-1930s at the time when it was decided by the then Fianna Fáil government to give pensions to those who had seen service in the War of Independence, lists of members for each company were drawn up. Mick Hilliard explained:

> These lists refer to one specific date, 11 July 1921, the day of the Truce, only members of the IRA on that date were to be included. They were drawn up following consultations between former IRA officers at various levels. It should be remembered that there were sometimes disputes as to a man's membership so that the final lists represent a consensus of opinion amongst the

officers. But there are instances of men who did not join up until after the Truce being included.

Incidentally, inclusion on such a list did not automatically mean the granting of a pension since each individual case had to be assessed by a referee to see if their activities merited such.

These records were later kept in the Department of Defence, but somehow copies of a number of them found their way to the Meath County Library in Navan. These give an accurate record of the strength of certain companies. In each of the following cases, to allow for the possible discrepancies mentioned above, numbers have been rounded off to the nearest five.

Navan	50	Dunmoe	15	Martry	25
Trim	35	Rathkenny	20	Bohermeen	20
Kilmessan	40	Clongill	15	Commons	30
Kiltale	20	Castletown	15	Dunderry	25
Kilberry	25				

The following figures, again rounded off to the nearest five, come from the memories of those spoken to:

Ballinlough	25	Whitegate	25	Carnaross	30
Oldcastle	20	Stonefield	15	Moylough	10
Ballinacree	10	Dunboyne	20	Kilcloon	10
Kilbride	25	Skryne	10	Moynalty	25
Kells	60				

These account for twenty six companies, about half of those in the county, and gives a total of 620 men. Excluding the two large companies in the towns of Navan and Kells, the average membership of the other rural companies is just over 20. Allowing for another 28 units, we have seen that there were certainly fifty in all, and taking the same average of 20 this would give another 560 Volunteers. This leaves a total of 1,180 and certainly a figure in the region of 1,200 may be taken as a very accurate estimate.

What was the strength of the British forces encountered in Meath by these men? Again it is possible to get a fairly good idea using as sources the memories of the IRA veterans as well as occasional references in contemporary local newspaper reports. Taking the military first, the situation roughly was this:

Navan	300 Leinster Regiment
	(*already based there before the Troubles*)
	150 Cameronians
Kells	150 South Wales Borderers
Dunshaughlin	100 South Wales Borderers
Oldcastle	50 (Regiment unknown)
Total:	750

Taking the RIC proper we have seen in the second chapter that there were about thirty barracks in the county in 1916. Those in the towns would have had a garrison of ten to twelve men, but in the case of the barracks in the rural areas they consisted of no more than a sergeant and three or four constables. It has also been seen how by 1919–20 most of these smaller stations were being abandoned as the police moved into the towns or just held the occasional rural barracks as at Longwood or Slane or Dunshaughlin. There is no indication though that RIC strength was significantly increased at this time in the county. Thus if we allow an average of five men for each of thirty barracks this would give a total of 150 RIC.

As regards the Auxiliaries it has been shown how the company of a hundred made their mark in the Trim area. It should be borne in mind that these men were not based exclusively in Trim; the whole idea of the Auxiliaries was to have a very mobile group moving quickly through the countryside in Crossley Tenders. So doubtless the company imposed on Trim inflicted themselves on the people of neighbouring counties such as Kildare, Offaly and Westmeath. A number of Auxiliaries do, however, seem to have had a permanent base in Navan, as Bobby Byrne recalled that sometime at the turn of the year 1920–21 the Navan Company received information that what is now the Newgrange Hotel was about to be commandeered as a barracks for British forces. He also remembered that for several nights some members of the company, with several tins of petrol, lay in wait in the grounds of the Church of Ireland, just opposite, with orders to burn down the hotel at the first signs of an attempt to occupy it. This vigil was called off after a time, but not long afterwards another building, what are now the offices of Navan Chamber of Commerce, just across the road from the hotel was taken over by about a dozen Auxiliaries and fortified with barbed wire and steel shutters.

Assessing the number of Black and Tans in Meath presents a problem. As stated earlier, many of those spoken to tended to use the term to cover all crown forces. Séamus Finn says that there were groups of the infamous Tans in Navan, Trim and Athboy; to these may be added Dunshaughlin, Kells and Oldcastle. The Black and Tans were meant to augment the RIC and there were probably no more than eight to ten in each group. This would give a total of about fifty for the whole county.

To summarise then the numbers of crown forces in Meath in 1921:

Military	750
RIC	150
Auxiliaries	100
Black & Tans	50
Total	1,050

Numerically speaking rebel and crown forces in the county were almost evenly matched, but there the similarity ended. In terms of training, experience, weapons and transport, the police and military enjoyed huge advantages. Conversely, the IRA suffered in these respects and there were other handicaps. Pat Fitzsimons felt that what was lacking in Meath was a "good young officer, aged about thirty, someone like Tom Barry". Jimmy Sherry thought that the terrain of the county was not conducive to the type of guerilla warfare carried out successfully elsewhere; and then there was the obstruction of spies and informers.

Still, given all these drawbacks, could more have been done by the Meath Volunteers? Originally, as has been seen, there were six battalions in the county. It would be difficult to fault the men of the Fifth Oldcastle Battalion. Their activities have been chronicled almost exhaustively in this section; the reason why so much attention has been focused on this part of the county is not in any way due to the fact that men such as Peter O'Connell, Charlie Conaty, Owen Clarke and Jack Lynch proved both articulate and clear-minded about the events of over sixty years ago but rather because this battalion area was actually the scene of more Volunteer activity than any of the other five. The Second Trim and Sixth Navan areas have also been dealt with in some detail, as have the Fourth Kells, if somewhat less so. In the case of the Third Athboy battalion area, it has hardly been mentioned at all because in the various sources – local newspaper accounts, statements to the Military History Bureau, reminiscences of IRA veterans, the memoirs of Séamus Finn (himself an Athboy man) – used to build up a picture of these years there is little or no indication of disturbances in this area between 1919 and 1921. The First Dunboyne area was also fairly 'quiet', but Peter Moran suggested a possible reason for this:

> Dunboyne was the home of Seán Boylan and as such it was the centre of a battalion, the brigade and later the division. It wouldn't have been wise to have attracted too much attention to the area; if large numbers of police and military were based here it would have disrupted the workings of the Volunteers in the entire county.

Peter's brother, Nick Moran, recalled that in Dunboyne itself the most serious incident came just before the Truce when two Black and Tans from Dunshaughlin, who used to drink in Kelly's pub, were ambushed one night on their way out to the Dublin Road. Both men managed to escape without injury. "The area around here", said Peter Moran,

> was used as a supply centre for weapons for the whole divisional area. This was another reason why it would not have been a good idea to attract attention. There were four major arms dumps around, in Dunboyne itself, Cornelstown, Leixlip and Batterstown.

At company level there is little doubt but that the most active unit in Meath was that in Carnaross. It was almost a family affair, with seven Farrelly brothers, five Dunne brothers, another family of four Dunnes, the Lynchs, the Dalys and the two Tevlins making up most of the company. These men carried out the ambushes at Dervor Hill and Drumbaragh as well as being involved with other companies at Sylvan Park. Both Peter O'Connell and Charlie Conaty had great admiration for the Carnaross men whom Benny Carolan described as "a belligerent lot." The neighbouring companies at Stonefield, to which Charlie and Peter belonged and which suffered the loss of Séamus Cogan and Patrick McDonnell, Ballinlough and Whitegate also played a brave part in the struggle.

Two other companies merit a special mention. In the Trim area, the Lalors, Sherrys, Mooneys, O'Hagans, Hynes and others mentioned in the course of this account kept up a constant harassment of British forces until the arrival of the Auxiliaries in the town at the beginning of 1921. And Patsy Bennett's Commons Company with the Stapletons, the Byrnes, the Hylands, Loughlin O'Rourke, Patrick Boyle and others also proved themselves an active combination.

As regards other companies the fact that they may not have played so aggressive a part as those singled out should not be put down to any timidity on their part. We are back again to the shortage of arms and ammunition. Many companies carried out tasks such as intercepting the mails, enforcing the Belfast Boycott, blocking roads, demolishing bridges and doing police duties, thus filling the vacuum left by the RIC in the rural areas from the start of 1920.

But to return to the original question posed: could the Meath IRA have done more in the war? On the basis of the evidence provided in this chapter each reader may decide for him or herself. Certainly, if the efficacy of an army is measured by the amount of blood it spills, then the Meath Volunteers of 1919–21 would be deemed a complete failure: for the period November 1919 to July 1921 the number of British fatalities was, as stated earlier, just one soldier and two police as against two IRA dead. Perhaps this may seem derisive to some, especially those whose republican activities have never extended beyond singing rebel songs in lounge bars.

On the other hand, it may be instructive to paraphrase what Peter O'Connell, in the course of a discussion once wisely said: "Just because we were an army didn't mean we had to go round shooting people all the time. We could get our way by other means. We didn't want to kill anyone."

6

January 1919 - July 1921:
The Troubles (2):
Constitutional Resistance

Time and again in the twentieth century it has been shown that guerilla warfare, as carried out by the Volunteers between 1919 and 1921, cannot succeed unless it enjoys at least tacit support from the community at large. In Ireland a programme of passive resistance and civil disobedience complemented the military struggle. This was carried out under the aegis of Sinn Féin and it succeeded in not just undermining the British administration but also in replacing it with native institutions. Local government bodies, the police force and the court system all gradually fell victim to the 'subversion' of Sinn Féin. This chapter attempts to chronicle these developments of a purely non-violent nature.

In Meath in the early months of 1919 opposition to Britain focused on demands to free the prisoners who had been arrested and detained since the mysterious 'German plot' of the previous May. The reason why this campaign now gained in momentum was because many of the newly-elected Sinn Féin representatives were, in fact, in jail and so could not be present when the first Dáil assembled in the Mansion House, Dublin, on 21 January. In Meath well attended meetings were held in all the towns with priests often being amongst the platform speakers. The main speaker in Kells was Fr Farrell, the republican-minded parish priest of Carnaross. In Oldcastle it was Fr Barry, a man whose main interests centred on the activities of the Back to the Land movement and who was now making one of his rare ventures into the mainstream political affairs of these years. In Navan and Trim the main speaker was new T.D. Eamon Duggan.

These meetings, while useful in mobilising public opinion, were hardly a cause of alarm to the authorities. Therefore, at the end of January, Sinn Féin decided to apply a bit more pressure and a directive from its Central Executive called on members to put a stop to hunts all over Ireland. Hunt meetings were of course very much the preserve of the titled upper-classes and high-ranked army officers, as well as those aspiring to either or both of these, and the natural political leanings of these groups would be to Unionism and Dublin Castle. In Meath the first clash came when the Meath Hunt assembled at Rathkenny on 1 February 1919. The hunting party at first ignored the opposition of the assembled crowd, mostly members of Kilberry Sinn Féin Cumann, but apparently the Hunt Master had second thoughts and after consulting with Joseph Ryan, a prominent local Sinn Féiner, he called off the fixture.

Better documented is the case of the Ward Union Hunt which was disrupted on two separate occasions during the month of February. In his statement to the Bureau of Military History Seán Boylan recorded both incidents in some detail. Before this, Boylan stated, he had gone to several places where hunt meetings had been scheduled to take place but had then been cancelled "as a ruse to wear us out and confuse us." Eventually he received genuine information that on 19 February a meeting would assemble at Dunshaughlin workhouse. Boylan continued:

> With twelve Volunteers I arrived there just as they had assembled with the stag in a box cart. I approached the Master, a Mr Levins Moore, and told him that we had come to enforce the Sinn Féin and Irish Government's ban on hunting.

Boylan recalled a brisk verbal exchange which ended with Moore saying that "the land is ours, we will hunt it, what can you do?", to which Boylan pointedly replied: "If everyone had their own land your people would not have much." Boylan had a long memory too. When the Whip, James Brindley, remarked "I think you are strangers", he was answered with, "We were not strangers in 1798 when you burned the house over our heads in Bonaravia, Dunboyne". He was referring to an ancestor of his who was evicted and whose house was burned at that time. After a while those in charge of the Hunt agreed to cancel the event but "in reality", said Boylan, "they had secretly arranged with the officers present to ride us down." Boylan's account of what then happened went as follows:

> I had placed six men in front of the box cart and six behind. There was a movement from the rear and a shout: "Charge, let him out", meaning the stag from the box cart. Some of my men in the rear of the box cart were knocked down in the charge. A 'lady' came straight for me. I jumped to the left and shouted: "One side, madam." She said, "Have we no right to the road?" I said, "Every right but not on top of us." One of my men in front of the box cart opened fire and shot a horse in the flank ... a stampede followed and the Master, Levins Moore, who had been in the front of the charge returned to me and said, "You have shot Mr. Nugent's horse." I said, "He is lucky he was not shot himself." He asked to be given the box cart and stag. I replied, "You won't have the cart now but I guarantee that the cart and the stag will be delivered safely at the kennels". Mrs Sam Watt, wife of the Captain, said, "I will identify the man who shot the horse." I said, "If you do, we have made arrangements to deal with informers." There were shouts of "Disarm him." I said, "The first one to move I will drop you." Shortly after, those of the hunt party who had remained to the end rode off ... when they had gone I sent an escort of Volunteers with the box cart and stag to the kennels at Ashbourne. Next day Mrs Sam Watt changed her mind in Dunboyne RIC barracks. When asked if she could identify the man who shot the horse she replied that she could not.

The stopping of the hunt was carried out by members of the Dunboyne and Kilcloon Volunteer companies. Boylan recalled that the men involved were Barney Dunne, Christopher Lynam, James Maguire, Michael O'Toole, Peter Keating, James Farrell, Joseph Gaynor and Nicholas Moran (all Dunboyne) and Michael Felix, Frank Carolan, Stephen Darcy and Peter Callaghan (Kilcloon).

Round two of this confrontation came exactly a week later, on Wednesday 26 February, at Batterstown. The previous Monday Boylan had finalised a document addressed to the Master and Members of the Ward Union Hunt. This read as follows:

> Acting on instructions from the Central Executive of Sinn Féin and endorsed by the constituency committees of north and south County Meath, we, the landholders and residents in the Ward Hunt area, hereby call on you and your supporters not to hunt or trespass the lands in our possession until all Sinn Féin prisoners are unconditionally released.

This was signed by Elizabeth Boylan, John Bruton, Edward Cussen, Patrick Kelly, John Farrell, Frank Farrell, Patrick Smith, Laurence Ward, Michael Kelly, John Lumley and Jim Quinn. That evening Boylan showed the document to Levins Moore at his home in Ashtown, county Dublin, but it made no impression and he said that the Hunt would go ahead on the Wednesday. On that day a large crowd gathered in the Batterstown area. The *Meath Chronicle* of 1 March 1919 estimated there were two hundred and fifty would-be hunters, forty RIC men, (Boylan gives a figure of sixty), and two lorry loads of military. Boylan recalled making his way through the police cordon by travelling in the motor car of the county councillor from Clonee, Patrick Moore. On reaching the village he:

> approached Lord Fingal, acting Master, and read the contents of the document to him. He said, "When the farmers and people who supported them forbid us to cross their lands, we have no alternative but to abandon the meeting, but we are not taking dictation from political parties."

Even forty years after the event as he gave his account to the Bureau of Military History Seán Boylan was still clearly relishing his success in forcing the Hunt to call off its meeting on that day, notwithstanding the presence of a very large force of police and military. He recalled being surrounded by correspondents of over a dozen newspapers to whom he said that he intended to frame the document and next day his photograph was in all the daily newspapers showing him reading the document to Lord Fingal. Later that week he remembered attending a meeting in the Mansion House where:

> they all gave me a great welcome and called on me to address the meeting. Mick Collins told me, "Anyone but yourself would be doing three years in jail."

There were no more hunts held in the county for the rest of the year and even Fairyhouse Races which were organised by the Ward Hunt Committee were also abandoned for that year.

During February motions of support for the obstruction of hunt meetings were passed by the RDCs of Oldcastle, Trim and Dunshaughlin. At the end of January a meeting of Kells UDC received a Sinn Féin deputation consisting of Pádraig de Búrca, John Brennan and Christopher McCabe and agreed to their request for the cancellation of Lloyd races pending the release of the prisoners. Navan UDC was less enthusiastic about the matter. On 4 February it passed a resolution condemning "the foolish action of a section of the people in Meath in stopping the hunts". Another motion was passed immediately afterwards calling on the government to release the prisoners but one suspects that this was a feeble effort, to use a relevant metaphor, to hunt with the hounds and run with the hares.

Generally speaking, however, no radical changes were evident in the attitudes of the local councils towards the rapidly developing national situation. From January 1919 to June 1920, when the local government elections of that year were completed, the minute books as well as the more detailed accounts of meetings published in the local press show that in the case of practically all of these councils they concentrated on the mundane business of local administration, making little or no reference to political affairs. By 1919 most of these bodies had distanced themselves from the Home Rule party but they also stood aloof from Sinn Féin, and their hostile attitude to physical force republicanism has been seen in the wake of the killing of Constable Agar in Ballivor in October of that year. During this period of a year and a half the premier body, Meath County Council, made only one noteworthy allusion to the national question when in March 1920 it passed a motion (there were only two dissenters) expressing:

> our disapproval of the government action in trying to enforce on Ireland, contrary to the wishes of the vast majority of the people, a Home Rule Act.

In truth this was much the same as the resolution, quoted earlier, that had been passed almost four years previously.

Navan RDC was the only council which consistently touched on the national issue and their deliberations reflected the uncertainties of the time. Remember that this was the same body as was elected in 1914 when, in common with all the others in Meath, it was an unyielding supporter of John Redmond and Home Rule. By June 1919 the members were voting to give an official address of welcome to Eoin MacNeill, a man who was by now a minister in the soon to be outlawed Dáil, on the occasion of his visit to Navan to open the Meath Féis. The wording of the address had strong republican overtones as it invoked Robert Emmet's memory and looked forward "to the day when this country shall take its place amongst the nations of the earth."

At the following month's meeting, when a communication was read from the Local Government Board reminding the Board of Guardians (basically the same membership as the RDC) that 19 July was to be celebrated as a day of peace and that the board was free to give extra food to the workhouse inmates, the members resolved to take no action on the matter because, as one of them put it, "we have no peace here; it ought to be part of the peace that we should have the government of the country in our own hands." In September the council attributed the current unrest to "repression and misgovernment" and unanimously recorded its protest at the policies "adopted by the Viceroy Lord French, which is reducing society in this country to chaos." In March 1920 the councillors expressed their:

> utter contempt and condemnation for the so-called Home Rule
> Bill which Britain proposed to impose on the country despite
> the fact that the measure has been repudiated in advance by all
> Ireland, both north and south.

One member stated that it was only through Sinn Féin that "they could obtain anything, whether Dominion Home Rule or a Republic."

In April 1920 a large number of prisoners in Mountjoy Jail embarked on a hunger strike in demand of special treatment. Nationwide there was massive public support for these men, and the country responded much the same as it had at the time of the conscription crisis two years earlier. Meath was no exception and indeed several men from the county were amongst the striking prisoners. On Tuesday and Wednesday, 13 and 14 April, nationalist Ireland came to a standstill. "One is met with the same story everywhere", a reporter for the *Drogheda Independent* of 17 April wrote, "shops closed and business suspended: as a moral protest it is an amazing spectacle carried out at a night's notice and a moment's deliberation".

In Navan the factories and mills were closed by order of the trade unions, schools were shut, no trains ran, rosaries were recited in public, shops were opened for only one hour in the morning and any firms suspected of carrying on trade were 'visited' by pickets. It was the same scene in the other towns. Public meetings were held with local politicians and the clergy to the forefront. In Navan a resolution condemned "the cowardly brutality of the self-styled government". The local councils all issued messages of solidarity with the prisoners. At a meeting of Navan RDC Christopher Owens stated that:

> the deeds of the British Government in this century have capped
> and exceeded those of the Spanish Inquisition ... the policy
> seems to be to make all Irishmen rebels and they have succeeded.

The furore ended on the Wednesday when the government capitulated and agreed to release up to seventy of the prisoners. Amongst the Meath men freed at this time were Frank Loughran and Patrick Clinch of Navan, John Mangan of Bective and later on, Frank O'Higgins of Kilskyre and Patrick Gilsenan of Killallon.

It may be of interest that not long after this, on 23 May, but otherwise far removed from these turbulent events, Oliver Plunkett, one of Meath's most famous sons, was beatified in Rome. It was a sure sign of the times, however, that the *Meath Chronicle* editorial of 29 May tended to stress his political rather than his spiritual role in the Ireland of his time. It reminded readers that a descendant of Oliver was Joseph Plunkett, who had been executed following the Easter Rising, and it concluded that "Ireland still stands enchained as she did in Essex's time".

Anti-British feeling was certainly running very high at this time and it was evident even in small things, such as when a self-styled Navan Vigilante Committee had announced on 20 March that newsagents in the town had agreed to cease selling those English newspapers which depended for their material on:

> the lurid details of the off-scourings of English courts, divorces and scandals ... and other excrescences which English society at present reeks of.

Despite this hostility to Britain the councils maintained their links with the Local Government Board in the Custom House despite the fact that a Dáil Department of Local Government headed by William T. Cosgrave had been set up over a year before this. Not even Sinn Féin's success in securing a presence on the three UDCs following the first phase of the local government elections in January 1920 had changed the policy of adhesion to the British administration.

No local elections had taken place in Ireland since 1914; the war forced the postponement of the triennial elections scheduled to have been held in 1917 and subsequently they were called off in both 1918 and 1919. The urban elections held on 15 January 1920 were the first in Ireland to be conducted under the proportional representation system. In the lead up to these elections lectures were given in Navan, Trim and Kells to educate the people in the intricacies of PR. The arrangement by which the Trim UDC (9 members) and Kells UDC (15 members) used heretofore to have one-third of their seats up for election every year over the three year cycle now was ended; all the seats were to be filled at the one contest, as had always been the practice in Navan. It has been pointed out earlier in this account that candidates seldom, if ever, gave their party allegiances after their names, since so great was the domination of the Home Rule Party of nationalist Ireland and its local councils, that to do so would be superfluous. But now in 1920 for the first time party designations were given after the names of the candidates.

In the lists of election results that follow the following abbreviations are used: 'S.F.' for Sinn Féin, 'Lab.' for Labour, 'T.T.' for Town Tenants, 'For.' for Foresters, 'F.U.' for Farmers Union and 'Ind.' for Independent. The symbol (o) after a name stands for an outgoing member of a council (as far as this can be ascertained). The compiling of these lists was entirely dependent on the local newspapers so that where there are gaps in the information they are due to gaps in these sources. In the tables which follow (as well as in those which will be later given for county and rural district councils), the candidates' names above the line are placed in the order in which they reached the quota and were elected on successive counts. Below the line the unsuccessful candidates are given in the order of first preference votes they gained; indeed in all cases the votes column refers to first preferences only.

NAVAN URBAN DISTRICT COUNCIL

Navan North (8 seats)

Electorate: 602   **Valid Poll: 347**   **Quota: 40**

NAME	OCCUPATION	ADDRESS	PARTY	VOTES
Laurence Clusker	Bootmaker	O'Growney Tce	T.T.	94
Seán MacNaMidhe	Sawmill manager	Canon Row	S.F.	68
William Breakey (o)	Merchant	Trimgate St	Ind.	38
Stephen Walsh	Labourer	New Lane	Lab.	24
Thomas Fitzsimons	Gentleman	O'Growney Tce	T.T.	6

Edward McCann	Labourer	St Patrick's Tce	T.T.	17
Michael O'Donnell	Chemist	Brews Hill	S.F.	20
Hugh Durr	Tailor	Trimgate St	S.F.	18
Joseph Murray	Labourer	St Patrick's Tce	T.T.	16
Richard McCauley	Shopkeeper	Market Sq.	Ind.	14
James Clark (o)	Farmer	Canon Row	F.U.	8
John Kielty	Draper	Trimgate St	S.F.	7
Thomas Reilly (o)	Victualler	Market Sq.	Ind.	7
Joseph Finnegan	Merchant	Trimgate St	Ind.	6
Michael Gaynor	Labourer	St Patrick's Tce	S.F.	3
John Hyland (o)	Coachbuilder	Trimgate St	Ind.	1

Navan South (7 seats)
Electorate: 523   **Valid Poll:** 305   **Quota:** 39

NAME	OCCUPATION	ADDRESS	PARTY	VOTES
John Spicer (o)	Miller	Belmont	Ind.	71
Joseph Rourke	Bootmaker	St Finian's Tce	T.T.	42
Larry Clarke	Clerk	Brews Hill	S.F.	39
James Boylan	Labourer	Limekiln St	S.F.	23
Joseph Maguire	Newsagent	Trimgate St	Ind.	25
Peter Fox	Labourer	New Bridge	Lab.	13
Eugene Gilsenan (o)	Grocer	Ludlow St	Ind.	18
Patrick Clinch	Shopkeeper	Bridge St	S.F.	22
James Coldrick (o)	Victualler	Watergate St	Ind.	12
James Reilly	Carpenter	Academy St	For.	10
Thomas O'Reilly	Merchant	Trimgate St	Ind.	7
Bernard Reilly	Victualler	Bridge St	Ind.	7

Joseph Keappock (o)	Merchant	Trimgate St	Ind.	6
Pat Loughran	Draper	Market Sq.	S.F.	6
John McEvoy (o)	Merchant	Market Sq.	Ind.	2
Thomas McKeever (o)	Draper	Market Sq.	Ind.	2

Although the fact that a total of thirty two candidates contested the fifteen seats was a healthy sign (in 1914 twenty-seven candidates contested the same number of seats), the combined total valid poll of about 58 per cent was disappointingly low. Outgoing members did poorly with only three being re-elected. It will be noted that all but one of the ten outgoing councillors seeking to be returned used the designation 'Independent'. In all the local elections of this year this description was usually used by those who had served on the councils at the time of the Home Rule, UIL, AOH monopoly of these bodies. With the emergence of new parties and groupings these candidates now found themselves politically disinherited.

The Town Tenants Association was a national organisation which aimed to obtain purchase schemes similar to those available to agricultural tenants, as well as having courts to decide fair rents. In 1919 there had been a prolonged dispute between the Navan branch and the urban council regarding the fixing of rents in some areas of the town. This ended late in May when a settlement was agreed. The tenants had been represented in the talks by Laurence Clusker and Joseph Rourke, both of whom were now elected to the body with which they had been in conflict just a few months earlier. In all there were four Town Tenants' representatives elected, the same as the number of Independents.

Of the five Sinn Féin members, Clarke, MacNaMidhe and Boylan have figured on various occasions earlier in this account. The Labour Party won only two seats but probably was hampered by the presence of the Tenants' candidates.

KELLS URBAN DISTRICT COUNCIL

Kells North (8 seats)
Electorate: 394   **Valid Poll:** 290   **Quota:** 33

NAME	ADDRESS	PARTY	VOTES
Michael Skelly (o)	Climber Hall	S.F.	49
John Reilly (o)	Carrick St	Ind.	44
Christopher McCabe	Maudlin St	S.F.	35
Patrick Connolly	Church Lane	Lab.	31
James Sweeney	Maudlin St	S.F.	10
Matthew Gartland (o)	Carrick St	Ind.	20
Charles O'Hea (o)	Newmarket St	Ind.	14
John English	Carrick St	S.F.	17
Patrick Morgan	Suffolk St	D.S.S.F.	21
Patrick Fox	Market St	Ind.	17
Thomas Fox	Carrick St	S.F.	12
Farrell Tully	Maudlin Road	S.F.	8
William Cooke (o)	Castle St	Ind.	6
John Smith	Fair Green	Lab.	6

Kells South (7 seats)
Electorate: 293   **Valid Poll:** 242   **Quota:** 31

NAME	ADDRESS	PARTY	VOTES
John Cooney (o)	Farrell St	Ind.	45
John Brennan	Kenlis Place	S.F.	41
Richard O'Reilly	Kenlis Place	D.S.S.F.	37
Patrick Hopkins	John St	Ind.	32
Bernard Fitzsimons	Bective Sq.	S.F.	15

E.P. Magee	Farrell St	Ind.	15
Nicholas Tully (o)	Farrell St	Ind.	17
Joseph Lynch	Farrell St	Lab.	11
Patrick Collins (o)	Church St	Ind.	8
Patrick Eustace (o)	Cannon St	Ind.	7
Michael Flanagan	Bective St	S.F.	7
Thomas Skelly (o)	Bective St	Ind.	7

The total valid poll in Kells was over 77 per cent. Outgoing members, all but one of whom styled themselves 'Independent', did much better than in Navan with six out of ten being returned. There was also one new independent member, making a total of seven in this group. Of the six Sinn Féin councillors, Brennan and McCabe had been on the delegation that had successfully requested the previous council a year earlier to cancel the Lloyd races as a gesture of solidarity with the interned prisoners. Labour fared badly with only one member being successful. 'D.S.S.F.' stood for the 'Discharged Soldiers' and Sailors' Federation' and is an indication that the recruiting campaign for the First World War described earlier must have met with a fair degree of success in Kells at least.

TRIM URBAN DISTRICT COUNCIL			
(9 seats)			
Electorate: 460	Valid Poll: 254	Quota: 26	
NAME	ADDRESS	PARTY	VOTES
Patrick Proctor	Loman St	Lab.	48
James Higgins	Market St	S.F.	47
J. J. Reilly	Market St	Comm.	47
Thomas Creighton	Emmet St	Lab.	42
Francis Matthews	Haggard St	Lab.	19

Bernard Reilly	Market St	Ind.	18
Patrick McCabe	Kells Road	Lab.	6
Michael Hynes	Market St	S.F.-Lab.	2
Robert Allen	High St	S.F.	16
Michael Giles	Market St	S.F.	5
James O'Hara	High St	Comm.	3
Daniel Kiely	Emmet St	S.F.	3

The valid poll here was just over 55 per cent. According to the *Meath Chronicle* not one member of the old council even offered himself for re-election. The most striking feature in Trim was the achievement of the Labour Party. Although Hynes gave a dual allegiance, his identification with Labour meant that the party had an overall majority, holding five of the nine seats on the council; as well as that it won over 45 per cent of the valid votes compared to a paltry 9 per cent in Kells and only 6 per cent in Navan. The two Sinn Féin members, Higgins and Allen, were members of families who were to have their homes and businesses burned out when Trim was looted and terrorised later that year in September. The abbreviation 'Comm.' stands for 'Commercial' and doubtless represented some kind of businessmen's grouping.

The *Meath Chronicle* editorial of 14 February 1920 included the following:

> In most cities and urban centres representatives pledged to the Irish cause have been elected chairmen, proof that the electorate have placed their confidence in men who were right on the main point and have revivified and renewed their pledge so gloriously given at the parliamentary election in December 1918 ... the electorate is unrepentant and has shown its determination to pursue to the bitter end its course for Irish freedom.

It is significant that the writer made no reference to the particular situation within his own county. This omission may not be very strange, however, since Sinn Féin could hardly be euphoric about the way things had gone for them in the three UDC elections. Granted this was the first entry of the party into the local hustings but given the decisive victories of Duggan and Mellows in the parliamentary elections just over a year earlier, party members were probably hoping for a better showing. The overall situation was that they controlled none of the councils and only in Navan were they the biggest grouping. Vote-wise the Sinn Féin performance was only mediocre, winning 36 per ent of the valid poll in Kells, 32 per cent in Navan and 28 per cent in Trim; overall this represented about 33 per cent of the valid votes cast but less than 20 per cent of the electorate. The townspeople of Meath could hardly be said to have "placed their confidence in men who were right on the main point."

Despite this, however, when the new councils convened at the end of January two of them elected Sinn Féin men to the chair. In Kells John Brennan defeated John Cooney who had sat on the previous body. This passed off quietly but in Navan there was quite a commotion at the inaugural meeting. The 'old' members were sticking together as Gilsenan proposed and Breakey seconded that John Spicer retain the position of chairman, a position, according to the *Meath Chronicle* report of 7 February 1920, he had held for twenty five years. When, however, his nomination was countered by Boylan and Clusker who proposed MacNaMidhe, Spicer withdrew. Clusker indeed was not impressed with the reasons Gilsenan gave for retaining Spicer, one of which was that "he would conduct business in the usual way". The *Drogheda Independent* of the same date quoted Clusker as saying that:

> if Mr. Spicer conducted business only in the usual way I do not think he will be a most satisfactory chairman as in the past for want of his attendance at several meetings there was no quorum ... it was hard on the officials going around the town trying to get a meeting together.

Spicer, to judge from press accounts, seems to have ended his long service to the council and town on a not very gracious note. The *Chronicle* recorded that when the members decided that future meetings would be held at night-time, rather than in the afternoons as had been the custom, Spicer "thumped the table in rage." Later, after withdrawing his name as a candidate for the chair he left the meeting only to return to let it be known that he was "never coming into this room again." In February he resigned his seat on the council altogether. The new chairman MacNaMidhe stated that:

> if conditions were at all normal I would be the last to oppose Mr. Spicer ... but the present time is abnormal; bayonet force and brute force have taken the place of moral force ... the chairmen of public bodies ... could not be entrusted in a national emergency to safeguard the national interest."

Another Sinn Féin member, Michael O'Donnell, became vice-chairman.

The position as regards Trim is unclear since the council's minute books could not be located and, for no apparent reason, their meetings were seldom if ever reported in the local newspapers (although Trim RDC and Board of Guardians meetings received adequate coverage). However, it is known that the new chairman was J.J. Reilly, the Commercial candidate.

The accession of two Sinn Féiners as chairmen of their urban councils brought no change, drastic or otherwise, in these bodies' dealings with the Local Government Board. Correspondence and communications continued as the councillors fretted about the routine business of local administration, grants and rents, health and housing. There were to be no echoes of the worsening national crisis in the councils' chambers for another six months. But if the local government system remained intact, already by then the British institutions of law and order in the county were being seriously undermined almost to the point of non-existence.

In the previous chapter it has been shown how from the early months of 1920 the RIC were beginning to abandon many of their smaller barracks and to concentrate their numbers in the towns and in a few remaining rural outposts such as Longwood and Crossakiel. About twenty of the deserted barracks in the county were burned in April and May by the Volunteers in order to prevent their reoccupation by the police. With the departure of the RIC from large stretches of the countryside there seems to have been an increase in the crime rate in the first quarter of 1920. Evidence of this comes from the meetings of the Spring Assizes in Trim early in March. The assizes was the highest court in each county; it sat once every three months and dealt with the more serious crimes such as murder, arson and robbery, lesser offences being dealt with by the petty- and quarter-sessions. The assizes was the occasion of the coming together of the Grand Jury, made up of Justices of the Peace. The Grand Jury which convened in Trim in March 1920 was the last effective meeting of this body in Meath. Those present constituted a who's who of the county's gentry class: amongst them were Sir Nugent T. Everard, Sir John Dillon, Rear Admiral Tisdall, Major W.G.R. Tisdall, Major Henry Sterne, Major Allan Montgomery and the quixotically-named Lieutenant-Colonel Dashwood Tandy. They heard from the Lord Chief Justice, who presided, that since their last sitting on 1 December there had been "a recrudescence of crime from which they were for many years happily free": the number of 'specially reported' cases in the three months was forty-three, as compared to only nine in the corresponding period a year earlier.

This upsurge in crime probably hastened what was coming anyway, a native system of law enforcement involving a police force and courts. The police were drawn from the ranks of the Volunteer companies and it soon became the practice of many battalions to include a police officer on its council. It has been seen that it was while carrying out police duties that Séamus Cogan met his death in Oldcastle on 22 July 1920. The republican or Volunteer police, as they became known, began to enforce law and order from about April onwards and over the next year they dealt with offences ranging from the trivial to the most serious, while in the process dispensing a brand of justice that was sometimes primitive but often practical.

One of the first reported cases concerned goods stolen from the Church of Ireland in Navan in May; the local police soon recovered them and arrested the guilty person. In a similar case and around the same time, the parish priest of Kildalkey was given back property that had been stolen from his church over two years before. The Volunteers acted as stewards at race meetings as at Bellewstown in July and at Lloyd in September. At the latter, the *Chronicle* reported, they policed the course and the roads and arrested several pickpockets. That ancient and much-honoured Irish custom of late drinking also came under the scrutiny of the new police. It seems that since the withdrawal of the RIC the licensing laws, or, at least, their observation, had become very lax in rural areas.

In July the police took it upon themselves to have the pubs closed at a 'respectable' hour in Mullagh and Carnaross after the fairs there. Several drinkers who insisted that they had not enough were forcibly removed and marched to their homes. In September Kells Volunteers issued a proclamation for their area regulating the hours for sale of alcohol and prohibiting Sunday drinking altogether. Fines of five shillings for drunk and disorderly behaviour were regularly reported in the local newspaper. The police were also involved in enforcing the Belfast Boycott. Dealers from Belfast were frequent buyers at the cattle markets in Navan. In September they were ordered to leave the town by the local Volunteers who also checked the trains at the Great Northern Railway to ensure that no cattle were destined for Belfast. Truancy was also dealt with. When, in June, a number of boys absconded from Trim Industrial School they were soon located in Castlerickard by the republican police.

Much more serious than all of these was the robbery of silverware and other valuable items from Tobertynan House, the residence of the Duc de Stacpoole, in the Longwood area. The house was also looted as the six intruders destroyed chinaware and oil paintings, smashed windows and furniture and fired shots into the ceiling before their departure on the night of Sunday, 16 May. The Duc himself was away from home at the time but it was said that his housekeeper had been so terrified that she went insane and had to be taken to Mullingar mental hospital. "This was only one of many similar incidents", stated Seán Boylan, who directly involved himself in the pursuit of the criminals. A few days later he met the Duc de Stacpoole in Trim and told him that the Volunteer police would soon restore his property to him. When de Stacpoole told him that the RIC were working on the case Boylan astounded him by saying that "they will do nothing; they are in collusion with the robbers."

Within a week six men were arrested, most of whom admitted their guilt and disclosed the whereabouts of the stolen goods. These were part of a gang, according to Boylan:

who had been terrorising the countryside for some time to the knowledge of the RIC, who took no action in the hope that the robberies would be blamed on the IRA and thus bring discredit on them.

Boylan stated that some of the property was recovered from a hiding place within view of Longwood barracks and he even went so far as to aver that one of the robbers had been advised by an RIC sergeant as to how to dispose of the silverware: "he signed a statement to that effect. I sent one copy to Michael Collins and one to the Duc de Stacpoole." Boylan told the latter that the RIC was "more concerned with arresting us than with restoring your property." Within a fortnight the Volunteers had recovered all the missing items and dealt some summary justice to those who had admitted guilt. They were stripped and flogged; receiving two cuts of a horse whip each, as well as being forced to work on a farm for three weeks.

When the case was finished, de Stacpoole offered Seán Boylan and his men £5, which was refused because, Boylan told him, "We are acting on behalf of the Irish government ... you ought to join us." The Duc demurred but published a letter of appreciation. Boylan heard but could not verify that, on account of this, the British government later reduced de Stacpoole's pension. It is clear that Seán Boylan set great store by this episode and he said that Michael Collins later remarked that their success:

> had done a lot to discredit all the false propaganda emanating from the British government and had brought credit to the IRA in the eyes of the people of both this country and England.

On 10 May, about a week before the looting of de Stacpoole's home, an incident occurred at the other end of the county which was to present the republican police force with their biggest case in this period. On that date a young man in his early twenties named Mark Clinton was shot dead while ploughing on his uncle's land at Cormeen, Moynalty. Although Clinton was a member of the Volunteers there was no political motive in his killing. "The trouble arose over a land dispute", remembered

Charlie Conaty, "the Clintons had secured the disputed land in face of strong local opposition." Two horses had been shot first just as they were being attached to the plough; it is said that that was all that was intended to be done as a warning, but that one of the gunmen on impulse decided to finish it and turned his rifle on Clinton.

What happened next gives a fair indication of the intense bitterness that can be engendered by agrarian disputes. Speaking at the inquest the dead man's father, when asked was it English soldiers who shot his son, replied, "No, but I wish it were ... it was his own neighbours." He went on to say that his son had been shot in the back but managed to turn around and could see his killers. Before he died he told his father that there were five of them but would not give their names. The father then went on to describe the indifference of some neighbours in nearby fields who completely ignored Clinton's dying calls for a drink of water.

Addressing himself to this inhumanity on the following Sunday Bishop Gaughran was his usual straight-talking self. He told his congregation in Mullingar Cathedral that:

> that parish is now stained with the sins of Cain and Achab and as the blood of Abel and Nabath cried out for vengeance so too will it be in this case if God's anger is not appeased ... the circumstances of this murder as revealed by the inquest fills me with horror. To refuse a drink to a dying man and above all to refuse to send for a priest at a moment when a poor soul was in such imminent peril, are features so unIrish that I thought they could be found only in some country like Zululand.

The Volunteer police took an immediate interest in the case although it was almost a month before the *Meath Chronicle* reported, in its issue of 19 June, that a number of men from the Cormeen area were "blindfolded, handcuffed and, like the four men arrested in the previous week in connection with the same matter, removed in a motor lorry to an unknown destination." (An 'unknown destination' was a code word for the improvised detention centres used by the republican police, usually disused farmhouses where Volunteers took turns in guarding the prisoners). In all about a dozen men who became known as 'the

Cormeen gang' were arrested over the next couple of weeks. Some of these were ex-British soldiers and trained snipers.

They were taken to the house of Harry Dyas at Boltown, Kilskyre, where Volunteers of the Fifth Oldcastle Battalion kept guard over them. Both Charlie Conaty and Peter O'Connell spent time on these duties. Peter distinctly recalled arriving with some of the arrested men at Dyas's house very early one morning and seeing a very large crowd just dispersing after a furtively-arranged cock fight which had gone on all night. With more pressing tasks on their minds, the Volunteers turned a blind eye to this activity. (Peter also remembered that it was at this time that he drank his first pint of stout for which he paid two old pence). After a time the prisoners were transferred to the Bohermeen company area and Patsy Bennett recalled doing guard duty over some of them in a house in Cortown.

It was almost the end of June, however, before the alleged ringleader was caught. This was William Gordon, an ex-army sniper of Killagriff, Trohanny, Bailieboro. Most of those who remembered this case were agreed that it was Gordon who actually shot Clinton, another member of the gang having killed the horses. Seán Boylan stated that Gordon "received the sum of £2 for the deed." Gordon remained free until the RIC arrested him on a charge of possession of arms and ammunition without a permit but after a brief hearing in Navan he was set free. Seán Boylan happened to be in Navan on GAA business on that day. A sympathetic *Meath Chronicle* reporter named Seán Hayes kept him in touch with the trial and reported Gordon's acquittal to him. Boylan stated that he then:

> issued orders that all roads leading from the town were to be patrolled by Volunteers and that all pubs were to be searched and, under no circumstances, was Gordon to be allowed to escape.

Word was then received that the wanted man was drinking in the Flat House pub in Railway Street. A number of Volunteers, amongst them Paddy Kelly of Johnstown and Michael McKeon of Navan, entered the pub, spotted Gordon and engaged him in conversation. It seems that they used the pretence that they were going to Bailieboro and offered him a lift but then, with Gordon's guard down, they produced guns and forced him outside into a waiting car. Gordon was taken to a house in Salestown, Dunboyne where he was soon joined by those arrested earlier and all now awaited trial by an IRA military court.

The personnel of this court were appointed by the Volunteers' headquarters staff in Dublin. There were three judges, all of whom were officers of the Dublin Brigade. The prosecution counsel was Séamus O'Higgins of Trim, while Séamus Cogan acted as the prisoners' counsel. The trial was held on a Sunday evening early in July and, according to Seán Boylan, Gordon:

> confessed to the crime and even admitted attempted murder in two other cases as well as to the burning of two homes. He was found guilty and sentenced to death.

This verdict was communicated to both Volunteer headquarters and the Dáil cabinet, the latter ordered a second trial. This was held a fortnight later with the same officers except for Cogan who was now dead. The same verdict was returned, and this time there was to be no reprieve for Gordon.

Seán Boylan recalled bringing a minister of religion to "give spiritual consolation" to the condemned man, who was a Presbyterian. Boylan remembered that Gordon told the minister "that he was not sorry and that he would do it again." "During his period of arrest," said Boylan, "he kept slips of paper with the names of those who had arrested him and kept him prisoner." When the minister pleaded for mercy for Gordon and said that he would arrange for him to be sent to the USA Boylan refused the request point blank saying that he would soon return "to hunt down everyone connected with his arrest and trial and have them arrested by the British." Gordon was executed at Castlefarm, Dunboyne, and his body was disposed of in a local quarry.

As for the other prisoners they were dealt with immediately after the second trial. The man who had shot the horses was sentenced to life expulsion from Ireland and all the others were deported for periods ranging from three to fifteen years, "their cases to be reviewed," wrote Boylan, "when the occupying forces had left the country." They were deported in batches of three and four from Dundalk, Drogheda and the

North Wall in Dublin. Peter O'Connell remembered a bizarre sequel to this episode when about fifty years later the man sentenced to life in exile returned to his native locality and entered a public house in which, unknown to him, was a close relative of Mark Clinton who had been shot dead all those years before. It seems that somebody warned the visitor who left and was never seen in the area again.

While the Volunteer police sometimes administered their own somewhat perfunctory justice, often they referred their prisoners to the newly-created network of Sinn Féin courts. Parish and district courts were rapidly supplanting the petty and quarter sessions in the course of 1920. These were held openly usually in parish halls and their proceedings were extensively reported in the local newspapers. The justices or judges invariably were drawn from the ranks of local councillors, other notabilities and even the Catholic clergy. From the lists of advocates given in the local newspapers' reports of these courts there seems to have been no problem in luring solicitors away from the old system. The courts dealt with minor offences ranging from theft to rowdyism and from drunkenness to wife desertion, five shillings being the standard fine in the latter two instances.

Hand-in-hand with these went the Arbitration Courts which dealt with land disputes and related problems. A typical arbitration court held in Navan in mid-July gave rulings about an equitable price for meadows and the sale of hay and dealt with sheep stealing. Several cases dealt with during this year concerned objections laid before the court by the Back to the Land movement in regard to land division. Cases often bordered on the farcical. For instance, in August, the court in Navan heard a plaintiff named Magee alleging that a man named Sherlock had kicked and otherwise ill-treated his goat, thereby breaking his back; Magee was allowed £2 damages. On the same day, the death of a dog run over by a motor car was considered. The defendant was exonerated, since the dog was adjudged to have been out of control at the time but, with Solomon-like wisdom, the judges ordered the driver of the car to supply the plaintiff with a pup in lieu of the dead dog.

The authorities made but token efforts to break up these sittings. An arbitration court in Navan on 4 October was visited by a group of military and police; the arbitrators were searched and some records and documents were taken away. But there were no arrests and, the *Meath Chronicle* reported on 9 October 1920, that the whole thing was "conducted in the best of good humour." When the police departed the court resumed its hearing of about thirty cases and was not interfered with again.

A report on the scheduled September sitting of Moynalty Petty Sessions gives strong evidence of how the old British administration of justice was rapidly being rendered impotent. Having first noted that the RIC barracks had been burned several months earlier, the *Meath Chronicle* account of 11 September continued that when the court was due to start it was found that there was no policeman with the key to open the courthouse. When approached the local agent refused to hand over the key since rent was due on the building. The courthouse owner, when contacted, consented to open it; even then there was only one case to be dealt with and the Resident Magistrate openly admitted to the reporter that "the bench is paralysed." It is fair to conclude that by the autumn of 1920 all over Meath the king's writ had ceased to operate.

The Local Government Act of 1919 made some attempt to grapple with the problem of the sprawling network of county and rural councils, and it was the new set-up which was used in the elections to these bodies held on Wednesday, 2 June 1920.

Taking the county council first it will be remembered that up to this it was composed mainly of twenty-one members each of which represented one of the twenty-one county electoral divisions into which Meath was divided at the time of the Local Government (1898) Act. There were still to be twenty-one such members but for electoral purposes the county was now divided into five electoral areas each to return a number of councillors. The Navan and Kells areas were to elect five members each, Trim and Slane four each and Dunshaughlin three. The full results of these elections are given hereunder:

MEATH COUNTY COUNCIL

Navan Area (5 seats)
Electorate: 5,414   **Valid Poll:** 3,273   Quota: 546

NAME	ADDRESS	OCCUPATION	PARTY	VOTES
P. O'Growney (o)	Castletown	Farmer	S.F.	773
P. Clinch	Navan	Shopkeeper	S.F.	654
P. Kane	Bohermeen	Farmer	S.F.	563
T. Crahan	Wilkinstown	Farmer	S.F.	420
Major Gerrard	Wilkinstown	Farmer	F.U.	263
P. McDonald	Athlumney	Insurer	S.F.-Lab.	157
T. Bowens	Hayes	Labourer	Lab.	103
J. Spicer (o)	Belmont	Miller	F.U.	93
P.J. Butler	Staffordstown	Farmer	F.U.	85
A. McCann	Ardsallagh	Farmer	F.U.	80
C. Owens	Hayes	Farmer	F.U.	32
J.J. Madden	Oristown	Farmer	Ind.	20
J. McGlew (o)	Castletown	Farmer	Ind.	20
C. Smith	Robinstown	Farmer	Ind.	8
C. McGrath	Kilcarn	Labourer	Ind.	2

Kells Area (5 seats)
Electorate: 5,342   **Valid Poll:** 3,544   Quota: 592

NAME	ADDRESS	OCCUPATION	PARTY	VOTES
John Brennan	Kells	Ironmonger	S.F.	924
Thomas Clinton	Moynalty	Farmer	S.F.	737
Thomas McCabe	Kilbeg	Quarry owner	S.F.	686

Thomas Reilly	Nobber	Farmer	S.F.	337
James McDonnell	Crossakiel	Farmer	S.F.	286
John Cooney	Kells	Merchant	Ind.	417
Patrick Sheridan (o)	Oldcastle	Farmer	Ind.	124
Richard McDonnell	Kells	Solicitor	Ind.	33

Trim Area (4 seats)
Electorate: 3,954   **Valid Poll:** 1,491   **Quota:** 299

NAME	ADDRESS	OCCUPATION	PARTY	VOTES
James Boggan (o)	Enfield	Farmer	S.F.	415
Patrick Proctor	Trim	Labourer	S.F.-Lab.	406
Michael Peppard	Clonard		S.F.	355
Patrick Conlon	Kildalkey	Farmer	S.F.	92
Michael McGarry (o)	Kildalkey	Farmer	Ind.	93
Simon Herbert (o)	Hill of Down	Farmer	Ind.	76
Edward Conlon (o)	Clonard	Farmer	Ind.	54

Slane Area (4 seats)
Electorate: 4,414   **Valid Poll:** 1,770   **Quota:** 355

NAME	ADDRESS	OCCUPATION	PARTY	VOTES
Richard Langan	Bellewstown	Union official	S.F.	489
Edward Collins	Laytown	Land steward	S.F.	345
Laurence Rowan (o)	Stackallen	Farmer	S.F.	343
James McGough	Slane	Farmer	S.F.	301
Arthur Matthews (o)	Mitchelstown	Farmer	Ind.	292

Dunshaughlin Area (3 seats) Electorate: 3,640	Valid Poll: 1,782		Quota: 446	
NAME	ADDRESS	OCCUPATION	PARTY	VOTES
Patrick Moore (o)	Clonee	Farmer	S.F.	588
Thomas Plunkett	Dunshaughlin	Labourer	S.F.-Lab.	576
Martin O'Dwyer	Clonee	Farmer	S.F.	475
Patrick Ward	Dunshaughlin	Labourer	Ind. Lab.	143

It can be clearly seen that, as in the urban elections five months earlier, outgoing members fared poorly. Only eleven even bothered to offer themselves for re-election and of these only four were successful (this may be contrasted with the fact that of the thirty-one members of the newly constituted council which met in June 1914, twenty-six had sat on the outgoing body). It was no coincidence either that these four were offering themselves as Sinn Féin candidates since even a passing glance at the above tables show that Sinn Féin won a sweeping victory. The party, in fact, put up just twenty-one candidates, although three were also Labour men, for the twenty-one seats and were victorious in all but one instance.

The exception was in the Navan area where the Farmers Union candidate, Major T.C. Collins-Gerrard, to give his full name, edged out McDonald. Gerrard, in fact, was best known in Meath at that time as the owner of a horse named Troytown which a couple of months before had won the Aintree Grand National. As a matter of interest Troytown was, up to this point, only the second Meath horse to achieve this. The other was called Manifesto and had won the National in 1897. The owner was Harry Dyas, the Kilskyre man whose house had been used as an 'unknown destination' for those suspected of complicity in the Clinton killing in May 1920.

To return to the election results and equally emphatic of Sinn Féin's dominance was its share of the vote. Although there was a valid poll of only 52 per cent the party won over 83 per cent of this. This includes the votes of the three men designating themselves Sinn Féin-Labour.

Independents, often outgoing men, won less than 10 per cent of the valid poll. The Farmers Union offered candidates in the Navan area only while Labour generally left the way clear for Sinn Féin. Although there was a low turnout of voters one good thing about the new system was that all the seats were contested, unlike the apathy prevalent up to this when, to take 1914 for instance, contests were necessary to fill only nine of the twenty one elective seats.

Turning now to the rural district councils the system here had also been reformed. One council, Edenderry No.3, had in fact been abolished altogether and the area formerly under its jurisdiction was now transferred to Trim RDC. In the case of the remaining seven the mode of election was changed in line with the county council. Up to now the arrangement was that a council area was divided into a number of district electoral divisions each of which returned two members, with the council as a whole having the right to co-opt up to three extra members if it so wished. All the rural district councils, with the exception, as has been just mentioned, of Trim, still administered the same areas but the role of the district electoral divisions was now changed. As with the county council these divisions now were combined to form electoral areas, each of which returned a number of councillors. Navan, for instance, was composed of the Painestown, Castletown and Navan electoral areas returning three, three and five members respectively and giving a total of eleven seats on this RDC.

One result of this change was that the number of members on each council, with the exception of Ardee No.2 which remained the same, was greatly reduced, in some cases drastically so. This was a much needed reform since, as has been seen earlier in this account, absenteeism from council meetings was rife, cancellation of meetings for want of a quorum was commonplace and the policy of co-opting new members, even if such could be found, made little improvement. Indeed as late as December 1919 Navan RDC was discussing the advisability of co-opting five new members. Even when they did agree to do so one member declared that they could get "no one from the Rathkenny area even though I have asked several." When the chairman suggested getting some women members an unidentified voice was reported as objecting that, "you cannot smoke then!"

In numerical terms the membership of the rural district councils was reduced as follows: Navan from 27 to 11, Kells from 50 to 21, Trim from 40 to 22, Oldcastle from 19 to 6, Dunshaughlin from 24 to 12 and Drogheda (Meath) from 12 to 6. In the tabulated election results which follow hereunder gaps in the information regarding voting figures and party affiliations are due to the same gaps in the local press reports. While the reading of these results may be tedious work it is felt necessary to include as full an account as possible, since the consequence of these elections were to prove of vital importance in ending the British hold on the local government network in both county and country.

NAVAN RURAL DISTRICT COUNCIL (11 Seats)

Navan Area (5 seats)

Electorate: 1,560   Valid Poll: 942   Quota: 158

NAME	OCCUPATION	PARTY	VOTES
James Mallon	Farmer	S.F.	241
Patrick Cowley	Farmer	S.F.	233
Thomas Foley	Farmer	S.F.	105
Edward Daly	Labourer	S.F.-Lab.	121
James Harford	Labourer	S.F.-Lab.	102
John Carty	Farmer	Ind.	101
Hugh Murtagh	Farmer	Ind.	20
John Meleady (o)	Labourer	Ind. Lab.	13
Chris McGrath	Labourer	Ind.	6

Castletown Area (3 seats)

Electorate: 1,042   Valid Poll: 602   Quota: 151

NAME	OCCUPATION	PARTY	VOTES
James Ginnity	Labourer	S.F.-Lab.	248

Laurence Rowan (o)	Farmer	S.F.	144
James Tallon	Labourer	S.F.-Lab.	133
Patrick Hoey	Farmer	Ind.	44
Patrick Smith	Labourer	Lab.	33

Painestown Area (3 seats)
Electorate: 955   **Valid Poll:** 473   **Quota:** 119

NAME	OCCUPATION	PARTY	VOTES
Thomas Bowens (o)	Labourer	Lab.	162
Joseph Ledwidge	Flax worker	S.F.-Lab.	118
James Kelly (o)	Clerk	S.F.-Lab.	68
Thomas McGruder	Farmer	Ind.	51
Christopher Owens (o)	Farmer	Ind.	42
William O'Neill	Labourer	Ind.	14
Patrick Dunne	Farmer	Ind.	9
Michael Carter	Farmer	Ind.	4
Patrick Wogan	Merchant	Ind.	4
John Doggett	Labourer	Ind.	1

Council Result: 6 S.F-Lab., 4 S.F., 1 Lab.

KELLS RURAL DISTRICT COUNCIL (21 Seats)
Kells Area (5 seats)
Electorate: –   **Valid Poll:** 623   **Quota:** 105

NAME	ADDRESS	PARTY	VOTES
James Dardis	Staholmog	S.F.	139
Patrick Harte	Greetiagh	S.F.	121
Chris. McCabe	Kells	S.F.	94

William Smith	Cookstown	S.F.	71
Philip Tevlin	Dulane	S.F.	84
James Harte	Ballybeg	Lab.	75
J.J. Madden (o)	Oristown	Ind.	25
Philip Reilly	Staholmog	Ind.	14

Kilskyre Area (5 seats)
Electorate: –   Valid Poll: 659   Quota: 111

NAME	ADDRESS	PARTY	VOTES
Francis Higgins	Balnagon	S.F.	168
Michael Farrelly	Cloonagrouna	S.F.	159
John Keogh	Ballinlough	Ind.	88
James Fox (o)	Girley	Ind.	104
William Dooley (o)	Fordstown	S.F.	72
Bernard Harte	Balrath	S.F.	41
James Lynch	Fordstown	Ind.	27

Nobber Area (5 seats)
Electorate: –   Valid Poll: 535   Quota: 90

NAME	ADDRESS	PARTY	VOTES
Peter Connolly	Meath Hill	S.F.	123
John Hughes	Posseckstown	S.F.	98
Thomas Lynch (o)	Ardmabreague	S.F.	98
Laurence Smith	Posseckstown	S.F.	69
Michael Monaghan (o)	Nobber	Ind.	76
Laurence Carolan	Ardagh	Ind. S.F.	36
James Weldon (o)	Rahood	S.F.	35

Moynalty Area (6 seats)

There was no contest here since only six candidates, all of them labelling themselves Sinn Féin-Labour, were nominated and thus were returned unopposed. They were:

NAME	ADDRESS
Michael Lynch	Skearke
Peter Lynch	Newcastle
George O'Connor	Moynalty
Bart. Reilly	Kilbeg
Hugh Smith	Deerpark
William Tobin	Moybolgue

Council Result: 12 S.F., 6 S.F.-Lab., 3 Ind.

TRIM RURAL DISTRICT COUNCIL (22 Seats)

Athboy Area (7 seats)

Electorate: 1,443   **Valid Poll:** 803   **Quota:** 101

NAME	ADDRESS	PARTY	VOTES
Séamus Finn	Athboy	S.F.	117
Thomas Gilroy	Athboy	S.F.-Lab.	96
Thomas Brown	Ballivor	S.F.-Lab.	93
Patrick Corrigan	Kildalkey	S.F.	72
James Gilsenan	Higginstown	Ind.	67
James Farrell	Higginstown	S.F.-Lab.	75
Patrick Carey	Greenanstown	S.F.-Lab.	67
Simon Murray	Moyrath		47
Thomas Yore	Athboy		41
William Loughran	Ballivor		29
Edward Matthews	Kildalkey		28

Matthew McNamee	Kildalkey		28
Patrick Sheridan	Rathmore	.	22
Patrick Conlon	Kildalkey		17
Chris Proudfoot	Athboy		4

Ballyboggan Area (3 seats)
Electorate: 785   Valid Poll: 358   Quota: 90

NAME	ADDRESS	PARTY	VOTES
James O'Reilly	Kinnegad	S.F.-Lab.	209
Patrick Coughlan	Clonard	S.F.-Lab.	123
Charles Kingston	Hill of Down	Ind.	16
John Langan	Clonard	Ind.	10

Enfield Area (3 seats)
Electorate: 738   Valid Poll: 273   Quota: 56

NAME	ADDRESS	PARTY	VOTES
Joseph Maguire	Enfield	S.F.	98
Peter Maguire	Longwood	Ind.	63
James Ivors	Longwood	Lab.	24
Thomas Pender	Enfield	Lab.	40
John Flynn	Rathcore		22
Patrick Fagan			15
Christopher O'Neill	Enfield		10
James Keegan	Killyon		1

Summerhill Area (4 seats)
Electorate: 1,005   **Valid Poll:** 348   **Quota:** 71

NAME	ADDRESS	PARTY	VOTES
Patrick Duffey	Summerhill	Transport	95
John Shanley	Rathmolyon	Transport	90
John Treacy	Rathmolyon	S.F.	65
William Keogh	Summerhill	Transport	50
John Cusack	Rathmolyon		24
Joseph Shannon	Springvalley		24

Trim Area (4 seats)
Electorate: 809   **Valid Poll:** 445   **Quota:** 90

NAME	ADDRESS	PARTY	VOTES
Christopher Matthews	Commons	Lab.	165
Patrick Callaghan	Tullaghanstown	Ind.	60
John King	Oakstown	S.F.	60
John Mangan	Kilmessan	S.F.	75
John Masterson	Clonmacduff	Lab.	70
J.J.Maguire	Trim	Ind.	30
John Gaughran	Commons	Lab.	•5

Council Result: 8 S.F.-Lab., 2 Ind., 1 Lab., 1 S.F.

DUNSHAUGHLIN RURAL DISTRICT COUNCIL (12 Seats)
Dunshaughlin Area (8 seats)
Electorate: 1,957   **Valid Poll:** 998   **Quota:** 112

NAME	ADDRESS	PARTY	VOTES
Bart Fitzsimons	Branstown	S.F.-Lab.	187

Thomas Dungan	Killeen	S.F.-Lab.	163
James Kearns	Roberstown	S.F.-Lab.	153
John McCormack	Pelletstown	S.F.-Lab.	76
William Doran	Kilmessan	Ind.	102
Mark O'Neill	Kilmessan	Lab.	73
Margaret Murray	Dunshaughlin	S.F.	63
Patrick Duffy	Ballybin	Ind.	73
Christopher Russell	Ashbourne	Ind.	51
Patrick Ward	Dunshaughlin	Ind. Lab.	35
Joseph White	Ballybin	Lab.	22

Dunboyne Area (4 seats)

There was no contest here since only four candidates were nominated. All represented S.F.-Lab. They were:

NAME	ADDRESS
Seán Boylan	Dunboyne
David Hall	Cultromer
James Mangan	Kilmore
Michael Reid	Dunboyne

Council Result: 8 S.F.-Lab., 2 Ind., 1 Lab., 1 S.F.

OLDCASTLE RURAL DISTRICT COUNCIL (6 Seats)

Oldcastle Area (6 seats)

Electorate: –   **Valid Poll:** 1,172   **Quota:** 168

NAME	ADDRESS	PARTY	VOTES
John Hand	Oldcastle	S.F.	308
James Smith (o)	Halfcarton	S.F.	208
Thomas McCabe (o)	Moate	S.F.	119

Francis Reilly	Boolies	S.F.	155
Frank Gilsenan	Gibbonstown	S.F.	103
Thomas Carr	Rathbrack	S.F.	129
Thomas Gibney (o)	Milltown	Ind.	76
Patrick Sheridan (o)	Boolies	Ind.	35
Thomas Glennon (o)	Galboystown	Ind.	20
Luke Caffrey (o)		Ind.	14
Morgan Ryan (o)		Ind.	5

Ardee (Meath) (6 seats)

Information here is very sketchy. There was one electoral area with ten candidates vying for the six seats. The local press gives only the names of the successful candidates and makes no reference to party affiliations. The elected members and their votes tally, on a quota of 69, were:

NAME	ADDRESS	VOTES
Michael Markey	Parsontown	129
Matthew Downey (o)	Grangegeeth	90
George Taaffe	Bigstown	53
George Garland	Howthstown	40
Nicholas Slevin	Mentrim	40
Thomas Kieran (o)	Balrath	38

Drogheda (Meath) (6 seats)

Again information is sparse. Fourteen candidates contested the six seats in the one electoral area. There was a valid poll of 876 giving a quota of 126. But the size of the electorate and individual voting figures for each candidate are not given. Neither are the names of the defeated contestants nor the party designations of these elected:

NAME	ADDRESS
Michael Connor	Duleek

Edward Collins	Corballis
James Deery	Donacarney
Patrick Dunne	Collierstown
William McGrane	Stamullen
Robert Moore	Robinstown

Boards of Guardians

It will be remembered that the Boards of Guardians, which administered the workhouses, were made up of the local RDC members, except that in Navan, Kells and Trim, the urban electorates were entitled to vote a number of additional members on to them. Thus there were also urban elections of a sort on 2 June.

Navan (4 seats)
Electorate: 1,124   **Valid Poll:** 584   **Quota:** 118

NAME	PARTY	VOTES
Patrick Clinch	S.F.	234
Laurence Clusker (o)	Ind.	99
John Spicer (o)	Ind.	76
James Hilliard (o)	S.F.	55
James Boylan	S.F.-Lab.	51
Joseph Keappock	Ind.	25
Joseph Rourke	S.F.-Lab.	17
Pat. Sheridan (o)	Ind.	16
James Ross (o)	Ind.	6
Alfred Walsh (o)	Ind.	5

Kells (5 seats)

Electorate: 687   Valid Poll: 466   Quota: 79

NAME	PARTY	VOTES
John English	S.F.	87
Nicholas Tully	Ind.	57
Matthew Gartland	Ind.	56
Bernard Fitzsimons	S.F.	51
Michael Skelly	S.F.	43
Joseph Lynch	S.F.-Lab.	47
Patrick Collins	Ind.	44
James Sweeney	S.F.-Lab.	36
Richard O'Reilly	D.S.S.F.	30
Thomas McManus	Ind.	15

Trim (3 seats)

Only three candidates were nominated and so were returned unopposed. They were:

NAME	PARTY
Michael Gorman	Ind.
Patrick Mooney	S.F.
Patrick Proctor	S.F. Lab.

These three were new guardians since none of the outgoing ones presented themselves for re-election.

What conclusions may be drawn from the foregoing mass of figures, names and parties? First of all a few general observations: as in the case of the county council, the voter turnout was only mediocre; for Navan RDC the level of valid votes was 57 per cent, for Dunshaughlin 51 per cent, while for Trim it was a lowly 47 per cent. Figures are not available for the other councils, but the *Drogheda Independent* of 12 June states that for the county and rural district councils elections combined there was a poll of 56 per cent. We have already seen that the county council contest on its own was 52 per cent which would leave the total rural council figure at much the same level (which in turn would be consistent with the Trim, Dunshaughlin and Navan figures).

Against that, however, the new system of electoral areas ensured that in all but two out of the seventeen areas there were contests for the seats. Contrast this with the farcical situation in 1914 when contests were necessary in only thirteen out of the eighty nine district electoral divisions, into which Meath was divided for the purposes of the rural council elections.

What were the political results of the elections? The *Meath Chronicle* was in little doubt. On its usually nondescript front page its issue of 5 June carried the following headlines: 'Smashing Sinn Féin Victory in Meath', 'National Majority On All Boards', 'Clean Sweep In Some Areas.' The hyperbole continued the following week when all the election results were known: 'Meath Solid for Sinn Féin', 'National Candidates Win Easily', 'Huge Majority on all Boards', 'Great Sweep in County Council'. The editorial writer exulted that:

> with almost unanimous voice the royal county has declared for
> a republic ... the rural councils are manned almost exclusively
> by Sinn Féin.

The *Drogheda Independent*, still suspicious of Sinn Féin, was more restrained. Only a year and a half before, in an editorial on 25 January 1919, it had referred to the first Dáil meeting as:

> a splendid display of spectacular politics that will prove impotent
> ... its legislation will not secure adhesion from the general body
> of Irishmen.

Now its editorial of 12 June conceded that "the majority of those who have exercised the franchise are in favour of Sinn Féin or republican policy." The comments which followed were more explanatory of this development rather than approving of it:

> It may be said that politics may have little or nothing to do
> with the business for which county councils, rural councils and
> boards of guardians are elected ... in a well ordered state and
> under normal conditions such a contention would be perfectly
> reasonable. This country however is neither well ordered nor are
> conditions prevailing normal; on the contrary a condition of
> governmental topsy turveydom is the outstanding feature of the
> Irish situation at the moment; in such circumstances it is natural
> that voters should concentrate on high politics when exercising
> the local government franchise and should avail of the occasion
> to give their views on the all compelling Irish national question.

This was a grudging blessing, if indeed a blessing at all.

And yet it would be difficult to quarrel with the euphoric expressions
of the *Chronicle* headline writer. The county council was almost the
monopoly of Sinn Féin. As regards the rural district councils they held an
overall majority in Kells and Oldcastle and in alliance with Labour they
controlled Navan, Trim and Dunshaughlin and, while party affiliations
are lacking in the cases of Ardee and Drogheda, the subsequent actions
of these two councils indicate that they too were of the Sinn Féin
persuasion. Furthermore, the outcomes of the three urban boards of
guardians' elections would have served to have consolidated the party's
control of these three bodies. It should perhaps be explained that the
Sinn Féin-Labour alliance meant basically that while the Labour Party
wished to keep its own identity, it agreed with Sinn Féin policy on
the national question. This would manifest itself at local level by the
two parties combining to free the councils from the grasp of the Local
Government Board and deliver them to the suzerainty of the Dáil.

In voting terms, for those councils for which figures are available,
Sinn Féin's performance could hardly be faulted: the party won 87 per
cent of the valid poll in Oldcastle, 77 per cent in Kells, 75 per cent in
Navan, 64 per cent in Dunshaughlin and 50 per cent in Trim, (although
this last figure may be understated since party affiliations could not be
ascertained for many of the defeated candidates for this council). These

percentages would be consistent with the 83 per cent won by the party in the county council election. Much more interesting and significant are the statistics of the Boards of Guardians elections in Navan and Kells. Remember that these were the same two bodies of voters who elected the urban councils in January. On that occasion Sinn Féin won just 32 per cent of the valid poll in Navan and 36 per cent in Kells; now only five months later it took 61 per cent and 57 per cent respectively. All the foregoing percentages refer to Sinn Féin candidates plus Sinn Féin-Labour candidates. The use of the dual designation did not mean that those adopting it were primarily Labour men. Sinn Féiners with no connection with Labour often adopted the label as a gesture of goodwill towards the party which was showing solidarity with them on the issue of national sovereignty. For this reason it would be impossible to assess the Labour performance *per se*; the only observation that may be made is that in the rural council elections for which information is available twelve candidates labelling themselves either 'Labour' or 'Independent Labour' went forward and only five were successful. An interesting development was the success of 'Transport' candidates in the Summerhill area of the Trim council; these represented the ITGWU which since 1918 had been organising itself in Meath in opposition to the longer established Labour Union. (This development will be examined in more detail in the next chapter). Overall, Independents fared only indifferently in both the RDC and Boards of Guardians' elections. One noteworthy point is that of almost two hundred candidates for the three types of elections only one was a woman – this was Margaret Murray who was elected to Dunshaughlin RDC.

Still the most salient feature remains the performance of Sinn Féin which now held the same kind of stranglehold on the local government bodies enjoyed just a few years earlier by the supporters of the now almost defunct Home Rule Party. It may have been noticed that amongst the newly elected rural councillors were Seán Boylan (Dunshaughlin) and Séamus Finn (Trim), the two leading figures in the county's Volunteer movement, as well as John Keogh (Kells) who was soon to succeed Séamus Cogan as O/C of the Fifth Oldcastle Battalion. Boylan and Finn indeed were soon to be members of the county council, where they could number other Volunteers amongst their colleagues. These new men, avowed revolutionaries, were in stark contrast to the tame constitutionalists and upholders of the status quo which they replaced. Long-serving public representatives such as Thomas Halligan, P.J. Kennedy, Edward Kelly, Patrick Boyle and Sir Nugent Everard, to name but a few, were now consigned, to adapt Trotsky's famous phrase, to 'the dustbins of local history'.

The inaugural meeting of the new county council was held in the County Hall, Navan on Saturday, 19 June. Of the twenty-one elected members only the sole Independent, Major Gerrard, was absent. These were joined by the ex-officio members, namely, the seven new chairmen of the RDCs: James Ginnity (Navan), George O'Connor (Kells), Séamus Finn (Trim), John Hand (Oldcastle), David Hall (Dunshaughlin), Michael Markey (Ardee) and John O'Farrell (Drogheda). The last named was a co-opted member of his rural council. All seven were committed to Sinn Féin policies.

A new chairman, Patrick Clinch, was elected without contest. Clinch was a Dublin man who had fought in the Easter Rising, had been interned for a while afterwards and, following his release, had moved to Navan where he ran a newsagent's shop called 'Siopa na nGael' on Ludlow Street. In January 1920 he had been an unsuccessful Sinn Féin candidate in the Navan UDC elections. In April he had been one of those released following the hunger strike in Mountjoy Jail and now in June he found himself enjoying respectability as a member of Navan Board of Guardians as well as county council chairman. He was, incidentally, also involved in his local Volunteer company. The new vice-chairman of the county council was Martin O'Dwyer.

The council's next business was to co-opt two more members. Their unanimous choices were Seán Boylan and Seán MacNaMidhe whose Sinn Féin and republican leanings have been clearly evidenced already in this account. Next came the resolution which repudiated the Local Government Board. It was moved by Clinch and seconded by O'Dwyer:

> that this council, being the elected representatives of the county
> of Meath, hereby recognises the authority of Dáil Eireann as the
> duly elected government of the Irish people and undertakes to
> give effect to all decrees promulgated by the said Dáil.

The motion was passed unanimously. In the course of June and July the same resolution was to be passed by the RDCs and guardians of Navan, Trim, Kells, Dunshaughlin and Oldcastle; by the Drogheda (Meath) council on 10 July and by the Navan and Kells UDCs on 20 July. As regards Ardee RDC and Trim UDC information could not be obtained on this matter but there is certainly no reason to believe, nor did anything happen subsequently to indicate otherwise, that they too did not follow suit.

The county council meeting continued with unabated zeal. The members resolved that business should be conducted as much as possible through Irish; that bills, cheques and signatures were all to be written in that language; that all applicants for jobs under the councils should have an adequate knowledge of Irish; and that henceforth the council should be properly known by the Irish version of its name, 'Comhairle Chontae na Midhe'. Indeed over the next year press reports of the council's meetings were headed by the Irish name and the same happened in the cases of most of the subsidiary councils.

It was also resolved that the republican flag be hoisted over the County Hall when the council was in session and that the Volunteers should not only be thanked for their supervision of the local elections but that an extra rate of one and a half pence in the pound be struck for their upkeep. The council even resolved to recognise Irish time only, since as one member put it, "God's time is good enough for the Irish people and we're not going to change our clocks at the whim of a foreign government." A further motion was sponsored by Finn and Boylan to the effect that:

> this council instructs the secretary not to supply statistics from which income tax gatherers can get information for raising this tax and that we refuse to supply particulars of officials' or employees' salaries for this purpose and that we place every obstacle in the way of the tax gatherers.

This motion was passed with the usual acclaim.

There was a slight crack in the united front when it came to appointing the council's various sub-committees. When two of the previous council members, Rowan and Boggan, proposed that Sir Nugent Everard be retained on the agricultural committee they were rounded on by James Ginnity and David Hall who introduced a blunt counter-proposal that "Everard be not a member of the committee". Ginnity alleged that when a labour strike was in progress a year earlier, Everard "tried to get the army of occupation to crush the transport workers", and Hall similarly claimed that he had "approached Dublin Castle for the protection of the armed forces." "He is no great friend of Ireland", concluded Ginnity, and, while a couple of councillors magnanimously recognised Everard's work in the agricultural sphere, the counter-proposal stood.

Thus ended the first meeting of the council. The next few meetings continued in a similar vein. In July, for instance, the council's officials were warned not to have communications or dealings with the LGB and that "those not obeying this directive are liable to dismissal or suspension." On 9 August a call was made on "those in Meath who hold Commissions of the Peace under the British government to resign same", while later that month a conciliatory gesture was made, on the suggestion of the Dáil's Ministry of Labour, towards RIC men who had left the force and that they "be given a chance to become loyal citizens and find suitable work." Those citizens of the Labour Party who had already proven their loyalty to Sinn Féin were now rewarded with a council motion to "employ none but trade union labour in council departments."

Further confirmation, if such is needed, of the new outlook of the local councils can be seen in an item of the business of Dunshaughlin RDC in July. It was proposed that "the resolution passed on 9 May 1916, condemning the Easter Rising be rescinded." The resolution referred to had recorded the then councillors' "abhorrence of the recent rebellion in Dublin and throughout the country whereby many innocent and inoffensive people have lost their lives." This was now deleted from the minute book with the vice-chairman explaining that those who had passed it originally were to be excused on the grounds of ignorance of the facts. At about the same time a member of Navan RDC inquired if a similar motion of condemnation of the Easter Rising was on that body's minute books but was assured that it was merely a resolution of sympathy. In late July almost all councils extended sympathy to the relatives of Séamus Cogan while in September they adjourned as a mark of support for the hunger-striking Terence McSwiney.

It must be understood, however, that all these resolutions, orders and activities of an overtly political nature formed but a fraction of the business of the various councils which, heady revolution or not, had to contend with the routine tasks of administering their areas. In so doing some of these councils by the end of 1920 found themselves running into certain difficulties. At first the authorities reacted very cautiously to their rebellious behaviour; a number of circulars and letters from the LGB warning that grants and other monies were liable to be cut off was their only response for the first five months. Then on 22 November a number of RIC men called to the county hall and took away minute books, files pertaining to the finance committee, letters from the Dáil, rate collectors' statements and so on.

A week later the police returned and took away more documents. It was probably from this time onwards that the county council began to meet in secret. Séamus Finn recalled meetings being held in the homes of councillors Martin O'Dwyer in Clonee and Patrick Kane in Bohermeen and later in the South Dublin Union on St. James Street. Attendances, never great since the initial enthusiasm of the summer months, now plummeted, The nine meetings held between August and December attracted an average attendance of only eleven members out of a total of thirty. Only one of these meetings, however, had had to be cancelled for want of a quorum of eight councillors but now in 1921 of the ten meetings scheduled between January and the July Truce only five went ahead, and in the cases of two of these it was only with the special permission of the Dáil representative who overlooked the fact that there was no quorum in either instance.

While it may be said that absenteeism was as much an affliction of the revolutionaries as of their predecessors it should, in fairness, be pointed out that men such as Boylan and Finn were by this time more preoccupied with the military struggle, that at least three county councillors, Ginnity, Thomas McCabe and Patrick Hopkins, who had replaced MacNaMidhe in September, were in jail for much of this period and that several others were doubtless reluctant to appear in public lest they should suffer a similar fate.

Police harassment and poor attendance at meetings were handicaps enough for the county council but another headache presented itself in the form of the attitude taken by its most important official, the county secretary John Grennan. It seems that Grennan had maintained correspondence with the LGB despite the council's breaking of links with this body in June. At the council meeting of 25 October the secretary's dissidence was first raised, following a report from the Finance Committee "that he had refused to give an undertaking as to the discharge of his duties." After some discussion the thirteen members present all agreed that Grennan be suspended and his case be considered. Grennan claimed in his defence that relevant sections of the Local Government (1898) Act "require me as secretary to perform certain duties." He also alleged that the real reason for his suspension was his refusal to take a republican pledge. This was denied by chairman Clinch who, in a letter to the *Meath Chronicle* of 7 May 1921, explained that:

> the action taken against Grennan was because of his persistent refusal to obey the orders of the authorised committee of the council in regard to matters of public administration.

By this time Grennan's fate remained undecided and there seems to have been reluctance on the part of the council to take the ultimate decision of dismissal. Suspension or not he seems to have continued with his work and the council's minute books in fact record his attendance at council meetings during this period. Not that the secretary was in any way repentant. In February, for instance, he refused to allow a Dáil representative to examine the council's books and it was this which once again brought the simmering pot to the boil. At the meeting of 18 February a motion that the "secretary of the council be hereby dismissed on grounds of disobedience" was carried by seven votes to two.

But the story did not end here as the resilient Grennan continued to turn up at his office insisting that he could not legally be dismissed without the concurrence of the LGB. Early in April he once again refused a Dáil emissary access to council papers following which he received a letter from the council ordering him to quit his office at once.

Probably wisely in the circumstances he obeyed this order, stating that "rather than risk my personal safety by staying in office I will resign." One cannot help feeling that, politics aside, John Grennan was a man of conscience whose stand at the time cost him both public opprobrium and financial loss. When, the following September, the council was read a letter from him tendering his resignation and asking for his pension the councillors were dismissive towards both him and his service of over twenty years.

By the turn of the year 1920–21 the county council and some of its dependant rural councils were labouring under yet another difficulty – money or, to be precise, shortage of it. It was no idle threat on the part of the LGB when in August they informed the county council that:

> no loans or grants from public funds for any purpose shall be made to any local authority who will refuse to submit accounts to audit and conform to the rules and orders of the LGB.

One decision of a financial nature taken by the first council meeting in June was not to defend claims made under British statute for malicious injuries. When decrees were given it would be the council's attitude that it could not meet them. It seems that there were indications that the British authorities were about to seize the councils' money in the banks so that at the meeting of 25 August it was decided "to cancel the appointment of the Hibernian Bank (Navan branch) as treasurers of this council."

In effect, this meant that the council withdrew about £50,000 from the bank and placed it in the care of trustees. The LGB retaliated in September by refusing to pay over £40,000 worth of loans and grants. This loss was made up by the securing of extensive credit over the next few months; the hope was that the crisis would ease when the following year's rates became available.

On 26 November, however, the county's rate collectors, following protracted pressure from the LGB, met and agreed to obey an order from that body directing them to cease paying over the rates to the council's trustees. Instead, they put the money into their own accounts. At the county council meeting of 13 December the members were informed by the supposedly suspended Grennan that their financial position was a "deplorable state of affairs." The council's commitments to its rural councils and boards of guardians could not be met while wages could not be paid to the gangers and road workers. Because of the stoppage of all work on the roads the council meeting of 31 January reluctantly agreed to reappoint the Hibernian Bank as its treasurer. There was no sacrifice of principle here since no recognition of the LGB was involved. The rate collectors now began to lodge their monies in the Hibernian Bank and the crisis gradually came to an end as there seems to have been no attempt on the part of the authorities to seize the money for meeting malicious injury claims.

The *Meath Chronicle* on 5 February 1920 stated that:

> practically all public bodies in the county financed through the county council have been affected by the financial crux which has become more acute during the last few weeks.

At a meeting of Kells Board of Guardians it was acknowledged that but for the work of the St Vincent de Paul Society and the generosity of local rural council chairman George O'Connor, the workhouse outdoor relief programme would long have ended. There were similar sentiments expressed in Dunshaughlin while at a meeting of Navan RDC in late January the idea was even mooted that they should return under the aegis of the LGB. This suggestion was defeated by six votes to two, with James Hilliard reminding his colleagues that "to go back now would make us traitors to our country."

The Navan urban councillors, however, did not show the same resistance to temptation for it was the financial exigencies of this time which was the root cause of this council embarking on a remarkable series of changes of direction in their allegiances. In the space of only fourteen months the Navan body contrived to switch from the LGB to the Dáil, back to the LGB again and finally back to the Dáil! This was the only instance of a Meath council breaking ranks with Sinn Féin and it was such a controversial issue that it is deserving of close consideration.

It was at their meeting of 20 July that Navan UDC had resolved:

to acknowledge the authority of Dáil Eireann as the duly elected government of Ireland and to undertake to give effect to all decrees and orders promulgated by said Dáil.

Eleven of the fourteen members, (nobody had yet been co-opted to replace John Spicer), were in attendance and the vote in favour was unanimous. For the next four months the councillors adhered to this line. As with all the councils they still received communications from the LGB but these were ignored. For instance, on 17 August, a letter from Dublin Castle requesting assurances that the council's accounts be submitted to LGB audit and that the orders be conformed with was marked 'read'; and on 19 October a strong warning from the same source that loans and grants were about to be withheld received the same response. During this period also, on 23 August, the council decided, in conformity with the Dáil's Belfast Boycott, that the Belfast Bank be removed as its treasurer.

By mid-November, however, some of the councillors began to have second thoughts. The council chairman, Seán MacNaMidhe, attended no meetings between 9 November 1920 and 12 April 1921 because he was, for most of this time held in detention. His place as chairman was taken by Michael O'Donnell, the Sinn Féin councillor, who had been appointed vice-chairman at the first meeting in January 1920.

At the meeting of 16 November a letter was read from the Inspector of Taxes asking if the council would give information regarding its liability. It was proposed and seconded by two of the Town Tenants' representatives that this information should be given and there was a counter-proposal from two of the Sinn Féin members that it should not. The counter-proposal was carried, but only just, by six votes to five with two abstentions.

Later at this same meeting acting chairman O'Donnell took the initiative in breaking from his own party's policies when he proposed that a resolution passed at an earlier meeting to the effect that no repayments be made on LGB loans be now rescinded, "in justice and fair play". The *Chronicle* report of 20 November further quoted him as saying:

If the money was not paid the houses were there as security and could be seized at any time and ... the tenants ... thrown out on the street. Their waterworks could be seized and the supply cut off.

When Sinn Féin member Hugh Durr asked the chairman to adjourn the matter for consideration for a fortnight, he was refused. Durr then stated that "this is not a question of repayments; this is a question of Ireland against England". Another Sinn Féiner, James Boylan, told his colleagues that "any man who does not adhere to Dáil Eireann is not worthy to call himself an Irishman ... you are traitors to your country." These emotional outbursts, however, could not prevent the motion being carried by eight votes to four with one abstention. Those who voted against were Durr, Boylan, Larry Clarke and Joseph Rourke, who was elected as a Town Tenants' member but was also involved in Sinn Féin. Following the vote Boylan told his colleagues that "this council is a disgrace to the rest of Ireland."

Further disgrace was to follow. The position now was that Navan UDC, implicitly at least, had returned to the LGB fold. Some of the members were determined to make this recognition explicit and a special meeting, which could be held under Standing Orders if eight members gave notice requesting such, was called for Monday, 20 December. Twelve members were present and the business consisted of two resolutions. The first was that the resolution withdrawing funds from the Belfast Bank be rescinded, that the appointment of trustees to look after the money be rescinded, and that a bank be appointed as the council's treasurer. The second motion was that the council should:

> give the necessary assurances that monies coming to us from the Local Taxation Account be distributed to the services to which they are assigned by statute and that our accounts will be submitted for audit to the LGB whose rules and orders will be conformed to by us, any previous resolution on this subject to be rescinded.

Both resolutions were in the names of two Tenants' representatives, Edward McCann and Thomas Fitzsimons, and both were carried by a margin of seven votes. Neither the minute books nor the press reports record how each individual councillor voted nor do they give the total votes for and against but bearing in mind that there were only twelve men present and that the margin of victory was seven some juggling with figures will show that the most who could have voted against those motions was only two. This represented a major about turn on the unanimous pro-Dáil vote of exactly five months earlier.

Over the next few months it is interesting to note that the type of importuning letters once received from the LGB was now coming to the council from the Dáil Department of Local Government. One in January pointed out the "persistent difficulties sustained by all local authorities"; another in March adopted the same tone. In both cases the council ordered that 'no action be taken'. At the meeting of 4 March the clerk reported that Ledger and Rate Books had been removed from his office in the name of the IRA; again this is most ironic since it had been just four months earlier, in November, that the RIC had visited the same office and taken away books and documents of the then 'subversive' council.

In this period, the first half of 1921, one is also struck by how irregular and infrequent was the attendance of the Sinn Féin councillors, as recorded in the minute books. Most seemed to have lost all interest. They were probably boosted, however, by the return of Seán MacNaMidhe on 12 April. At once he resumed the chairmanship to which he had been re-elected despite his absence at the previous January's annual meeting. During a somewhat acrimonious debate on housing on 17 May the *Chronicle* of 21 May recorded the returned chairman taunting his colleagues that "behind my back a majority decided to recognise [the LGB]" and reminding them that "you cannot serve two masters." The next development came on 7 June when the meeting was read a letter from the Dáil regarding the Belfast Boycott and asking that they have no dealings with, or accept cheques from, the Belfast Bank which had first been ousted from this position on 23 August only to be reinstated on 20 December.

The labyrinthine series of twists and turns finally ended on 20 September and was reported in the Meath Chronicle on 24 September. At a meeting attended by only eight members, perhaps the others did not relish eating humble pie, MacNaMidhe proposed and Fitzsimons seconded that:

> recognising our error in returning to the Local Government Board established by the English Parliament in this country, we, the Navan Urban District Council now hereby formally renounce our connection with that body and solemnly pledge our allegiance for the future to Dáil Éireann, the Government of the elected representatives of the people.

This was passed unanimously. The timing of this repentance is doubtless explained by the great feeling of jubilation which was permeating republican Ireland since the Truce in July. In Irish eyes this was viewed as a major victory and those who had wavered in their convictions now probably felt distinctly uncomfortable in the immediate post-Truce euphoria.

But why in the first place had the council reneged on its commitment to the Dáil? The following exchange is taken from the *Meath Chronicle* report of the debate at the crucial meeting on 20 December:

> Mr. Durr: "Is this council to forswear its allegiance to Dáil Éireann?"
> Mr. Walsh: "We cannot carry on without money."

And at the meeting of 20 September just mentioned when the chairman said that they "could scarcely hold up their heads to the rest of the country", Laurence Clusker took exception and explained that the change of loyalties was to secure grants to give employment locally. It is fair to say then that it was a concern with employment rather than any inherent pro-British outlook which explains the original defection. Such a concern would be consistent with a council which included four Town Tenants men and two Labour men. Against that, it must be pointed out that other councils with similar concerns and difficulties during this time remained loyal to the Dáil throughout.

In the world of local politics, of course, memories are long and over the years this issue had been resurrected on several occasions and blame apportioned. Even almost fifty years later the matter was being alluded to by Séamus Finn at a County Council meeting and a public argument ensued between him and a Navan member of the council.

Still the loss of Navan UDC was only a minor setback for Sinn Féin. Politically they still reigned supreme. This was shown in May 1921 when the elections to the Southern Ireland Parliament were held. Sinn Féin in fact rejected the very nature of this parliament since it was only a Home Rule arrangement and it created a partitioned island. The party, however, decided to use the election machinery to show their overwhelming support and also to use the occasion as a means of constituting the Second Dáil. There were, in fact, no elections. In all but one constituency Sinn Féiners were returned unopposed. So it was in Meath-Louth, the two counties having been joined together to form one constituency, returning five members. The five were Eamon Duggan, Justin McKenna (a solicitor from Mullagh), and three Louth men: J.J. O'Kelly, Peter Hughes and Séamus Murphy.

In Meath, then, by the time the Truce was signed on 11 July, Sinn Féin controlled practically the whole local government apparatus, directed a police force (however rudimentary), had organised an efficient court system and was unchallenged at the polls.

7

1918-23

Other Troubles - Land and Labour

Concurrent with the political and military struggles described in the previous two chapters, county Meath also witnessed much activity and upheaval in the arena of labour relations and land redistribution. It is, in fact, difficult to separate the two since, as will later become clear, the men who engaged in labour disputes and strikes against the farmers of Meath were often the same men who peopled their local branches of Back to the Land, the movement which aimed to divide the estates amongst the landless. For the sake of clarity, however, it is best to deal separately with these two aspects.

Until 1918 the Meath Labour Union could still claim to be the county's premier workingmen's organisation, but by the end of that year it has been seen that it was being challenged by the encroaching ITGWU, which was beginning to poach members and indeed branches en masse from the MLU. C. Desmond Greaves, in his book *The Irish Transport and General Workers Union: the Formative Years* (Gill & Macmillan, 1982), has recorded that:

On 1 January [1918] the Meath Labour Union resolved that they would affiliate to the ITUC [Irish Trade Union Congress]. However, between January and April they read of the meetings in Dublin in support of the Russian Revolution. They concluded that Irish labour was heavily infected with socialism – as indeed it was – and on 2 April they reversed their decision, resolving instead to affiliate to a new organisation known as the 'Association of Rural Workers and Workmen's Labour Unions. (ps 192–3)

1917 was the year of the Communist Revolution in Russia which brought hope to the lower classes everywhere but which seems to have been regarded with suspicion by the MLU. This conservative stance was in sharp contrast to the radical leanings of the leaders of the Transport Union who, as will be seen later, made no secret of their desire to import Russian conditions into Ireland.

Founded principally by James Larkin in Dublin in January 1909, the ITGWU in its early years spread only to Belfast and counties Wexford and Sligo. In 1917 branches were set up in Waterford, Kerry, Wicklow, Offaly, Laois and Limerick but it was not until the following year that the organisation really took off. "Until 1918", according to David Fitzpatrick, "rural Ireland proved indifferent to the ITGWU's exhortations." (*Politics and Irish Life 1913–21*, p 241)

Manuscript 7282 in the National Library of Ireland provides a list of Transport Union branches between 1909 and 1922, giving the founding dates of each branch, the names of secretaries and in some cases the number of members in each unit. In Meath the first ITGWU branch was formed in Navan on 16 February 1918 with Stephen Walsh as secretary and with a membership of 191 by the end of the year. There was a lull in organisation for six months until Trim (Christopher Matthews as secretary – 50 members) and Oldcastle (Thomas Smyth – 80 members) were both formed on 13 August. Kells (James Sweeney – 50 members) and Dunboyne (J. Maguire – 187 members) soon followed on 3 September; Drumree (David Hall – 64 members) on 8 October, Athboy (Thomas Gilroy – 40) on 2 November and Enfield (James Foran – 27 members) on 3 December. Although not included in the Union's roll book of branches, a separate typed manuscript indicates that in 1918 there were units also in

Ardcath (50 members), Dunsany (70 members) and Slane (50 members). This total of eleven branches was still a good deal fewer than the twenty one branches represented at the annual general meeting of the MLU held in the Foresters' Hall, Navan, in January 1919. Delegates were present from Bettystown, Girley, Robinstown, Syddan, Dangan, Nobber, Bellewstown, Johnstown, Skryne, Ballivor, Castletown, Bohermeen, Wilkinstown, Yellow Furze, Duleek, Moylough, Navan, Cormeen, Drumconrath, Martry and Ballinlough. This was actually only one less than the number of branches in attendance at the corresponding gathering five years earlier, but there is little doubt but that the MLU must have felt itself under threat from the rapidly growing Transport Union. Already by that time it is known for certain that the Drumree branch had transferred almost in its entirety to the newcomer, and there may well have been others. Perhaps it was this fear of further disaffiliations which prompted the MLU executive to issue a statement of its objectives to the readers of the *Meath Chronicle* in the 11 January 1919 issue. Amongst the declared aims of the Union were:

> To improve the standard of living of its members and dependents by securing for them a living wage, shorter hours of work, more regular employment and proper opportunities for education and recreation by controlling the cost of the necessaries of life by means of cooperation, by acquiring lands for members ... to settle labour disputes by amicable agreement where possible . ... to take legal action for members for recovery of wages, compensation etc. To secure for the members the advantages intended for them by Statutes relating to wages and work-men's compensations ... [and] to assist ... the propagation of the Irish language and to aid the advancement of Irish industries.

While all of this was laudable enough it is quite clear that by this time the workers of Meath – and particularly the farm labourers – were finding the more aggressive approach of the Transport Union to be much more attractive to their needs. It was the failure of the MLU to secure a high enough weekly wage for farm labourers in August 1918 which had led to the disaffiliation of the Drumree branch. Further defections now followed. In January 1919 alone former MLU branches in Skryne, Kilmessan and Robinstown now transferred to the ITGWU. Manuscript 7282, the roll book of Transport Union branches, gives the dates of affiliation and secretaries of Meath units for the first four months of 1919. These were: Kilmessan, 14 January, John Mangan; Kilmore, 21 January, Patrick Fagan; Ashbourne, 28 January, James Brunton; Skryne, 4 February, Christopher Hughes; Robinstown, 18 February, J. Harford; Summerhill, 4 March, A. Young; Duleek, 18 March, P.J. Conlon; Ballinacree, 25 March, Thomas Smyth, this branch amalgamated with Oldcastle the following November, which probably explains why the same name is given as secretary for both units; Longwood, 25 March, John Nolan; Crossakiel, 15 April, C. Byrne. No further formations are recorded until August of that year. The local newspapers indicate that in the first half of 1919 there were also branches of the union in Loughan, Cormeen, Dunderry and Ratoath. That these are not recorded in the union roll book may be explained by the system of sub-sections operated by the ITGWU: thus Loughan was a sub-branch of Kells, as was probably Cormeen and Dunderry of Robinstown; Ratoath was possibly part of the Ashbourne branch and indeed by early 1919 Dunsany had become a sub-section of Drumree.

Although the first four branches of the Transport Union were set up in the county's four towns the majority of the membership was rural-based, and composed of farm labourers, as was also the case with the MLU. The same trend was evident elsewhere in the country so that David Fitzpatrick in this regard writes in *Politics and Irish Life 1913–21* (p 245) that:

> Despite inconsistencies in statistics, it is clear that by mid-1919 the ITGWU, had successfully transformed itself from a small body of urban militants to a mass organisation bearing comparison with bodies such as Sinn Féin.

The rural nature of the union in Meath can be seen through the notes column pertaining to the organisation in the local newspapers. For example, in the issue of the *Meath Chronicle* on 22 January 1921 the secretary of the Skryne branch requested that "all members who intend

Branches of ITGWU 1918-21.

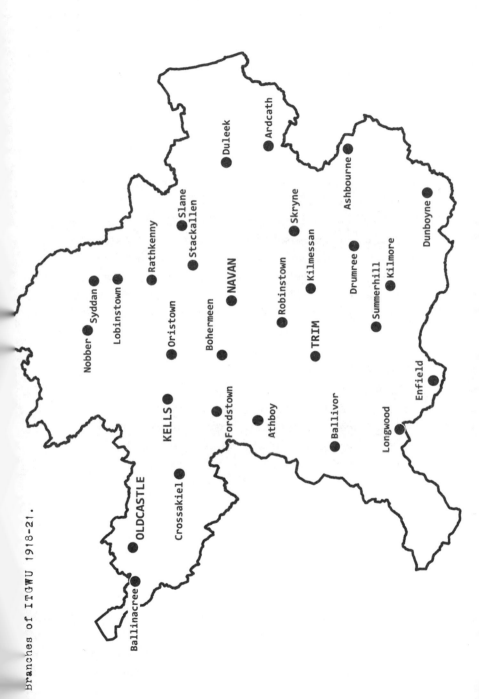

to graze cattle on the Union field this year are earnestly asked to hand in applications to the next meeting." One is also struck by the number of branches, particularly in the north Meath area, who gave as the venue of their meetings the local crossroads.

The growing confidence of the new union can be seen in what was probably the first ever Labour Day rally organised in Meath on 1 May 1919. Although the *Chronicle* of 10 May 1919 refers to a "monster demonstration in Dunshaughlin", it gives few other details of the event which received no mention whatever in the *Drogheda Independent*. The *Meath Chronicle* reported that "there were contingents from the surrounding districts of between 700 and 800 ... the red flag was borne in procession." There was a speaker from the Transport Union headquarters and a resolution was passed "that we, the workers of Dunshaughlin and district, hereby proclaim this day, May 1st, as a general holiday." It was indeed from this area of Meath, with Dunshaughlin as the focal point, that most labour trouble was to emanate over the next few years. The first clash, known in the union terminology of that time as the 'wages movement', was imminent.

At their annual conference on 7 January 1919 the Meath Farmers Union decided to incorporate itself into the Farmers Union of Ireland. "The farmers have had trouble with their labourers in the past and I fear confrontation in the future," one delegate presciently told his colleagues, before going on to stress the advantages of security in numbers. Thus it was not only the Transport Union which was spreading its net. David Fitzpatrick states:

> Farmers, first swollen by unaccustomed wartime prosperity, then menaced by wartime recession and by the mounting demands of men without property, organised themselves in defensive alliance to protect their wealth and social status.

In early 1919 the farmers' organisation in Meath seems to have been fairly haphazard. At the annual conference in February 1920 the secretary, Thomas Austin of Batterstown, stated in his report that a year earlier, when he had taken up his position, there had been only four working branches in the county, namely, Navan, Dunshaughlin, Kilmessan and

East Meath. He then recounted how, in the course of the year 1919, he had revived old branches or founded new ones in Kells, Trim, Oldcastle, Kilskyre, Rathmolyon, Athboy, Longwood, Ballyboggan and Drumconrath. Most, if not all, of these were in existence by the time the prolonged farm workers' strike got under way early in July.

The cause was of course the perennial one – wages. In September 1917 the Agricultural Wages Board had been set up with the function of fixing minimum weekly wages for farm labourers; initially it had settled on 25s for those in county Dublin, 22/6 for Meath and Kildare and 20s for the rest of the country. We have seen how in the summer of 1918 the Meath rate had been increased to 25/6, a figure which fell far short of the original MLU demand for 30s, and was thus a cause of much disgruntlement leading to defections and affiliations to the Transport Union.

Now in June 1919 the MFU was faced with two separate wages claims; from the MLU came the demand for 30s and a nine-hour day; from the Transport Union, a demand of 37/6 and an eight-hour day. The farmers quickly settled with the MLU but refused to deal with the Transport men. While negotiations were still going on a large labour demonstration was held on the Fair Green, Navan, on the last Sunday in June. This was organised by the ITGWU and was designed to impress, if not to intimidate, the farmers into concessions. The obligatory red flags were hoisted high, many with the inscription 'OBU' standing for 'One Big Union', a favourite union slogan of these years. The two main speakers were the Union's General Secretary, William O'Brien, and its Treasurer, Thomas Johnson. O'Brien told his listeners that soon "Ireland will be restored to the days of its communal traditions, conditions that are strongly reminiscent of the Russia of today." After thus making no secret of his admiration for Communist Russia, O'Brien then went on to castigate the farmers as "the biggest opponents of the amelioration of the conditions of farm workers", and then concluded with a somewhat dramatised warning:

> If the Meath farmers are alarmed because of our men walking under red flags with OBU on its folds it will be nothing to their alarm when they see the OBU of America and the industrial workers of the world bearing aloft the same flag.

Such visions and images do not seem to have mesmerised the county's farmers who held their ground on the wage claim. The farm labourers struck in the first week in July, coming out initially in the Dunboyne, Dunshaughlin, Drumree, Kilmessan and Ratoath areas. For the duration of the dispute, which was to last for almost two months, it was only the southern portion of the county which was affected, the sole exception being around the Duleek area where there was a Transport Union branch. From the outset the *Drogheda Independent* of 12 July 1919 was gloomy as to prospects for settlement, the editorial writer commenting that:

> The attitude adopted by the Farmers' Union is explicable only on the grounds of an attempt to smash the Transport Union and, unofficially, it is freely stated that that is the object.

The Union's strategy was to hurt the farmers by preventing them access to the stock markets in Dublin. Large parties of strikers were permanently based at the railway stations at Kilmessan, Drumree and Batterstown and turned back cattle and sheep destined for Dublin. On at least one occasion, in mid-July, this blockade was broken when, as the *Drogheda Independent* of 19 July reported:

> a large farmer in Drumree had a flock of thirteen sheep conducted to Drumree station by eleven RIC, including a sergeant and a head constable who drove back pickets with fixed bayonets.

Arising out of this incident ten local men were later charged at Dunshaughlin Petty Sessions with disturbance of the peace. Another baton charge by police against workers was reported in the Duleek area about this time also.

It was not only the railways which were blockaded by the strikers. The road to Dublin was also blocked by orders of a strike committee which issued permits to farmers who had settled with their workers on the union's terms. Soon large numbers of RIC were being drafted into the county at the request, according to the *Drogheda Independent* of 2 August, of the MFU. The barracks at Kilmoon was reopened and eight policemen were stationed there, and twenty RIC officers from Mayo were sent to reinforce their colleagues at Dunshaughlin. One of their tasks was to protect the workers on the estate of Lord Dunsany who had settled with them for less than the Union's demands; the men had resigned from the Union and were apparently incurring the displeasure of their former comrades. But the workers had their supporters too among the women employed at Sir Nugent Everard's tobacco facility at Navan, they donned red picket bands and came out in sympathy.

The two sides came together at the CYMS Hall in Navan on 18 July. By now the Transport Union had lowered its demand to 35s and was willing to accept the continuance of the nine-hour day. The farmers, however, refused to concede any more than that given to the MLU, that is, 30s. The meeting lasted only half an hour and was quite acrimonious: Eamonn Rooney, the Down-born, Drogheda-based union official mentioned earlier in this account, reportedly accused the Meath farmers of "treating their workers worse than the way negro slaves had been treated before their emancipation." A farmers' spokesman responded that the strikers would keep making demands "until the farmers cleared out and the land was taken over by the workers." The strike continued.

About this time Bishop Gaughran referred to the dispute in a very balanced sermon at a Confirmation ceremony in Mullingar. The *Meath Chronicle* of 2 August 1919 reports that he said:

> do not let the demand [of the worker] be extravagant for no man would pay wages that the industry ... would not yield ... on the other hand, the capitalists could not exact what profit they liked and put it in their own pockets.

An editorial in the *Meath Chronicle* on 2 August also adopted a moderate line, stating that "no body of employers and employees have such a union of interests as have farmers and agricultural labourers." The *Drogheda Independent*, on the other hand, made no secret of its support for the farmers, and its issue of 2 August commented that "the present demand is but one of a series intended to culminate in the final destruction of the farmer and the acquisition of their land ... by the labourer."

Nor had the vehemence of its anti-socialist stance lessened in any way since its attack on the Transport Union and its involvement in the 1913–14 Lock Out; excerpts from this have been quoted earlier but now the writer saw Bolshevism as the prime enemy, and an editorial later that month beseeched that "God forbid that such a regime would ever get a footing in the isle of saints to convert it into one of devils." Indeed, in its reporting of the Meath strike the *Drogheda Independent* at times tended to ridicule the workers. Thus, its issue of 16 August recounted a confrontation in the Kilmessan area between nineteen labourers and four farmers making hay and dismissed the whole affray as "a lively tussle for possession of hay forks." The same issue reported that in the Skryne area several acres of wheat had been cut down by 119 labourers, an amazingly precise figure, but that, when challenged by two constables and two sergeants, "the strikers slunk away."

As August wore on the strikers were proving a continuing irritant to the farmers. Roads remained blocked; auctions and markets were cancelled; the Agricultural Show scheduled for Navan in the middle of the month had to be called off by the MFU, and it was reported that Belfast drovers were refusing to handle Meath sheep.

By now also, however, the *Drogheda Independent* reported that four hundred military had encamped in the Navan Showgrounds, and that a large force of soldiers had taken over Dunshaughlin workhouse. And, according to the same source, blackleg labour was being drafted into the county in the form of five hundred labourers from Donegal who were about to arrive and be housed at the old mill in Kilcarn.

By the second week of August Eamonn Rooney let it be known that his union would settle for 34s and it was this figure which individual farmers now began to offer to their striking employees. It seems that many workers now resigned themselves to accepting this wage as the best on offer. The following figures were released by the union to the local press, and for each area they show the number of workers still on strike in the middle of August out of the total number of original strikers: Dunboyne, 38 out of 158; Summerhill, 74 out of 124; Kilmessan, 58 out of 103; Skryne, 54 out of 96; Drumree, 75 out of 135; Ratoath, 75 out of 120; Ashbourne, 30 out of 80; Robinstown, 40 out of 60; Trim, 60 out of 140; Kilmore, 20 out of 50; Duleek, 110 out of 130; Navan, 30 out of 103. These figures represent just over half of the total continuing in the dispute. At this point, on 16 August, Eamonn Rooney and the Navan Volunteers took a hand in matters, and the goods train was derailed a couple of miles outside Navan. This incident has been described earlier. At the time Rooney issued a statement:

> strongly protesting at the assumption by the press that the Transport Union was responsible for the wrecking of the goods train; there is absolutely no evidence that our organisation had anything to do with that occurrence.

History has, however, indicated otherwise.

It cannot be said for certain whether it was this incident which shook many, if indeed any, of the remaining strikers out of their intransigence. It is probably more likely that the gradual return to work just continued unabated. C. Desmond Greaves suggests that by now the farmers were as eager to secure a settlement as were the workers because they "were anxious to get animals to the Dublin Horse Show." (p 246)

The protracted dispute formally ended on Monday, 25 August, following a conference of interested parties at the offices of the Department of Agriculture in Dublin. Those parties were the ITGWU, the Farmers Union of Ireland, the MFU and the MLU. The settlement was for 34s, or 32s plus £4 harvest bonus, the continuance of the nine hour day and overtime to be paid at 1s per hour. These terms were to remain in effect until the following April.

Thus ended the wages movement in the Meath of 1919. David Fitzpatrick in *Politics and Irish Life 1913–21* (p 272) suggests that one important outcome of the struggle was that henceforth "organised farmers were no longer in a position to treat farm workers with condescension". He also refers to 1919 as "Irish Labour's most triumphant year", an achievement which in most part he attributes to the large scale demobilisation after the First World War and the consequent swelling of union ranks with veterans, men "unpractised in the habits of deference."

To what extent, if any, war veterans were involved in union ranks in Meath cannot be said, but it is certain that the days of the deferential and respectful approach by labourers to farmers were numbered. In this respect it may be stated that the real loser in Meath was the MLU.

Although its members gained the benefits of the deal agreed on 25 August it was as a result of the endeavours of the Transport Union men. While the Transport Union continued to grow, Nobber (with a sub-section in Kilmainhamwood) had affiliated on 5 August, and Ballivor on 28 October, and there was a steady growth right through 1920, the MLU was clearly a spent force.

Just before the conclusion of the strike in August a meeting of the Labour Union was attended by delegates from only ten branches, as compared with twenty one in January. And although a number of branches managed to linger on until as late as 1923, the MLU as a body was never again to engage in wage bargaining with the farmers after 1919. Indeed, the whole predicament of the MLU can be seen in a report in the *Meath Chronicle* of 10 September 1921 regarding the September 1921 meeting of the MFU. At the close of the meeting a deputation was received from the MLU asking that a wages arrangement made with the Drumconrath branch be adjusted upwards in line with a later and more favourable settlement concluded with the Transport Union. This was granted by the farmers, but long gone were the days of the back door 'cap in hand' style of pay bargaining.

In the years after 1919 one is struck by the way in which the wages movements and other union activities often were embellished with the paraphernalia and rhetoric of socialist revolution. Even in Meath the demand for a higher wage occasionally seemed to assume the form of a crusade for communism. There was, as has been seen, the proliferation of the colour red. 'The Red Flag', apart from being the standard of international socialism is also the title of that movement's anthem, and it is interesting that this song was written by a Meath man. Jim Connell (1852–1929) was born in Kilskyre but spent most of his life working as a docker and a labour activist in Dublin and London, where he died. 'The Red Flag' was written some time in the 1880s.

The OBU, a frequent slogan and inscription on the red flags, referred to the avowed aim of the Transport Union to organise all workers into 'One Big Union', that is, the ITGWU itself. C. Desmond Greaves traces the adoption of this policy to a union document regarding organisation that was issued on 1 July 1918 and that declared in part that "the days of the local society are dead; the day of the craft union is passing; the day of the OBU has come." (p 208). At this time the OBU concept was prevalent in Britain, on the continent and in the USA, and represented a form of syndicalism, the ultimate aim of which was, in its simplest and most simplistic manifestation, to paralyse capitalism with one mass strike. We have seen how the OBU slogan wafted its way into Meath on the folds of the red flags of 1919.

The term 'comrade', the standard form of fraternal greeting among socialists, was also in common usage amongst the working men of Meath in these years. It is often to be found in newspaper columns devoted to the various Transport Union branches, as for example in this excerpt from the *Meath Chronicle* of 2 December 1922: "At the annual meeting of Crossakiel branch Comrade Roche was re-elected president and Comrade Murphy vice-president."

This was no more than a ritual imitation of international socialist practice, although it is something of a novelty to see it cropping up in the unlikely setting of rural Meath.

Things became more serious, however, whenever union leaders or organisers visited the county. Amongst these were Thomas Johnson, William O'Brien, Eamonn Rooney and Cathal O'Shannon. We have already seen that O'Brien made no secret of his admiration for events in Russia when he spoke in Navan in June 1919. In October when Rooney addressed a meeting in Kells he referred to land ownership and gave a strong hint that if he and his comrades had their way, then the strong farmers and graziers of Meath might find themselves dispossessed; the *Meath Chronicle* of 18 October 1919 quoted his warning that:

> The question of the ownership of land was not an issue in the strike, but ... it would be well if the workers firmly realised that there was no absolute right of property in land, and that it would be very difficult indeed for any of the present old Meath settlers to prove their claim to those estates on moral grounds, because private ownership of land in Meath had its origin in Cromwell's confiscation and, although the present owners had not actually confiscated the land themselves, nevertheless it was stolen property ... the people's right to land was not weakened by the lapse of years or of centuries.

Most extreme of all was Cathal O'Shannon who in these years held various positions in the labour and trade union movement as well as being editor of newspapers such as the *Watchword of Labour* and the *Voice of Labour*. O'Shannon made no secret of his communism and, as David Fitzpatrick puts it, "the language of the Bolshevik revolution was to linger on in Irish Labour circles for many years, tirelessly reiterated by Cathal O'Shannon, communist editor of Labour newspapers." (*Politics and Irish Life 1913–21*, p 255).

O'Shannon was an occasional visitor to Meath although one such visit in April 1920 was both enforced and unwelcome. This was when he was deported from an international labour meeting in London and charged in Kells with making a seditious speech. Exact information is sketchy on this but it seems that the speech had been delivered in Kells in the previous January during the lead up to the urban elections; the theme seems to have been the same as that used by Rooney and just quoted, namely, land ownership and its attendant evils.

O'Shannon was a great admirer of the soviets, those councils of workers, peasants and soldiers from which Lenin and his followers had launched themselves into power in Russia in 1917 and which had soon become synonymous with the form of government there. Speaking at a meeting of the Irish Socialist Party in the Trades Hall, Dublin, late in March 1920, O'Shannon told his listeners that they had:

> to consider whether there is foresight or imagination enough to set about establishing the machinery for the Soviet Republic in Ireland...a revolution which brought about change in the political order would be of no use ... what was wanted was a social and economic revolution ... the soviet is the most revolutionary government yet evolved.

The declaration of soviets was a not uncommon occurrence in Ireland in these years. There were no reports or sightings of such in Meath. The nearest was just over the county boundary in Drogheda. This was declared on Wednesday, 14 September 1921, when about forty Transport Union men who had been on strike for several weeks took over Drogheda foundry and began to work under the direction of a foreman from Dublin. The revolutionary fervour seems to have been short lived. The *Drogheda Independent* of 17 September 1919 reported that, on the following day, "the RIC ordered the men off the premises … the workers went away peacefully enough." This was perhaps typical of the Irish soviets: only that which operated in Limerick in April 1919 seems to have had any substance. The use of the term 'soviet', however, would, as David Fitzpatrick puts it, "lend rare glamour to strikes and sit-ins", (*Politics and Irish Life 1913–21*, p 255), the aims of which were simply to improve working conditions and increase wages.

Red flags, soviets, the demand for the OBU, the term 'comrade' and so on, all for the most part represented a mere playing at revolution. Granted that to extreme socialists – O'Shannon, O'Brien and Rooney – the game was deadly serious. But to the farm labourers of the Transport Union, in which these three men were leading figures, in Meath who engaged in the strikes of 1919 and of other years, the objective was to secure a decent wage. In less contentious times some of the Transport men used their muscle for even more basic purposes, as when the *Chronicle* of 24 April 1920 reported that:

> Dunboyne workers through their local ITU branch secretary served notice on nine local publicans that they would not pay more than 6d. for a pint of porter … the publicans held out for only a week.

This was a far cry from Trotsky's fomenting of permanent communist revolution.

After the upheavals of 1919, the years 1920 and 1921 were relatively calm from a labour viewpoint. 1920 began with the UDC elections in January, when organised labour made its first real breakthrough in gaining representation on local councils and boards. In the national context Labour won 18 per cent of first preferences and 21 per cent of the contested seats. In Meath the relevant figures were 14 per cent and 20 per cent respectively. Of the eight Labour candidates elected between the three councils all were Transport Union members, as were a number of other councillors standing for Sinn Féin and the Town Tenants. In the local elections in June, Labour performed miserably, according to

David Fitzpatrick. The details of the county and RDC contests have been given in the previous chapter, and the results in Meath generally bear out Fitzpatrick's verdict, although 'miserably' may be too strong an adverb in that county's context.

Before this, in mid-April, had come the great national shut down in support of the hunger-striking prisoners. This episode has been recounted earlier, and it is certain that without Labour's backing it would not have been possible. The socialist historian C. Desmond Greaves sees this as "[the] great event which marked the highest point in the Irish national liberation struggle." (*The Irish Transport and General Workers' Union: The Formative* Years, p 265). The stoppage was applied faithfully in Meath. At least one Transport Union official from the county was among the protesting prisoners. As the *Chronicle* reported on 24 April 1920, the Meath road workers section passed a motion of congratulations to their secretary Eugene Englishby "on his hunger strike against the forces of capitalism and tyranny."

From an organisational point of view the Transport Union continued to expand in 1920 with new branch affiliations from Castletown (B. Monaghan, secretary) on 20 January; Syddan (Michael Markey) on 24 February; Oristown (Thomas Englishby) on 30 February; Stackallen (James Ginnity) on 27 April; Bohermeen (Patrick Harte) on 1 June and Fordstown (James Lynch) on 6 July. But the rate of expansion was far slower than what it had been for the previous two years. In fact, there were to be no further new branches for the rest of 1920 and only one, Rathkenny on 29 March, for the whole of 1921.

This slowing down was undoubtedly due to the harassment of the Union and its officials during the Troubles. C. Desmond Greaves states that out of a total of 583 branches, 115 collapsed during these years. The slow down in new branch affiliations is not the only indicator of the Union's difficulties in Meath in 1920–21. In the union roll book, which dates to March 1922, the Meath branches at Oldcastle, Longwood, Castletown, Stackallen and Bohermeen were all deemed 'dead' by this date. Further symptoms of the malaise came in the incidence of amalgamations as rural branches, probably depleted of members, were compelled to join with larger units in the towns. Thus in the course of 1920, Duleek joined with Drogheda, Longwood with Trim and

Ballinacree with Oldcastle (before its own demise).

It is interesting that from January 1920 Meath had a representative on the Union executive of nine. This was Dunshaughlin man, Michael Duffy, a member of the Drumree branch. Born in Clonsilla, county Dublin in 1883, Duffy had been educated in the national schools of Kilskyre, Cortown, Ratoath, Clonsilla and Castleknock. The family settled in Dunshaughlin about the turn of the century and Duffy was in the employ of Meath County Council from 1911 to 1922. In this latter year he was elected to the Senate by the Dáil and was to remain a Senator until the dissolution of that body by de Valera's government in 1936. Duffy later worked for Cement Ltd., where he was in charge of labour relations.

On the wages front settlement was reached amicably in April 1920 with the farm workers' pay rising to 40s per week in the south and east Meath areas, and to 37/6 in the rest of the county. At the annual meeting of the MFU in January 1921 the secretary in his report expressed the hope that "the last has been heard of the taunt 'anti-labour' which had been thrown at the association." But agreement on pay for this year was not to be reached until after much threatening noises from both sides. Initially, on 7 April, the farmers were insisting on a cut of 2/6 per week. This led the Drumree branch to declare a half-holiday for the labourers in its area. The *Meath Chronicle* of 7 May 1921 reported that at a public meeting to protest at the proposed wage reductions Michael Duffy warned: "The workers were not seeking trouble ... but ... if the farmers persisted in their present attitude they would be responsible for inflicting on Meath a calamity compared with which the struggle of 1919 would be like child's play."

Talks broke down in the middle of July and the MFU instructed individual members to settle on their own terms. A strike due to begin on 25 July was averted by the intervention of a Dáil arbitrator who persuaded the farmers to maintain the same rates until 1 November; from then until 31 January 1922 the union was prevailed upon to accept wages being cut to 38s in south and east Meath and 37/6 in the rest of the county.

Over the next two years farm labourers' wages continued to fall. Perhaps this was due to the disarray in which the Transport Union found itself, or perhaps it may be attributable to the dissolution of the Agricultural Wages Board on 1 October 1921. In February 1922 talks broke down between the two sides and Meath witnessed another strike. It is noteworthy that on this occasion the strike was concentrated in the north Meath area around Kells and Oldcastle which had been quiet in 1919. It is also interesting to see that by now the Volunteers in some areas were being seen as strike breakers. The *Meath Chronicle* of 11 March 1922 reported that the IRA had arrested four striking labourers in Fordstown who were being used to protect the property of a large farmer at Teltown as well as defending from attack non-union men employed on his land, and had recovered twenty-three head of cattle driven off land in Charlesfort. Labour and the republican movement had stood together in Meath during the troubled years but now a rift was forming. It is also probably more than just a coincidence that it was at this very time, March 1922, that leading figures of the MFU were prominent at a meeting in Navan which decided to set up a committee to raise money for the maintenance of the IRA. Some of those who had never been much enamoured of the republican struggle now found it easy to adjust themselves to the new regime.

Of course it would be unfair to single out the farmers as the culprits of these years. It is difficult to generalise but to keep some balance it may be worth quoting, by way of apologia, David Fitzpatrick's analysis of the farmers' role in these years:

> It was they who paid much of the cost of the revolution, they who housed the men on the run, their sons who staffed the IRA and their daughters who staffed the Cumann na mBan.
>
> (*Politics and Irish Life 1913–21*, p 279)

Electorally, Labour ruled supreme in Meath in 1922, and it is remarkable to think now that in the general election on 16 June of that year, that self-proclaimed and unashamed Communist Cathal O'Shannon won a runaway victory in the Meath-Louth constituency. Details and analysis of this election will be given in the next chapter.

Although farm wages fell slightly again in March 1923 it is a fact that the breakthrough of Labour, in both its political and trade union aspects, in the years after 1919 represents one of the most significant developments of this period. An anonymous letter published in the *Meath Chronicle* on 22 April 1922 combined the brashness of the new force with uncertainty as to the full extent of its power. The writer, who styled himself 'Red Flag', begins by asserting that "Labour Day will be observed as a general holiday in the Oldcastle district this year", but then hesitates to express the hope that "as this is the only annual holiday the workers practically take …. let us hope there will be no curtailment in their weekly wages in consequence." He then closes with a triumphal flourish thanking God that "the days of slavery are vanquished."

While attainment of a decent wage was an aim pursued zealously by the farm workers of Meath, what was of more fundamental importance to these men was the desire to own their own plot of land. The land hunger evident in the county between 1914 and 1918 intensified in the following years and with it came an increase in the branches and activities of the Back to the Land movement.

In the minds of the Back to the Land leaders there was no doubt as to the necessity for land reform in Meath. At a meeting called in April 1920 for the purpose of forming a branch in the Ratoath area the local priest, Fr Kenny, told his listeners that in the county about 90 per cent of the land was owned by only 5 per cent of the people. Two years later a speaker at a meeting of the organisation's executive put the same point in much earthier fashion when he complained that "while much progress has been made, nine-tenths of Meath is still owned by the bullocks."

The *Meath Chronicle* of 6 December 1919 reported on a meeting of the Navan branch that month where Mr J. M. Bell, a speaker from Dublin, described the system of landholding in Meath as "the rottenest bit of economics that was ever allowed to exist", and he berated the people of the county themselves for permitting this aberration. "There was little use", he stated, "in talking about a republic or the great British Empire or about colonial home rule … if they had hungry stomachs."

It would be difficult, however, to blame the landless men of Meath for lack of effort in the campaign to break up the ranches and estates in the county. Occasionally, as will be seen, their ardour actually carried them beyond the bounds of law. Organisationally, the Back to the Land movement was certainly on a sound footing. By the end of 1920 there were branches in Oldcastle (where it had begun in 1906), Ballinlough, Johnstown, Kilberry, Crossakiel, Boyerstown, Castletown, Navan, Rathaldron, Dunshaughlin, Kilmessan, Nobber, Warrenstown, Rathmolyon, Summerhill, Martry, Skryne, Duleek, Kilmainham, Ratoath, Curraha, Dunboyne and Tara. In addition there were, over the next two years, branches established in Trim, Yellow Furze, Batterstown, Rathfeigh, Garadice, Mornington and Cormeen.

For the years under review the earliest incidence of land trouble came in February 1919 when the long disputed Spiddal Farm in the Nobber area was found to be ploughed up. Arising from this eight men, described as "respectable farm labourers", were arrested and later jailed. The trouble stemmed from the purchase and division of the farm by the local Back to the Land branch and subsequent dissatisfaction amongst some of the members at the way in which the portions had been allocated. In particular, it was alleged that Dr Cusack, who had been the Home Rule Party's candidate in the general election shortly before this, had obtained for himself far more land than was proper and was being tainted as a 'grabber'.

Apart from that the local newspapers do not reveal many more cases of land agitation for the remainder of this year though, as 1919 drew to a close, the editorial writer of the *Drogheda Independent* of 13 December anxiously commented that:

> there is scarcely a district in Meath in which land trouble of some
> sort is not brewing or smouldering … in Navan, Ballivor and
> elsewhere auctions have been prohibited and abandoned.

In 1920 the smouldering tensions burst to the surface on several occasions. There were frequent cases of cattle drives in various parts of the county. In March the estate at Liscarton, just outside Navan, was the target of much destruction with twenty-four gates being taken from their hinges and trees being felled and carted away; also in the Navan area, another bout of vandalism included a grave being dug with a wooden cross at its head. In May five hundred cattle were driven off an estate at Curraha while in the same month three members of the Navan

Branches of Back to the Land, 1920-22.

Back to the Land branch were sentenced to a month's imprisonment in Mountjoy for refusing to give assurances of good behaviour.

Not that the Back to the Land organisation sanctioned such behaviour. Quite the opposite in fact, and in the case of the Curraha incident, for example, the movement's leaders deemed those responsible as being ineligible for any division of land in the future. At various monthly meetings in the early part of 1920 acts such as those described were condemned as "immoral", and as having being carried out by the "backers and hirelings of the ranchers." At the April meeting, the *Meath Chronicle* of 17 April 1920 reported a speaker, Mr Cumisky, as stating anxiously that "many people believed that Back to the Land was a ruffianly movement ... responsible for burnings and so on".

It was shortly after this that the organisation was restructured with a county executive of seven men at the helm. Their most urgent priority was, a spokesman emphasised, "to put an end to irresponsible actions on the part of individuals." The members of the executive were Terence O'Dea (Navan branch), William McDermott (Curraha), Patrick Timmons (Martry), Thomas Tormey (Summerhill), T. Cumiskey (Castletown), a Mr. Flood (Ballinlough) and a Mr. Loughran (Duleek).

The land agitation continued intermittently until the middle of 1921, and it was only then that some semblance of normality returned. At a meeting at the end of 1921, the secretary, Philip Myles, was referring to how the political and military Troubles had hampered the movement's activities when he stated that "the reign of terror had suspended our efforts for almost eighteen months." In spite of that, much progress was made in the years 1919 to 1923. Land division remained the paramount aim but this was to be carried out in an orderly way. The executive explained at a meeting reported in the *Meath Chronicle* of 8 April 1922 that:

> They had made it plain that they were not out for confiscation and were prepared to give full value for any land they got even though they might believe that it had come unjustly into the hands of the present owners.

Oldcastle was the most fertile ground for the Back to the Land's activities. Up to the end of 1919 well over 3,000 acres had been divided among one hundred and seventy new tenants. In March 1921 the local branch concluded the purchase of another 1,400 acres, formerly part of the McRory Estate, in the Ballinrink and Rathivor areas. This was divided into eighty allotments, nine going to ex-servicemen (British Army), eighteen to former estate labourers and the rest to small local landowners. These same three classes also benefited the following December when 500 acres, previously the land of Lord Trimbleston, were divided up in the Kilmainham area. In the course of the year 1919 the branch in Castletown succeeded in apportioning 250 acres into nineteen farms varying in size from four to twenty acres. These are but a few examples of the successes of the movement as recorded in the local newspapers for these years.

There are indications of strong support for land division coming from the Transport Union. This would be expected given the rural nature of the union, the branches of which were peopled with men of no property. The following extract is taken from the *Watchword of Labour*, 6 May 1920, the organ of the labour movement in 1919–20, and it refers to the activities of the Summerhill branch of the Transport Union:

> This County Meath branch has set a splendid headline in the matter of acquiring land for its members. After nine weeks of battling, four land gluttons had to unloose their grip on forty acres in the Garadice district and to be content with an acre apiece, four acres of the rest going to small farmers, while the remaining thirty two acres went to thirty two branch members. Another twenty acres on the same farm has now been given up and is ready for division among branch members.

Just the previous month, at a joint meeting of the Navan branches of Back to the Land and the Transport Union, those present resolved:

> that no member of the union shall take part in any work on the proposed new racecourse at Proudstown until Back to the Land has made final arrangements for the purchase of the Fitzherbert property for distribution amongst the landless men of the district.

Shortly afterwards the branch purchased over 400 acres and the way was then clear for the construction of the racecourse, the first meeting being held there on 16 September 1921.

The co-operation and good relations between the two organisations can further be evidenced from the Back to the Land executive meeting of June 1922. When a motion was forwarded asking the executive to request "all Labour and Trades bodies to get involved in the Back to the Land branch in their district for the betterment of the landless labourer classes," there was general agreement that this was already the case; the chairman said that "the best men in my district are the Transport Union men", while the secretary, Philip Myles, confirmed that in his area of Oldcastle, "the labourers always gave us whole hearted support."

In a modest way Back to the Land was a success because it did much to defuse the volatile feelings generated by land hunger in Meath. An executive meeting in May 1920 pointedly, and probably justifiably, commented that if a branch had been in existence in Cormeen "such a thing as the murder of Mark Clinton would not have happened because the people would have had a means to get justice." Subsequently, indeed, a branch was established in the area.

It is also worth pointing out that of the five major political or semi-political organisations in the Meath of 1913–14 (the other four being the United Irish League, the Ancient Order of Hibernians, the Meath Labour Union and the original Irish Volunteers), Back to the Land was the only one still thriving ten years later. Having survived the 'vampire' embrace of the UIL in 1914–15 as well as coming intact through 'the reign of terror' of 1920–21, now in May 1923, as Ireland's civil war was fizzling out, secretary Myles was looking to the future as he reiterated the principles that had guided the movement since its formation in 1906. At a joint Back to the Land and Transport Union meeting at Garristown he told those present that:

> we have great work to do in our own county Meath. If we work together, irrespective of party politics, we will accomplish our constant aim – a share in the land for every man willing and able to work and an increased and prosperous population.

8

July 1921 - May 1923:
From Truce to Treaty and Civil War

One immediate result of the Truce in Meath was the proclamation issued by the Competent Military Authority lifting the ban on association which had been in existence from the previous March. Commercial, sporting and social life now quickly returned to normal to judge from the notices sections in the two local newspapers. Fairs, markets, football matches, concerts, dances, céilís, Irish Ireland nights and aeríochts all resumed in a kind of collective joyous reaction to an end to the restrictions imposed by the hostilities. These activities, particularly those with Gaelic overtones, were often proclaimed with great gusto as people were summoned, in the name of the republic, to attend them, a clear indication of the triumphalist feeling then permeating the country.

In Meath this euphoria reached a climax early in September when Eamon de Valera paid a visit to the county to attend an aeríocht in Ardbraccan. This was St Ultan's aeríocht and patron day and its purpose was to raise funds for St Ultan's Hospital in Dublin, an institution that cared for sickly infants from the poorer areas of the city. Among de Valera's entourage were Maud Gonne and Countess Markievicz who were part of the platform party along with the usual array of local politicians and clergy. The speeches dwelt more on cultural matters, such as the revival of Irish, rather than on any political themes and the *Chronicle* referred to the occasion as "a red letter day in the history of Meath", giving the number at the gathering as ten thousand.

In this period, the second half of 1921, one is struck by a note of optimism and a sanguine look towards the future. This manifested itself in many ways. For instance at a sporting level it has been stated earlier that it was at this time, on 16 September to be precise, that the first race meeting at Proudstown was held, attended, wrote a local reporter, "by a vast crowd, a concourse scarcely ever equalled anywhere in Ireland." By now also the urban district councils were discussing plans for electrification of their towns, Navan UDC proudly boasting that already Trimgate Street, Brews Hill, Railway Street and Market Square had been rigged up to the new system. Another development saw an order from the Dáil to the county council instructing it to outline its plans to abolish the workhouses, those much hated and foreboding symbols of benign British paternalism. At its meeting of 17 October the county council finalised a scheme, later approved by the Dáil, to close down all five workhouses and their adjoining hospitals except for Navan, which was to become the county hospital, and Trim which was to be used as a county home for the old.

This same meeting called for the release of all internees, a reminder that the Truce signed on 11 July had stopped the hostilities but may not yet have ended them. There were still about a hundred Meath men being held in Irish and British jails as a result of activities arising out of the Troubles. The *Meath Chronicle* of 5 November 1921 reported one of the strangest ramifications of the War of Independence and uncovered a Meath connection with it. This was the mutiny by Irish soldiers of the Connaught Rangers based in India and it was brought on by their anger at reported British atrocities in their native land. A Navan man, Private John Fitzpatrick, related to the newspaper that in May 1920 he had been based in the Simla Hills in north east India and that when news came of continuing British oppression in Ireland a group of the soldiers arranged for mass to be said for the repose of the dead

Irish. After this Fitzpatrick and several others, including another Navan man named Thomas Murray, were arrested on a charge of sedition and imprisoned. The following November one of their number, James Daly from Westmeath, was executed. The rest were fortunate to be released since the advent of the Truce had been used by the authorities as a pretext for averting a court martial and the men were discharged from the army.

From 11 October 1921 a delegation of five Irishmen, one of whom was Meath TD Eamon Duggan, was in the process of negotiating for the formal end to armed hostilities and the future of Ireland. The outcome of these talks was the Anglo-Irish Treaty signed in London in the early hours of 6 December. The Treaty proved to be a controversial settlement, particularly in the article which provided for an oath of allegiance to be taken to the monarch and in that which decreed that Ireland should remain within the British Commonwealth. Dissatisfaction over the continuing partition of the island was also voiced but this was muted since it was generally expected that certain devices written into the Treaty would soon bring reunification. In the months to come, the Treaty was to divide Sinn Féin, the Volunteers and the general body of Irishmen. It was also to lead to a civil war.

In Meath both local newspapers welcomed the Treaty and expressed the hope that the Dáil would vote for its ratification. In its issue of 10 December the editorial column of the *Chronicle* read that:

> It is not necessary to say that Ireland owes a deep debt of gratitude to Arthur Griffith and his colleagues for their magnificent handling of the situation ... if the Treaty does not come up to what one would have hoped it gives the substance of that freedom for which Ireland endured its Calvary for the last four or five years ... Ireland now stands as independent before the world as England does.

These judgments were tempered with a warning that while:

> Utopia might be reached sometime it was not just yet and the only way to maintain the rights we have secured is to be ready to defend them.

The writer finished on the note which probably struck the most responsive chord among his readers, namely, that the settlement would mean that "the grim spectre of war has been removed from our doors." The *Drogheda Independent* issue of the same date was no less enthusiastic about the Treaty as the leader writer lyrically noted that:

after the long night of sorrow and suffering and striving, the Dawn of a better day has broken over this land of Destiny ... the universal feeling was one of profound relief and thankfulness to the God of Our Fathers.

"The Irish plenipotentiaries", he went on,

have earned the thanks of all their countrymen by their splendid fight to secure for their nation the essentials of freedom ... nobody should have any attitudes save those of endorsement and gratitude.

Similar sentiments were expressed by Bishop Gaughran in Mullingar when he stated that:

the settlement reached in London is one that ought to inaugurate an era not only of peace but of prosperity for Ireland ... if Ireland does not succeed now it will plainly be her own fault ... our country owes a deep debt of gratitude to the delegates.

Further support for the Treaty came at the end of the month when over two hundred of Meath's farmers met in Navan to consider the settlement. The gathering unanimously passed two resolutions, one calling for ratification and the other for unity. The latter motion was prompted by the split in the national movement, a division of opinion as to the merits of the Treaty, which saw de Valera taking a strongly anti-Treaty line that was backed by a sizeable contingent of TDs as the Dáil debated the document.

By this time also the local councils were getting down to discussing the Treaty. The first body to do so was Navan UDC at a special meeting called on 27 December. For a matter of such crucial importance to the country's future, it is remarkable that only five of the fifteen members were in attendance. These were Chairman Seán MacNaMidhe, Michael O'Donnell, Larry Clarke, Laurence Clusker and Peter Fox. At the outset the chairman introduced a motion advocating acceptance and warning against the dangers of a split in the movement. "Acceptance of the bargain is the only alternative to turmoil and chaos", he argued. He was seconded by O'Donnell who stressed that the settlement gave Ireland fiscal control, control of trade, commerce and industry, a voice in the League of Nations, the freedom to frame a constitution, to raise an army and to elect a parliament. Continuing with enthusiasm O'Donnell claimed that ninety per cent of the people were in favour of the Treaty and he then listed the Catholic clergy, the Protestant clergy, the farmers, the press, businessmen, the Jewish community and even the Unionists as amongst its supporters.

At this point a note of dissent was introduced by Clarke who raised a sensitive issue by stating that "those most in evidence as in favour were those who went back on Dáil Éireann when the Dáil and the country most wanted them". He went even further than this as he named O'Donnell as being "mainly instrumental in getting the council away from the Dáil." This was probably unfair and when Clarke offered a counter-motion, "that the council should not take any action on this matter until after the Dáil reassembles on 3 January", there was no seconder for it. The chairman's original motion was then passed and the meeting ended.

Three days later, on 30 December, came the special meeting of the county council. Once again, considering the gravity of the issue, the attendance was disappointing with only fifteen, or just half, of the members present. It may be pointed out in fact that this was even lower than the average attendance of seventeen over the seven council meetings since the July Truce. Five councillors did go to the trouble of sending apologies for their absence, amongst them being Seán Boylan who in his note urged acceptance of the Treaty.

Opening the proceedings chairman P.J. Clinch stated that while he was not totally satisfied with the Treaty he felt that "his ideals could easily be attained under it." This was the same argument put forward by

Michael Collins and other TDs during the Dáil debates, the so-called 'stepping-stone' theory, namely, that while the Treaty did not give total freedom it did give the freedom to achieve that freedom. Clinch also expressed concern at the prospect of further bloodshed if the document were to be rejected. In this respect he pointed to the actions of the leaders of the Easter Rising saying that "they had given up so as to avoid further bloodshed but this did not mean that they had compromised on their principles."

Following this the council's vice-chairman Martin O'Dwyer moved the motion urging ratification. The resolution read that "we, the members of Meath County Council, call on Dáil Éireann to ratify the Treaty as we believe it has secured the essence of freedom and we see no alternative to it except chaos which would be fatal to the best interests of the country in the present generation." O'Dwyer then went on to praise Eamon Duggan, "in the way he acted through the trying and difficult negotiations in London", and he concluded by stating that the council was voicing the views of 90 per cent of the people of Meath in calling on our other representative Justin McKenna to vote for the Treaty.

After a number of councillors had spoken in support of O'Dwyer's resolution, a counter-motion was introduced by David Hall urging that "the council take no action in the matter of the Treaty but that we leave it as a matter of national interest in the hands of the political representatives of the Irish nation." He further argued that the council had no political mandate and certainly should not be dictating to TDs. This viewpoint was backed by Patrick Kane who, in the course of his speech, launched into a long diatribe against the Irish press which he described as having always been "pro-British." Kane also raised the question of partition, a matter which received little debate at the time of the Treaty, and he asked if it was fair "to leave the Catholics to the mercy of their bitter enemies." "England in difficulties made this Treaty," he concluded, "would England out of difficulties abide by it?"

Both Hall and Kane were at pains to stress the point that they were not anti-Treaty as such, only against the council's decision to discuss it. But argument became very heated and on one occasion a voice was heard to assert that "if told to fight on again I will do so." Hall refused several requests to withdraw his motion in the interests of unity and when a division was taken his amendment was defeated by eleven votes to four with O'Dwyer's original motion being carried by the same vote. The eleven pro-Treatyites were Clinch, O'Dwyer, Collins, Boggan, O'Farrell, Langan, Peppard, O'Reilly, Markey, Proctor and McGough. The four dissenters were Hall, Kane, Ginnity and McDonnell.

In January 1922 the rural councils of Trim and Oldcastle unanimously passed pro-Treaty motions. Both bodies were adamant that in so doing they were voicing the feelings of the vast majority of the people in their districts. In Oldcastle, for instance, one councillor claimed that "95 per cent of the people in the area want the Treaty", while at the Trim meeting the *Drogheda Independent* reported similar sentiments being expressed as follows:

> Mr Farrell: "Everyone in Athboy is in favour."
> Mr Keogh: "Summerhill too — to a man and woman they are all in favour of it."

Kells UDC, with only one dissenting voice, also came out in favour at its January meeting. In regard to the other local councils neither newspaper columns nor minute books reveal their attitude to the Treaty but there is no reason to believe that they differed from the prevailing opinion.

This pro-Treaty stance was shared in Meath by the Sinn Féin party itself. Meetings were held early in January of both North Meath and South Meath Comhairle Ceantair. The former voted in favour of ratification, unanimously, according to the *Drogheda Independent*, and "by a big majority", according to the *Chronicle* of 7 January. South Meath Sinn Féin followed suit, with only one dissenter, reported the *Drogheda Independent* of 7 January, and by twenty-seven votes to three, reported the *Chronicle*. At a branch or cumann level the *Chronicle* listed eighteen units in the North Meath Comhairle Ceantair area that were pro-Treaty with only one, the Navan cumann, against. In the south Meath area the same newspaper reported that only the Dunshaughlin cumann had taken an anti-Treaty stand.

In Meath then there was a near unanimity of opinion in regard to the Treaty. The bishop, the two newspapers, the councils, the farmers and Sinn Féin itself all called for Dáil ratification. The issue was not so clear-cut, however, when on 7 January the Dáil voted by a margin of only sixty-four votes to fifty-seven, to accept the settlement reached on 6 December. Of the five TDs for the Meath-Louth constituency only one, J.J. O'Kelly, then Minister for Education, took the republican side. In its next issue of 14 January 1922, following this vote the *Drogheda Independent* editorial asserted that:

> the extreme republicans have nothing to offer beyond glorification of an ideal which is not now realisable ... the Irish people will not let go the substance of freedom which is theirs in order to pursue, and no one knows for how long, its shadow.

One consequence of the signing of the Treaty was an amnesty for internees and in December thousands of Irishmen returned home to heroes' welcomes. The *Meath Chronicle* in its various issues for this month listed about seventy names of men who were feted on their return in Navan, Kells, Trim, Oldcastle, Nobber and Dunshaughlin. In January, following the Dáil's ratification, about twenty more Meath men were freed.

Another result of the Dáil's vote of acceptance was the beginning of the transition of power from the British to the Provisional Government, which had been chosen from those pro-Treaty Dáil deputies to oversee the administration of the twenty-six counties until the Irish Free State would officially come into being on 6 December 1922. This transition manifested itself primarily in the handing over of police barracks and in the withdrawal of British forces and the RIC. Thus it was on 13 January that the hated Auxiliaries evacuated Trim Industrial School and took their leave of the town. A similar fate befell those members of the same force who had hastily improvised a barracks at Church View, Navan, during the Troubles. This process continued in Kells, Oldcastle, Athboy, Slane and elsewhere so that by the middle of March the *Meath Chronicle* of 18 March 1922 could report that:

> every police barracks in Meath is now cleared of the RIC ... the old regime has given place to the new ... the flag of green, white

and gold now proudly floats over fortresses hitherto sacred to the Union Jack.

The transition of power was not without its difficulties. From one point of view there was a determination amongst certain elements to fire what was literally a final salvo at the departing RIC. Thus, for example, in Skryne early in March a former constable was shot and wounded at his parents' home. Around the same time in Kells an exchange of words between ex-RIC men and some townspeople developed into something more dangerous with one of the police and a local youth receiving gunshot wounds. From another point of view, and a much more serious one for the future of the country, the handing over of power in many areas led to clashes for possession of barracks between rival factions of the IRA. The county of Meath witnessed several such confrontations which will be described presently.

In April, May and June attention focused on the campaign for the general election scheduled for the sixteenth of the last named month. This is often referred to as the 'Treaty election', and it gave an opportunity to the general public to register their views on the settlement of 6 December. The monolith of Sinn Féin which had practically monopolised the seats in the 1918 and 1921 elections was, by now, badly cracked so that pro-Treaty and anti-Treaty candidates carrying the same party name were competing for the attention of the electorate.

In what was a protracted campaign the most prominent visitor to the county was Cathal Brugha, one of the most trenchant figures on the republican side. Speaking to an estimated crowd of four thousand at the Market Square, Navan, on the second Sunday in April, Brugha told his listeners that the five delegates to the Treaty negotiations had been ordered not to come to any decision until it was first submitted to the Cabinet in Dublin. They had also been instructed not to sign anything that would keep Ireland as part of Britain or to accept any form of an oath of allegiance; the Treaty meant "changing Irish people into Britishers"; the permanent occupation of Irish ports would involve Ireland in future wars; the Governor-General, the king's representative in the country, would be "a symbol of servitude"; and partition would be a disaster for the country. As regards the pro-Treaty argument that the only alternative was a resumption of the war, Brugha countered that as long ago as the previous November Lord Birkenhead, one of the British signatories, had stated that Britain would never again resort to war in Ireland.

The same five Sinn Féiners who had taken the seats in the non-election of May 1921 were once again nominated. It has been seen that four of these, Duggan, McKenna, Hughes and Murphy, had voted pro-Treaty in the Dáil on 7 January, with only O'Kelly taking the republican viewpoint. The fact that there was now a contest in the Meath-Louth constituency, as it still remained, was entirely due to the decision of Labour to run a candidate. At the end of March a conference in Drogheda of trade union representatives from the two counties voted by 48 to 21 to enter the fray and, with near unanimity, selected Cathal O'Shannon as their candidate. O'Shannon, a radical socialist, was no stranger to Meath. By this time he held the positions of acting chairman of the Irish Labour Party and Trade Union Congress and of editor of the *Voice of Labour* as well as being an official of the Transport Union. Indeed it was prominent members and officials of the union such as Michael Duffy, Stephen Walsh, James Sweeney, Christopher Matthews and James Harford who directed his campaign in Meath.

The so-called Collins-de Valera pact, drawn up by the leaders of the two wings of Sinn Féin in an attempt to get the party to contest the election as a unified force, cleared the way for the strategy adopted by Labour. This pact, it was reasoned, removed the Treaty as an issue so that the election should be fought on purely domestic matters. So it was that when O'Shannon spoke in Navan a week before polling day the theme of his speech was totally different from that of Brugha given in April and so much so, in fact, that it was almost as if the two men were contesting two different elections. O'Shannon's only comment about the Treaty was to say that this election was not a vote on it; Labour had stood aside in both the 1918 and 1921 elections but now that the British were gone it was time to build a new state and it was from this fact that the real election issues arose.

These issues, such as housing and unemployment, were ones which affected people in their day-to-day lives. Since a native government now had control of finance it had the means of remedying these social ills; education should be free at all levels and teachers should participate on school boards; the new police force, unlike the RIC, must not be armed and should be under local control. Referring to the land question, an issue of primary importance to many in Meath, O'Shannon said that the Labour Party would continue the programme of redistribution and would show no mercy to the estate-owners, "the descendants of foreign free-booters in possession of hundreds of thousands of acres of grasslands".

On emigration he asserted that this could be ended by proper utilisation of the nation's resources to provide full employment and to support a population of eight million. In his one concession to the national question O'Shannon touched on the problems of partition and sectarianism in the north and his solution was the standard socialist one of Catholic and Protestant workers coming together in trade unions to fight the common enemy, the employers. In the Meath-Louth constituency Labour's emphasis on social and economic issues and its virtual disavowal of the national question did the party no harm whatever; in fact, as the following tables show, it carried it to a remarkable runaway victory:

Electorate:	62,000 (approximately)
Total Poll:	3,8010
Spoiled Votes:	1,509
Valid Poll:	36,501
Quota:	6,084

FIRST COUNT		
O'Shannon	Lab.	13,994
Duggan	Pro-Treaty S.F.	6,990
O'Kelly	Anti-Treaty S.F.	5,733
Hughes	Pro-Treaty S.F.	4,282
Murphy	Pro-Treaty S.F.	3,367
McKenna	Pro-Treaty S.F.	2,135

O'Shannon and Duggan having exceeded the quota were declared elected and O'Shannon's surplus was distributed as follows:

SECOND COUNT	
O'Kelly	+ 2,869 = 8,602
Hughes	+ 1,830 = 6,112
Murphy	+ 1,926 = 5,293
McKenna	+ 1,285 = 3,420

This brought O'Kelly and Hughes above the quota and the former's transferable surplus votes were apportioned thus:

THIRD COUNT	
Murphy	+ 929 = 6,222
McKenna	+ 492 = 3,912

Thus Murphy took the final seat.

The most striking feature of these figures is, of course, O'Shannon's huge vote. Although the poll was a mediocre 61 per cent, he won more than 38 per cent of the valid votes cast, a figure which represented over twice the quota, and was over 7,000 votes clear of his closest pursuer. This was a remarkable triumph for a man who, unlike his five rivals, did not enjoy the advantages of being a sitting deputy or a native of the constituency. As well as that it can be fairly stated that O'Shannon's well known radical views were far to the left of the voters who elected him. That his victory came as a major surprise is evidenced by newspaper comment at the time. The *Meath Chronicle* of 24 June 1922 admitted that "O'Shannon's vast poll came as a revelation to many", while even his own newspaper *Voice of Labour* conceded that "he astonished his friends and opponents," and went on to say that his victory was achieved in spite of:

a charge of atheism against him in certain districts, a charge that was wiped out by thousands of votes in two of the most orthodox Catholic counties in Ireland.

This result is perhaps better understood in the national context rather than in any circumstances pertaining to local conditions or the candidate himself. It should be remembered that this was the first general election ever contested by the Labour Party and although they put up only eighteen candidates seventeen of them won seats, the other losing out by only thirteen votes. This was a great achievement and in his book *Labour in Irish Politics 1890-1930* (p 162), Arthur Mitchell offers this explanation:

> The great success of the Labour candidates was partly due to their emphasising social and economic issues, problems which the other parties hardly touched on at all. More important was that many voters, tired of the wrangling over the treaty and fearful of violent developments, voted for candidates who were obviously peaceful and outside the dispute.

O'Shannon's stressing of social issues and his virtual ignoring of the Treaty has already been seen. At a time when this very issue of the Treaty was leading the country into what, in retrospect and probably also at the time, seems like an inexorable descent into civil war, the stance adopted by O'Shannon was undoubtedly the main contributory factor to his huge vote.

The five Sinn Féin candidates between them won 62 per cent of the votes, 46 per cent going to the four pro-Treaty candidates and just 16 per cent to the sole republican. This indicates that of those voters in Meath and Louth who regarded the Treaty as the priority issue in the election a majority of almost three to one were in favour. Further support for the settlement can be found in the way O'Shannon's surplus transferred to the other candidates, 64 per cent went to the pro-Treaty side, thus indicating that amongst Labour voters also a sizeable majority were pro-Treaty.

One problem in all of this is that these figures refer to Meath-Louth rather than to Meath on its own. The nearest one can get to establishing the sentiments of the electorate in each county individually is from an examination of the results of the next general election just over a year later in August 1923. By then Meath and Louth were two separate constituencies and the following table compares the results of the 1922 and 1923 elections, giving percentages of votes attained by each party:

Party	1922	Meath 1923	Louth 1923
Pro-Treaty S.F. (1923 Cumann na nGaedheal)	46	42.6	46.4
Anti-Treaty S.F.	15.7	16.9	27.4
Labour	38.3	22.6	10.3
Farmers		17.1	15.9
Other		0.8	

In Louth in 1923, Cathal O'Shannon finished bottom of the poll with only 2,517 votes. The three seats went to sitting deputies Murphy and Hughes, both now representing Cumann na nGaedheal, and the prominent republican figure Frank Aiken. With almost 74 per cent of the votes going to the rival Sinn Féin candidates it is fair to say that politics in Louth were now polarised, if it had not already been in 1922, since the bitterly divisive civil war.

A different picture emerges in Meath. Here the seats went one each to Cumann na nGaedheal (Duggan), Farmers (P.J. Mulvany) and Labour (David Hall) with the republican O'Kelly losing out. In Meath just less than 60 per cent of the vote went to those parties who had engaged in the civil war.

What can be inferred from these figures as regards the situation in Meath alone in 1922? Firstly, it is fair to say that in the light of O'Shannon's collapse in Louth in 1923 the majority of his huge vote had almost certainly come from the Meath area. Secondly, the appeal of anti-Treaty republicanism was limited to only about one in every seven voters in Meath. And thirdly, this point is emphasised by the performance in 1923 of the Farmers Party, closely identified with pro-

Treaty sentiments, which did not bother to offer a candidate in 1922.

While other conclusions may be drawn from the foregoing statistics there can be little doubt but that the most salient feature of the 1922 election results in Meath was the performance of O'Shannon and Labour. The *Chronicle* of 24 June commented jokingly that the county was no longer 'royal Meath' or, in Parnell's phrase, 'republican Meath' but rather 'red Meath'. The headline of this issue was 'Labour's Gigantic Triumph.' The issue of the following week dated 1 July carried a much more sombre headline: 'Irishmen fight Irishmen.' The civil war had begun.

As with Sinn Féin and the general public the IRA was divided over the Treaty. In general the headquarters staff in Dublin was in favour, a notable exception being Liam Mellows who emerged as one of the most intransigent opponents of the settlement, but amongst those officers who had borne the brunt of the fighting, especially in Munster, there was a predominantly anti-Treaty sentiment. Though several attempts were made to bring the two sides together, by the summer of 1922 no reconciliation had been achieved and the bombing of the anti-Treaty Executive's headquarters at the Four Courts in Dublin starting on 28 June, rapidly turned an uneasy peace into a full-scale civil war.

How did the Meath IRA react to the Treaty? Bobby Byrne recalled a meeting of Volunteers from all over the county being held at the Commons, Navan, on a Sunday afternoon early in 1922. Well over a thousand men were in attendance at the gathering, the purpose of which was to ascertain their feelings about the settlement and, Bobby concluded:

> those in favour of accepting the Free State arrangement were told to remain standing as they were; those against were directed to move one step forward; there was a majority of up to ten to one in favour of the Treaty.

Despite his graphic recollection of this meeting, no one else could corroborate Bobby's account, although many of the old IRA men spoken to conceded that it could indeed have happened. Most of these men remembered the Treaty being discussed at company level or even informally between individual members of the same or different companies. "We spoke of it amongst ourselves," said Peter O'Connell, "we never received a directive from battalion or brigade level."

In their own battalion area both Peter O'Connell and Charlie Conaty recalled that in each company only about a half-dozen men were against the settlement. A similar situation prevailed in the area of the Second Brigade, which was composed of four battalions encompassing what may be loosely described as central Meath, stretching from Trim in the south to as far north as Castletown. The position here was ascertained from papers deposited in the County Library, Navan, in 1935, probably by Mick Hilliard. These papers list by battalion and by company those officers and men who were members of the IRA on 1 July 1922, that is, at the outset of the civil war. These were, of course, the anti-Treatyites or 'Irregulars', since the pro-Treaty men had by now, as Mick Hilliard bluntly put it, either "joined the Free State army or gone home." The relevant number of officers and men was as follows:

First Battalion:	O/C Joe Lalor
	no other staff
Trim:	no names given
Kilmessan:	ten
Dunderry:	thirteen
Kiltale:	two

| **Second Battalion:** | No names given for either battalion or company level. |

Third Battalion:	O/C James Ginnity no other staff
Castletown:	one
Kilberry:	four
Rathkenny:	none
Clongill:	five

Fourth Battalion:	O/C Paddy Stapleton
	no other staff
Bohermeen:	two
Ardbraccan:	seven

Martry: none
Navan: twenty-seven

There emerges here a picture of a depleted IRA, suffering from paucity of both officers and, with just a couple of exceptions, men at company level. There is no documentary evidence available for either of the other brigades, the First centred on Dunboyne and the Fourth included Athboy, in which Meath men were organized, but there is no reason to believe that the situation in those areas differed substantially from that prevailing in the Second Brigade or, indeed in the Fourth Brigade in north Meath, where both Charlie Conaty and Peter O'Connell recalled an equally strong pro-Treaty sentiment.

The same picture emerges at an even higher level. In its issue of 25 April 1922, *An t-Óglach*, the organ of the IRA, accounted for each division of the army regarding its allegiance. It should be borne in mind that this publication, emanating from Volunteer headquarters, was a strong advocate of the Treaty. As has been seen earlier Meath was the kernel of the First Eastern Division which was made up of nine brigades. As regards the Divisional staff, *An t-Óglach* claimed it was "in its entirety loyal to GHQ", that is, pro-Treaty.

There is no reason to dispute this since, both then and in later years, men such as Seán Boylan, Séamus Finn, Séamus O'Higgins, Eamon Cullen and Pat Clinton were all noted advocates of the settlement and some of them were to be associated politically with the groupings which were soon to emerge from the pro-Treaty side.

Regarding the staff of the brigades which were relevant to the Meath situation, *An t-Óglach* gave the following assessment:

First Brigade: (Dunboyne)   All brigade staff except intelligence officer loyal; 3 out of 4 battalions loyal; remaining battalion staff disloyal but rank and file are with GHQ.

Second Brigade: (Navan)   All brigade staff and all four battalions loyal except one company with a local grievance.

Third Brigade: (Kells)   All staff, all six battalions and twenty- eight companies loyal.

Fourth Brigade: (Athboy)   All brigade and battalion staff and all company officers loyal.

The intelligence officer of the First Brigade referred to above was John Costigan who was soon to become involved in a controversial incident which will be dealt with shortly. The company of the Second Brigade which had what is described as "a local grievance" was almost certainly that in Navan. The nature of this grievance is unclear, but it may well have arisen from personal friction between the Navan officers and the Divisional staff. That there were differences was indicated on a few occasions but the reasons for them were either unknown or remained unrevealed. It is quite probable that the split over the Treaty served to accentuate this antagonism which dated back to 1920.

To return to *An t-Óglach* it must be pointed out that the claim that the only 'disloyalty' in Meath came from an intelligence officer and "a company with a local grievance" was incorrect. A number of men who, since the Volunteer reorganisation of a year earlier held officer rank at either brigade or battalion level, were already by now (April 1922), or were soon to become, firm opponents of the Treaty. Amongst these could be numbered Seán Farrelly of Carnaross and Paddy Stapleton of the Commons. But the prime example was Mick Hilliard who had been appointed Intelligence Officer of the Second Brigade in April 1921, but who now began to emerge as the leading republican figure within the county.

That the *An t-Óglach* article was substantially correct, however, can be evidenced from extracts from a letter and other documents dated 20 March 1934 and sent by Mick Hilliard to the Meath County Librarian of the time. Describing the disarray into which the IRA in Meath had fallen by the early summer of 1922 the writer states that:

> on 1 July 1922 the Meath Brigade was not a defined area and I was given charge of the whole county and instructed to organise it. The brigade and battalions were not up to strength, neither

was the organisation completed in the whole county. I formed an Active Service Unit and with its formation brigade organisation ceased almost to exist.

All the evidence then indicates that the great majority of Meath Volunteers took the pro-Treaty side. Many now joined the swelling ranks of the new Free State Army; others simply left their soldiering days behind and returned to normal life and work. Meanwhile on the anti-Treaty, republican side there was a great depletion in numbers and a breakdown in IRA organisation. This then was the position in Meath on the eve of the civil war but even before this full-scale conflict the county had witnessed a number of skirmishes between the opposing factions.

The first such incident occurred on Sunday, 23 April when the two rival groups clashed over possession of the former RIC barracks in Slane. That afternoon an officer loyal to the Four Courts Executive had ordered opposition troops to evacuate the building but later that day it was reoccupied by a pro-Treaty garrison. A shoot-out ensued, and it took a timely intervention by the local parish priest Fr Clavin to end the fighting with both sides agreeing to leave the building unoccupied.

Then, on the following day in Dunshaughlin, a prominent Free State Officer, was shot at point blank range and miraculously escaped death. Bernard Dunne of Dunboyne, adjutant of the First Meath Brigade, had just left Murray's shop in the village when he was confronted by a number of men who ordered him to give up his firearms. At a trial arising out of this incident over a year later in May 1923, John Costigan, the dissident intelligence officer mentioned earlier, admitted his part in the shooting. He testified that the shooting of Dunne, who was wounded in the right shoulder, was accidental and unintentional and happened when Dunne refused to halt. Costigan and his companions in fact came to the aid of the wounded man and even accompanied him some of the way to Trim where he was treated for his injuries. It was probably for this reason that Costigan was later found not guilty and discharged by the court.

At the time, however, the incident gave rise to much rancour in the locality. When it was discussed at the next meeting of Dunshaughlin

RDC the political differences engendered by the Treaty were clearly shown. One member stated that the assailants, who he claimed had played no part in the War of Independence, were now belatedly jumping on the bandwagon and "were worse than the Black and Tans." Another member countered by declaring that "the people who are to blame are the five men who signed that Treaty in London and no one else."

A further outbreak of violence came on the following Sunday night, 30 April, when once again rival groups fought what the *Meath Chronicle* of 6 May 1922 described as "a short but fierce gun battle" for Athboy barracks. The report recounted how the building occupied by Free State forces, was rushed by twenty armed men and that at one point a bomb was thrown through a window causing much damage. After half an hour the attackers retreated without serious casualties on either side.

Although no further incidents of this nature were reported for the months of May and June, the exchanges at Slane, Dunshaughlin and Athboy were very much the preliminaries to the main clash following on the shelling of the Four Courts. In Meath the *Chronicle* recorded the first stirrings of hostilities as its issue of 1 July, which, as has been seen, was headlined "Irishmen fight Irishmen", referred to "scenes in Navan of warlike character." It reported much movement of Free State troops by railway, the commandeering of cars, lorries and provisions in Skryne and Kilmessan, and the early arrests of several leading republicans in Navan and Trim.

It was around this time that Mick Hilliard's hastily-organised active service unit, alluded to earlier, came into action. Owen Heaney of Kilberry was one of the last, perhaps the very last, surviving members of this unit. Born in 1902 Owen, with his brother James, had joined the local Volunteer company in 1919 at the outset of the Troubles but "apart from carrying out raids for guns we were not very active during the Tan war," he recalled. Firm opponents of the treaty from the start, when the civil war began in Dublin, Owen and James, with a couple of others, made their way to Curraghtown House, Dunderry, halfway between Navan and Trim, where they knew Hilliard's group was based.

In the papers which he sent to the County Library in 1935 Mick Hilliard listed thirty-three members (excluding himself) of his unit. Under the heading 'Others' he added another fifteen names. The first list represents those men who occupied Curraghtown House early in July 1922. About half of these were from the Navan Company, with most of the rest being drawn from the companies in Kilberry, Rathkenny, Clongill and the Commons.

"We were reasonably well armed", remembered Owen Heaney, "but organisation was slack and we had no scouts out when we were surrounded by Free State troops on the second day that I was there." This was on Wednesday, 5 July, when at about five o'clock in the evening a large consignment, perhaps up to a hundred, of men from the First Eastern Division arrived on the scene. Owen continued:

> Paddy Stapleton, Christy Cregan and George McDermott were then sent out to parley with the Free Staters but they were shot at and McDermott was killed instantly.

McDermott, aged 34, was a native of the Commons, Navan, and had fought in the British Army during the First World War. The nature of his death caused much controversy and bitterness at the time with the Free State side counter-claiming that he had been shot at for ignoring a warning to halt.

The exchange of fire continued right through the night and into the next day until a ceasefire was arranged following the intervention of local clergy. By then, however, another man lay dead. He was a twenty-four year old Kildare man, Seán Nolan, a vice-commandant in the Free State forces. Charlie Conaty was present at Curraghtown and remembered speaking to Nolan shortly before his death: "he was not cautious enough," said Charlie, "he was shot as he tried to throw a grenade while clambering over a gate". Charlie was in Curraghtown as an officer in the Free State Army. He stated:

> I had no opinion about the Treaty myself. The only reason I supported it was because of a directive to do so from the IRB. I joined the army early in 1922 and was given the rank of captain and was in charge of the Navan and Kells areas.

A memorable day in Charlie's life was 7 February 1922 when he had supervised the handing over of the barracks in Kells from the RIC to the Free State Army. Curraghtown, however, saddened him, as it did many others, including Bobby Byrne of Navan and Johnny Bennett of Ardbraccan. Both of these men had joined the national army and were present at Curraghtown but shortly afterwards they returned to civilian life. Following the ceasefire, the members of the unit surrendered and were detained in Trim workhouse. The *Drogheda Independent* referred to most of these as "young boys" and the *Meath Chronicle* of 8 July 1922 listed their names as follows: Donal Quinn, Christy Cregan, Mick Hilliard, Edward Cahill, John Farrelly, Nicholas Naulty, Thomas Kinsella, Laurence McGovern, John Gaynor, Michael McKeon, Joseph Egan, Richard Doran, James Boylan, William Sullivan and Dónal O'Sullivan (all of these were of the Navan Company); Owen Heaney, James Heaney, John Shields, Peter Shields and John McKeon (Kilberry); Patrick Boyle, James Byrne, Patrick and Laurence Stapleton and William McGuirk (Commons); Michael Swan and James Hoey (Clongill); James and Matthew Ginnity (Rathkenny); George Cudden (Castletown), Gerald O'Reilly (Bohermeen) and C. Fagan (unknown). This is a total of thirty-two names, one shorter than the list given by Mick Hilliard himself. The two sources also show some changes in the personnel involved; Hilliard's list includes the names of J. Sweeney, J. McLoughlin, J. Lear and P. Whyte but not those of Val Stapleton, C. Fagan and Peter Shields as given in the *Meath Chronicle* report. In general, however, the two sources tally remarkably closely.

On the 15 July 1922 the *Meath Chronicle* published a letter from Mick Hilliard in which he berated the newspaper's account of the Curraghtown affair as "very garbled and one-sided", while claiming that the Free Staters had opened fire on his scouts without first calling on them to surrender. Referring to McDermott's killing, the writer said that it could easily have been avoided and that his men had their "opponents completely at our mercy but in our ranks were none but honourable men who would not be capable of such cowardly action."

The men of the active service unit, however, were not to remain in custody for long. After two weeks in Trim they were transferred to Dundalk Jail and it was from here that on 27 July a spectacular break-out was staged. Owen Heaney recalled:

Frank Aiken with many of his Louth followers were in prison there at the time with us. Only a few including Mick Hilliard, knew of the rescue attempt in advance. A man named McGill blew a huge hole in the prison wall and about two hundred of us got out. Most of the Curraghtown unit stuck together and a waiting lorry took us as far as Louth Village. From there we made our way by night across the fields to Mellifont Abbey. After that we broke up into smaller groups. I spent a few nights in a safe house in the Lobinstown area before going home.

Some never got home. The *Meath Chronicle* reported the recapture at Wilkinstown on 12 August of Michael McKeon, Paddy Stapleton, William McGuirk and Laurence McGovern. Others were not at large for long. On 12 September the same newspaper recorded the re-arrests at Kilberry of Dónal O'Sullivan, James Byrne, Michael Swan and Matthew Ginnity as well as about another half-dozen men. At around the same time in the Skryne-Rathfeigh area a major round-up operation netted up to fifty prisoners, mostly Kildare men, and many of them escapees from Dundalk a month earlier.

It was in September also that another effort was made to bolster the fragile structures of the IRA in the county. The previous attempt on 1 July had maintained the Meath Brigade as part of the First Eastern Division, with Mick Hilliard as Brigade Commandant, Ciarán O'Connell as Adjutant, Dónal O'Sullivan as Quartermaster, Tom Duffy as Intelligence Officer and, as seen earlier, Paddy Stapleton, James Ginnity and Joe Lalor as battalion commandants. This arrangement was now radically changed. "On 1 September, 1922", wrote Mick Hilliard, "north Meath was included in the Fourth Northern Division, when a further attempt was made to perfect brigade organisation."

The new brigade staff comprised Pat Farrelly as commandant and Mick Hilliard as adjutant with James Ginnity, Seán Farrelly, Brian McKeon (Crossakiel), Thomas Gargan (Virginia) and Peter McMahon (Tierworker) as battalion commandants. There is little doubt but that the Meath IRA was by now a mere skeletal structure, with little or no formal organisation, its membership constantly harassed and subject to arrests and re-arrests, with those who managed to stay free being constantly kept on the run.

For a couple of months, at least, some semblance of organisation was maintained. After the Dundalk break-out those men of the original active service unit that were still at large managed to regroup and for a while based themselves in a large unoccupied house near Whitewood Lake in the Nobber area. "It was decided to carry out an attack on Athboy barracks," said Owen Heaney, "and Michael Price was sent down from Dublin to lead it" (Price was later to become brother-in-law to the legendary Cork guerilla leader, Tom Barry). The operation was fixed for a date in mid-September. Owen continued:

> There were about thirty of us involved. We were very well armed, or so we thought, with five Lee-Enfield rifles, a Hotchkiss gun and a number of revolvers. We had also two cans of petrol to be used as bombs to blow through the steel shutters on the windows of the barracks. I was put to do guard duty at the corner of the building and when one of the petrol cans was being carried forward it exploded prematurely and threw me back on my feet. Then the shooting started and we found that the Hotchkiss gun was useless and that the rifles were in very poor condition. The whole thing was very badly organised.

The *Meath Chronicle* of 9 September 1922 reported that the firing lasted up to two hours before the attackers retreated, leaving one of the garrison behind them dead. "Athboy was the last operation carried out by the unit," said Owen,

> Even though I was living in my home area I managed to stay free for another couple of months. Then one day in November while digging potatoes with John McKeon we were arrested by Free State troops. While we had a clear view of the road from the field we were working in they came up the railway at Simonstown and from there through the fields. We were taken to Navan barracks but I could never stand being locked up and was determined to escape. One day in the exercise yard I picked up a small spike-shaped object and that night I began to dig through a wall in

the cell. I used to hide the rubble in my pillow and mattress. It didn't take too long and I soon had a hole big enough to escape through, even though I had to take off my coat to get out of it.

Owen had been only about a fortnight in detention and he now found it prudent to get well away from home. He went to the Castlepollard-Clonmellon area of Westmeath where he stayed for the duration of the civil war. Just before the cessation of hostilities in May 1923 he had one narrow escape when Free State soldiers accosted him one night near Oldcastle:

> They chased me on bicycles and I had to abandon my own bicycle and jump over a fence, into a field and up the side of a hill. There were bullets flying after me as I ran and I was sweating so much that I had to dump my trench coat. I got away safely but I was lucky because later I heard that the coat was found full of bullet holes.

Also on the run by this time were Matt Wallace and James O'Connell. Matt had been released from Dorchester Prison in January 1922, in the general amnesty that followed the ratification of the Treaty. "In jail I had heard nothing about the Treaty," said Matt,

> There was a warden on my cell and any time I asked him what was going on in Ireland he'd just look at me and say 'No news is good news, Paddy'.

He returned to Dún Laoghaire after an extremely stormy night's crossing and from there he took a train into Broadstone. Matt remembered:

> It was a Saturday morning and I knew that my mother would be coming into Dublin on the train to do some shopping. She got a great surprise when she saw me because nobody at home knew I had been freed.

He remembered that later that morning he was given £10 by a Prisoners'

Dependents group, "I bought myself a new suit and returned home in great style and to a great welcome."

Matt was completely against the Treaty and with the outbreak of civil war he was forced to go on the run for a second time. He was involved in some activities with a small number of other Irregulars in the area but late in January 1923, along with his brother Tom, he was arrested at home in Batterstown and sent to Trim and later to Dundalk and the Curragh detention centres.

James O'Connell remembered that of the Skryne Company only himself and one other took the anti-Treaty side. They took part in the seizure of the Millmount Tower in Drogheda, where many of Hilliard's unit had also been involved, at the outset of the Civil War but this had to be evacuated when the artillery was sent in. "After that," said James, "I stayed in various safe houses, often sleeping in sheds and outhouses at night time." He was arrested in February 1923 when Free State troops arrived at his home, where he was paying a short visit. Like Matt Wallace, he was sent first to Trim and then to Dundalk and then the Curragh. Both men remembered the horrible conditions then prevailing in the Irish prisons: "compared to Dundalk and the Curragh," said Matt, "Dorchester and Wormwood Scrubs had been like holiday camps." James in particular remembered with distaste the 'food' that was served to prisoners in Dundalk:

> They must have boiled the potatoes with the sack still on and, as for the meat, I always suspected that it was the leg of a horse or maybe even a dog that we were being given.

Meanwhile the civil war continued. Following the abortive attack on Athboy barracks in September 1922 the county witnessed only two more military operations worthy of note for the rest of that year. Later in September, the barracks in Oldcastle came under a heavy attack by machine guns and mines. Once again a local priest had to intervene and he persuaded the Free State defenders to surrender and hand over the building. Although no combatants were killed in this exchange, a local man named Edward Tuite, who lived close to the scene of the fighting, was struck by a stray bullet and later died from a haemorrhage. Then on 6 October it was the turn of Navan barracks to come under attack, a two hour assault at night ended as suddenly as it had begun with no casualties on either side.

By now the war was growing in intensity and bitterness. Already Collins, Griffith and Brugha were dead and the Free State Provisional Government now led by Cosgrave was about to implement its threats of executions of Irregulars. Politics and politicians now seemed powerless to end the conflict. In Meath the local councils were reduced to expressing their abhorrence of the war and its casualties. The death on 22 August of Michael Collins in particular had a profound effect: all the councils passed motions of sympathy, some of them at specially convened meetings while Navan urban council appointed four of its members to attend the funeral. The September meeting of the County Council called for an end to the war while in December the rural district councils in Trim, Dunshaughlin and Navan all adopted a resolution calling on "the leaders of the warring parties to meet and arrange a truce to permit the country to settle down to peace and prosperity." But this was of no avail. Coming into 1923, the January meeting of the Dunshaughlin RDC discussed a communication received from an organisation calling itself the Peoples' Peace League and then resolved to set up a branch in the area. The public meeting called to establish this was, apparently, a fiasco, as David Hall at a subsequent council meeting stated, that "the only ones to attend were four young men from Culmullin." In March the councils were circularised by the so-called Neutral IRA Men's Association, calling for an end to the war and it seems that at the end of the month a Meath Brigade of this organisation was set up. By then anyway the war was drawing to a close.

Since 8 January the republicans in Meath had been leaderless following the recapture of Mick Hilliard in the Moynalty area. Hilliard was caught in Maio at the home of Peter McMahon, who, it has been seen, was a battalion commandant in the IRA's Fourth Northern Division. In later years Hilliard was to marry McMahon's sister. Peter O'Connell recalled how on a few occasions towards the end of 1922 he had met Mick Hilliard cycling on the roads of north Meath. Peter recalled:

I had joined the Free State army in February 1922 and after doing an officer's course in Kilkenny I was made a captain. I was based in Kells but things were fairly quiet. I didn't see any point in trying to arrest Hilliard and in fact we used to stop and talk to each other on the road.

Taken to Trim following his arrest, Mick Hilliard was court-martialled and came perilously close to being executed on the charge of possession of firearms without authorisation. Charlie Conaty was a member of the court martial party and he remembered the occasion thus:

> A revolver had been found in a sack of meal in a shed at the McMahon's home and this was the basis for the charge against Mick. Most of the other officers on the court martial thought that this was evidence enough to convict him but I felt otherwise and said so and luckily the execution order did not go through.

Other Meath men were not so fortunate. Amongst the seventy-seven republicans executed during the Civil War were several with connections with the county. On 11 December Laurence Sheehy of Lobinstown and Terence Brady of Wilkinstown had been executed in Dublin on a charge of "treachery in assisting armed persons and in using force against national troops." A month later a similar fate befell Thomas Murray of Kilcarn, Navan, who was found guilty of "being in possession without authority of a revolver and six rounds of ammunition." Early in February, Clareman Con McMahon was executed in Limerick Prison. McMahon was alluded to earlier in this account as one of the earliest organisers of the Meath Volunteers after the 1916 Rising; his work as an insurance salesman had later taken him out of the county.

That the Free State authorities were in no way inhibited in using the severest of measures to break their opponents was shown in the aftermath of a double bank robbery in Oldcastle on 5 March. The two raiders made off with £400 but were caught almost immediately at Crossdrum, a mile outside the town. Within a fortnight both men, Henry Keenan of Newcastle, county Down and Michael Greery of Athenry, county Galway, were executed in Mullingar.

Faced with such intimidation, and leaderless since the re-arrest of

Mick Hilliard, what remained of the disorganised Irregular forces were now reduced to a series of pointless and often mindless acts of destruction against property, both public and private. In Meath in 1923 the railway system was a prime target. On 4 January the Nobber, Kilmainhamwood and Kingscourt stations were subjected to raids involving the setting on fire of signal cabins and carriages. On 23 January there was a similar incident at Kilmessan while on the following day the evening train from Dublin was stopped, and some of its carriages burned a mile from Drumree. In March the stations at Navan and Trim came under attack. On 10 April the train at Drumree was once again held up by armed men who then derailed it and, on the same night, the railway station at Athboy was demolished by a mine.

Other targets of destruction during this period were the post office at Kilmainhamwood where telephone communications were smashed on 4 January; Dunshaughlin workhouse, parts of which were destroyed by fire on two separate occasions, 9 and 14 February; and Summerhill courthouse which was gutted on 16 March.

Much more serious were the attacks on private houses. On the night of 5-6 April two houses in the Skryne area were visited by arsonists. At Lismullin the home of Sir John Dillon was badly burned with the loss of much valuable furniture and antiques. Sir John was then aged about eighty and had played little part in public life and, according to the *Meath Chronicle's* report of 14 April 1923 on the affair, he had been "justly regarded as an excellent employer. As a landlord, before he sold to his tenants, which he did early and readily ... he was one of the very best."

A mile away at Baronstown what was apparently the same gang later set fire to the home of Adderley Wilkinson. The flames were quickly contained, however, although this only resulted in a second arson attack a few nights later, fortunately little damage was done on this occasion either. In May two more houses were burned, one at Wilkinstown and the other at Tullaghanstown, Athboy.

By now the cycle of destruction and killing was shuddering to a halt. In Meath the last serious incident was a raid on the Civic Guard barracks at Dunshaughlin when, on 27 April, five men forced their way into the building, planted and detonated a mine, leaving the entire place in ruins. Remarkably, there were no casualties.

Ten years of social change, military turbulence and political upheaval in Meath ended with a whimper when, on 17 May, Ballybeg railway station near Kells was partially destroyed by fire. A week later, on 24 May, the republican Chief of Staff Frank Aiken called a ceasefire, thus bringing the civil war to an end.

Epilogue

Amongst those old IRA men spoken to when this account was being prepared the civil war was remembered with regret rather than with bitterness. Several took no part whatever in it. Benny Carolan of Kells said that he had "never held an opinion about the Treaty; I always feared that it would lead to war and I was proven right." For Paddy Lalor of Trim:

> Irish history ended on the day the Four Courts were shelled; I wanted no part in the civil war but despite that I was arrested and jailed for a few weeks by Free State troops. I had been soldiering for four years and was anxious to get back to the family tailoring business since a green flag wasn't going to fry food in the pan.

Although fellow Trim man Jimmy Sherry joined the Free State army he hated every minute of the war. "I favoured the Treaty," he explained,

> only out of loyalty to Michael Collins. He was a born leader and, if he were to go to hell, I would willingly have followed him there. I bore no grudge against the republicans I guarded at Trim and the only bitterness I bore was against a couple on my own side. These were men who had joined the IRA after the Truce and whom I saw deliberately shooting at and wounding Irregular prisoners in Trim. But after 1921 it was all about jobs in the army and the guards. It was no longer love of country.

The generosity of spirit shown by both Charlie Conaty and Peter O'Connell towards Mick Hilliard in 1922-23 has already been noted. Matt Wallace testified that such magnanimity continued through later years: "when we used to meet at our association of Old IRA men there was never any quarrel between those who had taken opposing sides in the civil war", he said.

Even in the immediate aftermath of the civil war the deliberations of the local councils provide much evidence that there was a willingness to let bygones be bygones. In the latter part of 1923 controversy focused on the continued internment of thousands of republican prisoners. At the county council meeting of October 1923 this matter was raised in the form of a motion calling for the release of all political prisoners. One speaker in favour, James McDonnell, said that the way these men – many of them on hunger strike – were being treated "would not be done by the Bazi Bazooks or would not be tolerated in Afghanistan or Turkey." Although some councillors spoke against the motion during a heated debate, in the end the resolution was passed with a comfortable majority.

Over the next couple of months similar resolutions were passed by Kells urban council and Dunshaughlin and Oldcastle rural councils and the editorial writer in the *Meath Chronicle* on 18 November commented that "every public body in Meath with one exception has subscribed to the demand for release of these men and women."

The one exception was Navan UDC. Here when the matter had first been raised at the October meeting the *Meath Chronicle* reported how one member had taken a copy of the motion and contemptuously flung it to one side, slamming those – that is, the Navan Sinn Féin club - who had forwarded the resolution with the words: "the cheek of those people to dictate to me, who was a Sinn Féiner before some of them were born." When the issue was raised again at the November meeting the same councillor stated that those who had sent in the motion were "enough to give one a fit of nausea" and continued that "some were in jail because it was the proper place for them and they should be kept there." He then wondered whether:

> the government should be asked to supply them with petrol to
> burn more houses, give them nippers to cut telegraph wires and

.45s to shoot people in the back as in Kerry, and give them the chance to burn and incinerate babies in their homes.

Although a number of other councillors let it be known that their sympathies rested with the internees the motion was ruled out of order and the debate ended without a vote.

In spite of a large amount of good will and a certain desire for reconciliation it was this kind of invective which was to remain to the forefront of Irish political life for decades to come.

Index